W9-AFI-449

THE VOICES OF THE DEAD

THE
VOICES OF THE DEAD
STALIN'S GREAT TERROR IN THE 1930s

HIROAKI KUROMIYA

YALE UNIVERSITY PRESS
NEW HAVEN AND LONDON

Copyright © 2007 Hiroaki Kuromiya

All rights reserved. This book may not be reproduced in whole or in part, in any form (beyond that copying permitted by Sections 107 and 108 of the U.S. Copyright Law and except by reviewers for the public press) without written permission from the publishers.

For information about this and other Yale University Press publications, please contact:
U.S. Office: sales.press@yale.edu www.yalebooks.com
Europe Office: sales@yaleup.co.uk   www.yaleup.co.uk

Set in Bembo by Carnegie Book Production, Lancaster
Printed in Great Britain by St Edmundsbury Press Ltd, Bury St Edmunds

Library of Congress Cataloging-in-Publication Data
Kuromiya, Hiroaki.
    The voices of the dead: Stalin's great terror in the 1930s/Hiroaki Kuromiya.
      p. cm.
    Includes bibliographical references and index.
    ISBN 978–0–300–12389–0 (alk. paper)
    1. Political persecution—Soviet Union. 2. State-sponsored terrorism—Soviet Union—History. 3. Victims of state-sponsored terrorism—Soviet Union—Case studies. 4. Soviet Union—History—1925–1953. I. Title.
    DK267.K85 2007
    947.084'2—dc22

                                                                                                  2007015570

A catalogue record for this book is available from the British Library.

Extracts from *Ukrainian Dumy*, translation © 1979 by George Tarnawsky and Patricia Kilina, are reprinted by kind permission of the President and Fellows of Harvard College.

10 9 8 7 6 5 4 3 2 1

Contents

List of Illustrations and Maps   vii

Introduction   1

1 Love with Foreign Diplomats: The Lives of Goroshko
and Vasil'eva   28

2 Informers: The Story of Moshinskaia and Others   47

3 A Monarchist's Swan Song?   64

4 'The NKVD is Satan': Priests and a Beggar   76

5 Ukrainian Peasants and Kulaks: Ubiquitous 'Enemies'   93

6 Ukrainian Bandurists: Singers of 'National Ballads'   108

7 Koreans and Chinese in Kiev: Improbable Spies   125

8 Foreign Connections: German, Latvian and Romanian Links   141

9 Consular Affairs: Fatal Visits   162

10 Across the Borders: Families Divided   183

11 Husbands and Wives: From Love to Death   198

12 POW: 'The Polish Military Organisation'   218

13 The Case of a Trotskii: What's in a Name?   239

Epilogue   253

Notes   268

Index   289

Illustrations and Maps

Illustrations

1 The site of the former NKVD building, Kiev, 2006
  (courtesy of Valerii Vasil'ev)   15
2 A record of execution (courtesy of Iurii Shapoval)   19
3 A monument in Bykivnia   20
4 A mass grave in Bykivnia (courtesy of Iurii Shapoval)   21
5 A cross in Bykivnia   22
6 A Polish intelligence report. From CAW, I:303.4.1929, 50/199   31
7 Goroshko's interrogation record. From Goroshko file, ark. 10   34
8 The Kiev Opera Theatre   40
9 Vasil'eva's interrogation record. From Vasil'eva file, ark. 7   43
10 Moshinskaia's trade union card, Moshinskaia file, ark. 49   50
11 A memorial in Bykivnia   57
12 Sigizmund Karlovich Kvasnevskii (courtesy of Yuri Shapoval)   59
13 Zhelikhovskaia's case file   67
14 Zhelikhovskaia's 'poem', Zhelikhovskaia file, ark. 30   71
15 The Vydubychi-Heorhii church   79
16 The Luk'ianivka cemetery   85
17 A Polish intelligence report, CAW, I:303.4.1929, 168/137   96
18 Bigotskii's signature, Bigtoskii file, ark. 8zv   103
19 A Polish intelligence report, CAW, I:303.4.1929, 7/164   106
20 Bandurists in 1939 (Muzei Teatral'noho, Muzychnoho ta
   Kinomystetstva, Kiev, f. N/V 6941)   111
21 Kopan's trade union card, Kopan's file, ark. 209   115
22 Balatskii's letter to Khrushchev, Balatskii file, ark. 46   121

23 Japanese military radio log, from *Rikugun mitsu dai nikki* (1938), vol. 16, 1423 (courtesy of Bōeichō Bōei Kenkyūjo Toshokan, Tokyo)   133

24 A memorial in Bykivnia   136

25 Kronberg's trade union card, Kronberg file, ark. 34   145

26 Kronberg's 1933 letter, Kronberg file, ark. 37   147

27 Zeibert's identity card, Zeibert file, ark. 32   151

28 Zeibert and her students, Zeibert file, ark. 35   152

29 Diktovskaia's pension book, Diktovskaia file, ark. 20b   171

30a and b   Marangos' interrogation record, Marangos file, ark. 16zv and 17   176–7

31 A memorial in Bykivnia   187

32 Al'bova's 'mug shot', Al'bova file, ark. 24   193

33 Nikołłaj/Mikołaj Szczepaniuk (courtesy of Iurii Shapoval)   196

34 Dzevitskii's trade union card, Dzevitskii file, ark. 24   201

35 Sosnovskii's trade union card, Sosnovskii file, ark. 32   206

36 Kurovskii's 'mug shot', Kurovskii file, ark. 24   210

37 A Polish intelligence report, CAW, I: 303.4.1929, 12   225

38 A memorial in Bykivnia   234

39 Trotskii's 'mug shot', Trotskii file, ark. 74   242

40 Trotskii's letter to Gorbachev, Trotskii file, ark. 184   243

41 A monument in the centre of Kiev (courtesy of Valerii Vasil'ev)   263

42 A grave pit in Bykivnia (courtesy of Iurii Shapoval)   264

43 Memorial to the victims of the Great Terror on the main site in Bykivnia   265

Illustrations 6, 17, 19 and 37 are reprinted by kind permission of Centralne Archiwum Wojskowe, Warsaw. Illustrations 7, 9, 10, 13, 14, 18, 21, 22, 25, 26, 27, 28, 29, 30, 32, 34, 35, 36, 39 and 40 are reprinted by kind permission of Tsentral'nyi derzhavnyi arkhiv hromads'kykh ob'iednan, Kiev.

Maps

1 Pre-1939 Eastern Europe (courtesy of Timothy Snyder)   3

2 Present-day Kiev   12

Introduction

The dead cannot speak. Can one retrieve their voices? Death under I. V. Stalin, the ruler of the Soviet Union from 1922 to 1953, has been written about, but the dead themselves remain elusive because their voices have been lost to us. The present book is an attempt to recover the voices of those executed under Stalin.

Millions of innocent Soviet citizens died unnatural deaths in the Soviet Union in the 1930s. Seven to eight million died of hunger in the Great Famine of 1932–33. Untold numbers of people also died in the brutal campaigns for the collectivisation of agriculture and the dispossession of peasants (de-kulakisation) that led to the famine. Many of those who survived died in exile. The infamous Gulag resembled a mass grave.

Fortunately, millions of people who shared the hellish lives of the 1930s survived the Stalin era. When the danger receded, they began to speak out. As a result, a fairly good picture of collectivisation, de-kulakisation, famine, exile and forced labour has become available.[1]

The Great Terror

This is not the case with the Great Terror of 1937–38. It is still a mystery, an enigma. During it, some 700,000 or so people (to be more exact, 681,692 people: 353,074 and 328,612 respectively for 1937 and 1938, according to official data) were sentenced to be executed for political reasons—as German, Polish or Japanese spies and, more generally, as 'enemies of the people'. Owing to the incompleteness of available data, the actual figures are almost certainly higher, probably close to one million.[2] The death sentences accounted for 44.66 and 59.29 percent of those arrested in 1937 and 1938 respectively. The corresponding figures for the preceding and succeeding years, 1936 and 1939, were 'only' 0.4 and 4 percent respectively. These 1937 and 1938 death sentences, according to official Soviet data, account for 91 percent of all political death sentences handed down between 1921 and 1940. The next most intensive year was 1930, the year of collectivisation and de-kulakisation, with 'merely' 20,201 death sentences.[3] The Great Terror was an extremely concentrated wave of purposeful mass killings.

It took place under the cloud of approaching war—war both in the east (against Japan) and in the west (Germany and Poland). The Soviet Union had since its foundation been living under siege: the country was surrounded by hostile capitalist countries. Japan's advance into Manchuria in 1931–32 dramatically escalated the Soviet fear of inevitable war. This was further reinforced by Hitler's ascent to power in Germany in 1933, even though Stalin did not recognise the threat represented by Hitler immediately. Stalin restored diplomatic relations with the United States in 1933 as a counterweight to the Japanese threat and sought diplomatic alliances with Western democracies. He was convinced, however, that these countries remained deeply hostile towards the Communist state. (Hence he kept open the possibility of a rapprochement with Germany.) It is not an overstatement to say that not a single country of import was sympathetic towards the Soviet Union except the People's Republic of Mongolia. Mongolia occupied a strategic position between the Soviet Union and Manchukuo, a puppet government set up by Japan in 1932 in northeast China. Although Mongolia had been ruled by Communists since 1924 (the Soviet Union was the only country that recognised the republic), even the Mongolian Communists did not always find common ground with the Soviet Union in matters of critical importance such as Japan's threat from the east. Therefore, in the summer and autumn of 1937 Stalin despatched a contingent of Soviet secret police operatives to Mongolia, had a Mongolian version of the *troika* (an extra-judiciary organ) formed there and engineered a Mongolian Great Terror in which tens of thousands were executed as 'Japanese spies'. The republic, under the rule of Horloogiin Choibalsan, closely followed Stalin's lead.[4]

Stalin and other Soviet leaders who ordered the mass killings justified them with reference to the coming war: they contended that the arrested

Map 1: Pre-1939 Eastern Europe.

were spies, defeatists and subversives—'enemies of the people': however cleverly they masked their political faces, in the event of war they would reveal their true colours. In Stalin's view, confinement and incarceration were not enough. In 1937–38 the secret police went after many of those who were already in prisons and labour camps and executed more than 30,000 of them.[5] Stalin used the Great Terror as a pre-emptive strike to prepare for war. Subsequently Stalin and his close associates conceded that evidence of disloyalty often did not exist and that some innocent people suffered in the process. Yet they firmly believed until the last days of their lives that the Great Terror was fully justified and that without it the Soviet Union would have been beaten in World War II.[6] The lives of individuals meant absolutely nothing to Stalin. It was politics and power that were absolute. The mass killings of 1937–38 were a purely political expedient.

Victims were arrested at night and, in most cases, executed shortly thereafter without so much as the formality of a trial: they were sentenced to be shot by extra-judiciary organs such as *troika*s and *dvoika*s, NKVD (secret-police) tribunals consisting of two or three people. Most of the arrested had been on the police register of the politically suspect and simply disappeared one night into a Stygian nether world, never to be seen again. In almost all cases, their families and relatives were misinformed, if they were informed at all, that the arrested had been sentenced to ten, twenty or twenty-five years in prison without the right to correspondence. In fact, they were shot and buried in mass graves. Whereas the phenomenon of the Great Terror of 1937–38 was well known at the time, operations were nonetheless carried out in strict secrecy. The orders for mass arrests and killings given by the Soviet authorities at the time did not become known until after the 1991 collapse of the Soviet Union.

These orders reveal prior planning. In fact, some specified 'target figures' for executions and imprisonments in each region and province of the country. Even though these quotas were strictly speaking 'upper limits',[7] they were soon replaced, with the sanction of Moscow, by even higher figures, a result of the competition among regional and provincial police to achieve ever greater results. Moscow remained in control, however, and in the autumn of 1938 Stalin intervened to end the operations.

It is not that those executed in the Great Terror never attempted to speak out. Many previous efforts have been made to retrieve their voices. Yet these relate almost exclusively to those with at least some degree of fame, who left behind speeches, novels, stories, diaries and other forms of self-expression.[8] Significantly, not a single convincing case of an actual foreign spy has been uncovered among them.

The vast majority of those executed in the Great Terror, however, were not famous but rather utterly unknown, 'ordinary' Soviet citizens: workers, peasants, homemakers, teachers, priests, musicians, soldiers, pensioners, ballerinas, beggars. They were targeted by a series of special-operation orders issued by the secret police and directed against specific groups of people such as ethnic minorities (e.g., Poles, Germans, Koreans, Latvians and Greeks), the de-kulakised, the clergy, criminals, those with foreign connections and others. The 'ordinary' people destroyed in the Great Terror have attracted the attention of no one outside their own families and relatives. In many cases, their families and relatives have long since disappeared. Some were themselves arrested and executed, but in many cases they were simply dispersed owing to a variety of circumstances (displaced by World War II, for instance). In such cases, no interest has ever been shown in their fate. No one exists to mourn or even remember them, let alone condemn their executions.[9]

The present book is a modest attempt to allow some of those executed in 1937–38 a voice. The focus is on individuals, in particular those whose lives meant absolutely nothing to Stalin: innocent people who were swept up in the maelstrom of political terror he unleashed. Most of the people discussed here are 'unremarkable': they left no conspicuous imprint on history. They were condemned to oblivion by Stalin. Curiously, however, Stalin once deplored the amnesia of the people:

> People have a bad habit of praising the living, of course if they are deserving, and of consigning the dead to oblivion. They commend idols, as they said in olden times, or leaders, as they say now, and express sympathy for them so long as, excuse me for my expression, they have not kicked the bucket [skovyrnulis'], but when they die, people sometimes forget them.[10]

Stalin made this remark in April 1941 concerning V. I. Lenin, the creator of the Soviet state, who had died in 1924. Approaching the age of sixty-three at the time, Stalin may well have been thinking of his own death as well. Whatever the case, Stalin never had second thoughts about physically destroying those who were not idols or leaders and consigning them to oblivion: they were merely among the numerous 'enemies' to be eliminated. At the time, while reviewing a list of those to be executed, 'Stalin muttered to no one in particular: "Who's going to remember all this riffraff in ten or twenty years time? No one. Who remembers the names now of the boyars Ivan the Terrible got rid of? No one."'[11] Undoubtedly, their weight in history is not comparable to that of an absolute ruler like Stalin. Indeed, biographies of Stalin are legion whereas those of 'ordinary' Soviet citizens are few and far between. I myself have recently joined the ranks of biographers of Stalin.[12] Yet I am convinced that the lives of the 'ordinary' people discussed in this book are no less memorable and no less worthy of being written about than that of Stalin, their killer. Without them, history is incomplete. Such incompleteness gives the reader a distorted picture of history. The lives of 'ordinary' people, in other words, are a vital part of history.

This book is meant to commemorate these forgotten lives. At the same time, it is also meant to elucidate the mechanism of Stalin's Great Terror and illuminate a slice of the Soviet society of the 1930s.

Sources

In most cases, the only sources available are personal files of the executed composed by the Soviet secret police (the NKVD). They are macabre documents. True, torture is not detailed explicitly in case files, but a careful reader can detect it taking place between the lines of the interrogation. Execution, by contrast, is plainly recorded. (Stalin explicitly sanctioned both torture and execution.)[13] The files contain records of interrogations by the Soviet secret police as well as other documents giving personal data (birth dates, addresses, families, trades, education). By carefully dissecting these files and seeking what little additional information is available on the executed, the present book attempts to retrieve their lost voices and reconstruct their life histories.

Reading these case files demands the utmost care and caution. In critical respects, they are more difficult to use than the records of the Inquisition to which Stalin's Great Terror is often compared. During the Inquisition of medieval and early modern Europe, trials took place and records were kept. Unlike in the Great Terror, interrogations were recorded by a third party, a notary, who was required to write down 'what he [the defendant] might utter during the torture, even his sighs, his cries, his laments and tears'. Generally, even though the trials themselves failed to prove witchcraft, the records of the Inquisition are a superb source which historians have put to use with much success.[14] By contrast, the records of the Great Terror appear to be little more than stacks of falsification. Certainly, they are not verbatim records of interrogation: often only a page of notes (or sometimes none at all if the interrogator failed to extract what he wanted from the arrested) was taken during an all-night session. In almost all cases, people were arrested on false charges of being 'enemies of the people'—foreign spies, anti-Soviet conspirators, members of 'counter-revolutionary' organisations and so forth. Some people were so frightened that they confessed to the fabricated charges of crime without resistance. Others fought and insisted on their innocence. Many were eventually broken by manipulation, intimidation, threat, physical and psychological torture and other methods of coercion.

As the present book shows, however, some people, including those who might appear utterly weak and helpless, fought to the end and refused to surrender. Even the secret police could not falsify the records in such cases. Unlike defendants who fell apart under pressure, it is relatively straightforward to retrieve the voices of those who stood their ground. Their consistency is tangible.

Confessions were a sufficient but not a necessary condition for guilty verdicts and executions. Without confessions and without any evidence of guilt, people were still convicted and executed. Often the police were overwhelmed by the number of cases and the need to meet the high quotas of arrests and executions handed down from above. Local police often picked on villages and settlements situated closer to their headquarters in order to fill the quotas more quickly. Those further afield escaped relatively lightly, at least in the short term. Forced to process cases in a conveyor-belt fashion, the police sometimes could not be bothered with extracting confessions. Nevertheless, confessions strengthened their cases, and the ability to beat them out of the arrested was in a perverse way highly regarded within the police.

Obviously the confessions of broken men and women do not reflect their true voices, in spite of the fact that secret-police interrogators recorded them in detail. Since at the time the slightest manifestation of doubt about the Soviet system and its leaders constituted a political crime, formulaic remarks such as 'The NKVD is Satan', 'The death of Stalin will save Russia' and 'People live better in the West than in the Soviet Union' were obviously inserted into interrogation records by the police to lend the confessions credibility. Such self-incriminatory confessions fill the files of the 'repressed'.[15] Without them, the charges would have been too far-fetched and baseless to have been believable. A careful perusal of the confessions, however, suggests that they were essentially fictions. Written by interrogators and signed by the accused under duress, they contain just enough detail to be credible to the unsuspecting reader. In some important cases, these confessions were afterwards widely propagated by the Soviet government.

It is possible to read deeper meanings into the confessions of the accused. Stalin's terror, like the Inquisition before it, was meant to extirpate 'heresy'. There was every reason for Stalin to believe that heretics abounded in the country. For one, the Soviet people in general lived very badly: the rapid industrialisation campaign launched in the late 1920s severely squeezed national consumption and latent discontent was palpable. For another, the violent practices of the Soviet government (such as collectivisation and de-kulakisation) alienated even its erstwhile supporters. The Great Famine of 1932–33 appeared to most to embody the mistakes and failure of Stalin's administration. Stalin insisted that although his critics had been decisively defeated by the 'success' of collectivisation, they had not given up the fight. They had gone underground and were seeking to undermine the Soviet system clandestinely. Therefore, revolutionary vigilance was needed. The implication was that it was not so much a concrete act of subversion as a state of mind that was under detection, for in the event of war these subversives would reveal their true colours and betray Stalin and the Soviet regime. They had to be isolated and destroyed. Every trick (including the third degree) had to be employed to reveal the hidden self of the accused. For a probe of the suspect's heretical beliefs to be successful, it had to yield a confession. Unlike the Inquisition, however, in Stalin's terror those who confessed and repented were not spared but executed.[16] Stalin suspected that their abjuration of heresy was merely a dissimulation, an art perfected by those who in fact refused to capitulate.[17]

A different view is offered by Arthur Koestler's *Darkness at Noon* (1940). Using Nikolai Bukharin (who was tried at the famous Moscow show trial in 1938 and executed) as the novel's hero Rubashov, Koestler, an ex-Communist,

depicts Bukharin's (Rubashov's) seemingly willing and evidently self-destructive participation in Stalin's bloody carnival as a capitulation induced by his own ideology: Bukharin accepted the Stalinist logic of sacrificing communists to the larger cause of the revolution and the survival of the revolutionary regime in the face of Nazism. Bukharin (Rubashov) acknowledges his (and his comrades') erstwhile fight against the communist (Stalinist) leadership as an unforgivable ('objectively counter-revolutionary') crime against the revolution itself. His confession of guilt was to be the last service to the revolution. Both Bukharin (Rubashov) and his interrogators believed, according to Koestler, that after the final victory of the revolution, their sacrifice would be given its due place in history.[18]

This interpretation does not seem to apply to any of the people discussed in the present book. None of them was a revolutionary like Bukharin and none thought in terms of his or her service and sacrifice to the Revolution.

Unfortunately, the confessions of the accused, particularly those made at the Moscow show trials in 1936–38 in which famous old Bolsheviks like Bukharin confessed to their 'counter-revolutionary' crimes ('conspiracies against Stalin'), and their dissemination by the Soviet government led many contemporaries to believe in the existence of numerous 'enemies of the people' (i.e., critics of the Soviet system) in the Soviet Union.[19] While one would hope that the same assumptions would not be made by historians, regrettably the latter often lack a 'feel' for the lives of the individuals who died under Stalin. Consequently, they fail to read the documents of the Stalin era in their proper context. It is easy to believe in the 'fiction in the archives', as Natalie Zemon Davis noted in reference to early modern French history.[20] Uncritical readings create overly simplistic pictures of the Stalin era: the Soviet people were either opposed to the regime or dedicated to it wholesale.[21] Even well-informed people who lived under the Soviet regime and who therefore do have a 'feel' for Soviet life under Stalin often fail to understand the complexity of life, creating anti-Stalinists out of loyal Soviet citizens.[22] Other scholars miss the deeply hidden private lives of individuals, asserting that there was no room for the private sphere in Stalin's Soviet Union.[23] Although pious believers in Stalinism were legion, critics of the Soviet system and its leaders undoubtedly existed. Otherwise the Soviet Union would have been a utopia for totalitarian leaders. Likewise, foreign spies did operate on Soviet territory, just as Soviet spies worked outside the Soviet Union. This was a universal fact of international political life. But that does not make every critic a spy or even an anti-Soviet element. History speaks to us from the pages of the case files and other police documents, but one simply cannot take their contents at face value.

In most cases, these files, the only records left about the dead, offer the reader subtle yet telling clues and hints about them. The records of interrogation normally weave elements of truth into a web of fiction to make it credible, while the fictions embedded in the records inevitably reveal themselves upon close inspection. This is where the judgement of the reader becomes crucial. A knowledge of the interrogation process, experience of reading these files and recognition of recurrent formulaic phrases regularly attributed to the accused are all essential to the process. This is a difficult and complex task, and one that I have made the central concern of the present book.

The key is in the detail, which may reveal, for instance, that the arrested knew nothing of the existence of the counter-revolutionary organisations to which they were accused of belonging.[24] Some accusations were so far-fetched that the arrested failed to comprehend them; even when broken, their confessions retain traces of disbelief and resistance to the absurdity of the charges. Contradictions abound. Since these files were composed by the police not for historians but for the extra-judiciary organs (such as *troikas*), no attention was paid to consistency in confessions and testimonies. For the historian, contradictions provide the key to retrieving the hushed voices of the arrested.

One method for separating fact from fiction is to compare the longhand and typed notes of a confession. In all cases, interrogations were recorded in longhand initially. The records of interrogations in which the accused denied the charges were not normally typed up afterwards, because they were not useful. (The vast bulk of the files used in the present book are handwritten, 'raw' documents.) In some important cases, however, the records of confessions were typed up. These were often intended for the eyes of the higher-ups. Furthermore, in almost all cases, the bill of indictment was typed. This sometimes falsely states that the accused confessed. By carefully comparing handwritten original documents against typed documents, one can detect the mechanism of terror and recover the silenced voices of the condemned.

Documents missing from case files can provide important clues too. Often, these concern police informers and provocateurs. A perusal of the files shows that certain documents mentioned in the bills of indictment are missing. Sometimes, the secret police note in the files that they are withholding documents for 'operational reasons'. In a few instances involving important espionage cases, the files indicate that the police sought to rewrite history completely by systematically hiding the use of agents whom they subsequently arrested as foreign spies. Thus, fragments of information buried in the case files can prove highly revealing.

In addition, post-Great Terror testimonies, if available, have been attached to the case files and prove very helpful. It turns out in many cases that the arrested were tortured and that the testimonies taken against them in 1937–38 were invented or forced from witnesses who subsequently recanted them. The post-Great Terror material reveals the mechanism of falsification and helps one to read the case files more discriminatingly.

None of the cases I have examined in this book carries any credible evidence of political 'crime', even in the broadest sense of the word employed by Soviet authorities at the time. (This included any remark critical of the Soviet government as well as jokes and rumours about political leaders.) As a result, all of the executed (and a few who escaped death) have since been 'rehabilitated'. The peculiar term 'rehabilitation' (*reabilitatsiia*) refers to the process by which accusations made against the arrested were proved to be baseless and the accused were thereby exonerated. This was dignified only by a declaration from the Soviet government, not a formal apology. Still, it was important in that the exoneration removed the taint of being an 'enemy of the people' from the accused and their families. As is true of all cases discussed here, the exoneration confirms that they were killed for no crime.

In fact, the subversive actions and remarks ascribed to the arrested were never proved. Any actual evidence of political opposition and resistance is difficult to come by in the police case files. The very absence of such proof tells us, however, that the Soviet people did not generally speak their minds regarding politics, whether or not emotion occasionally got the better of them and concealed political sentiments revealed themselves accidentally. By the time of the Great Terror people had come to live by and large according to the terms dictated by the regime and had learnt not to speak out. All non-official political sentiments were driven underground as a result. Such being the case, it is hard to give credence to the charges of anti-Stalin remarks regularly ascribed to the accused by their interrogators, often using identical phrases from one case to the next.

The police files are treacherous sources. Confessions and testimonies were generally invented by interrogators. The police beat confessions out of the arrested in order to confirm their own preconceptions

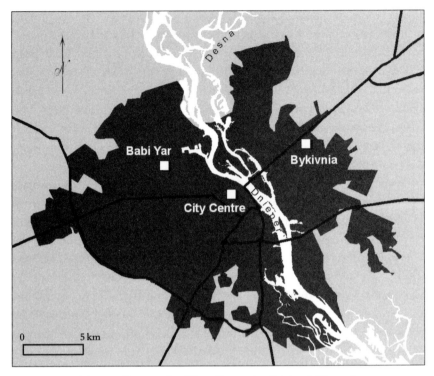

Map 2: Present-day Kiev (drawn by Richard Thurau).

about their 'enemies'. Naturally the contents of case files are formulaic, colourless and devoid of individuality. However, even such files, if handled with caution and care, throw up valuable clues through which one can uncover the lost voices of the dead. From dull and vapid files emerge concrete, individual and varied lives that have been condemned to oblivion.

The Case of Kiev

Almost all of the cases examined in this book come from Kiev (Kyiv in Ukrainian). The choice of Kiev is deliberate: for several years I have been allowed to travel there to read the police files of individuals who were victims of the Great Terror. This is due to the fact that, in general, today's independent Ukraine allows greater access to information than does Russia. Although these files are not altogether freely accessible, they are not entirely out of reach even of foreign historians. As such, Kiev and Ukraine make an excellent case study for Stalin's Great Terror.

At the time of the Great Terror, Kiev was the capital of the Ukrainian Soviet Socialist Republic, a constituent republic of the Soviet Union, and the third largest city in the country after Moscow and Leningrad. According to the 1937 census, the city of Kiev had a population of 775,856 and the Kiev Oblast' (of which Kiev was the capital) a population of 5,098,241.[25] Although there are few comparative studies, the nature of terror in Kiev was not very different from that in other places. Indeed, the Great Terror was no less great in Kiev than anywhere else in the Soviet Union. This was because the terror was enacted from above and closely monitored from Moscow.

How representative was Kiev of Ukraine as a whole? Ukraine in the Great Terror was not noticeably different from elsewhere in numerical terms. In 1937–38, 123,421 people were sentenced to be shot in Ukraine.[26] This figure accounts for 18.1 percent of the death sentences handed down in the country as a whole in the same period and is roughly commensurate with the relative weight (17.5 percent) of the population of Ukraine in the total population of the country (according to the 1937 census).[27] In Kiev, according to the available data, 3,555 people were executed in 1937 and 1938 in the secret police's prisons. There were 1,545 in 1937 as follows: 1 (April), 1 (May), 1 (June) 15 (July), 75 (August), 241 (September), 283 (October), 517 (November) and 411 (December); and 2,010 in 1938 as follows: 300 (January, including 2 on Russian Orthodox Christmas Day, 7 January), 261 (February), 108 (March), 268 (April), 503 (May), 30 (June), 5 (July), 49 (August), 212 (September), 245 (October), 26 (November) and 3 (December).[28] These 3,555 executions account for 2.9 percent of the total executions in Ukraine, a figure slightly higher than Kiev's share (2.7 percent) in the population of Ukraine as a whole. The data on executions in Kiev, however, are almost certainly incomplete. In addition, many people who held positions of responsibility in Kiev were taken to Moscow and executed there. Numerous politically suspect people were deported from Kiev and arrested elsewhere.[29] On the other hand, many in positions of responsibility in the provinces were brought to Kiev to be executed. In the end, Kiev is likely to be not very different from Ukraine as a whole.

To be sure, Kiev, like any other city, had its peculiarities. First, as the capital of Ukraine, it was not in Russia. Although the culture, language and customs of Ukraine were similar and closely related to those of Russia (and Belarus), so much so that Russians often regarded Ukraine as a mere province of Russia, Ukraine was not (and is not) Russia. Many Ukrainians believed (and still believe) that Ukraine is fundamentally different from Russia. Thus, supporters of Ukrainian nationhood criticised Russia by contrasting the supposedly democratic nature of the Ukrainian body politic (inherited from the Cossack era) with Russia's supposedly autocratic penchant and Poland's supposedly aristocratic traditions. Moreover, Ukraine was divided into the Soviet-ruled eastern Ukraine and 'Western Ukraine', at the time a region in Poland from which vigorous Ukrainian independence movements emerged. Kiev was Russian to the extent that the common language was Russian rather than Ukrainian and its culture, like that of other cities in Ukraine, tended to be Russian (and Polish and Jewish) rather than Ukrainian. Yet the surrounding countryside was, ethnically, predominantly Ukrainian and the Ukrainian peasants were regarded by Russian rulers with suspicion as bearers of Ukrainian nationalism and separatism. In other words, Kiev was an important 'Russian' island in a vast Ukrainian sea. Nevertheless, Nikita Khrushchev, a Russian, who governed Kiev and Ukraine from 1938 until after World War II, found the city to be diverse and unruly:

> The year was 1928, and in Kiev unemployed workers demonstrated, marching down the streets carrying the red banner. We brought them together in an old building of the Kiev City Duma, where there was a meeting hall that would fit four or five hundred people, and there they held a rally. Mensheviks and Socialist Revolutionaries were still active, and there were many Ukrainian nationalists. Trotskyist influence was also strong, and the Trotskyists were taking advantage of difficulties that existed in Kiev.[30]

Khrushchev's characterisation is misleading, because he used 'Mensheviks', 'Socialist Revolutionaries', 'Trotskyists' and 'Ukrainian nationalists' as political labels. Still, it is true that Kiev was a difficult place to govern. Before Khrushchev, during the Revolution and the Civil War of 1917–20, Kiev changed hands as many as twelve times, as the Kiev writer Mikhail Bulgakov describes in his famous 1924 novel *The White Guard*. Kiev appeared to Moscow as potentially vulnerable to Ukrainian nationalism, among other political deviations. L. M. Kaganovich, who governed Ukraine in the 1920s before Khrushchev, 'was fond of saying that every Ukrainian is potentially a nationalist'.[31] The head of the Ukrainian secret police, an ethnic Russian, contended in 1938 that '75–80 percent of Ukrainians are bourgeois nationalists'.[32] It was not until the 1950s that an ethnic Ukrainian assumed political leadership of Ukraine. The suspicion of nationalism surely affected Kiev's political life: accusations of Ukrainian nationalism were an important feature of the Great Terror in Kiev.

Second, Kiev was close to the Polish border (about 200 km), as one resident of the time noted.[33] It only became the capital of Ukraine again in 1934, replacing Kharkiv, a much more modern city which lies further east and which had a larger proletarian population. This change was prompted by concerns that the largest city in Ukraine, so close to the western borders, was not strong enough politically. By transferring the capital to Kiev, Moscow sought to strengthen it politically in preparation for war. This move was accompanied by extensive destruction of the old Ukrainian cultural and architectural heritage of Kiev, presumably

1: A cross dedicated to the victims of terror stands on the site of the former NKVD building in the centre of Kiev.

to deprive it of 'Ukrainian-ness' (which was 'bourgeois') and infuse the new metropolis with more 'Soviet-ness'.

Third, Kiev's proximity to the border also meant that it was ethnically diverse. Its heterogeneity was historical: population movements over many centuries had made the steppe land of Ukraine ethnically mixed. Although the presence of Russians (the master race, as it were, of the Soviet Union) did not pose a problem to the Soviet leaders in Moscow, that of other ethnic groups, particularly Poles and Germans, did, even though they were not numerous, in 1926 accounting for only 6.2 percent in the city, and for an even smaller percentage in the surrounding countryside. (In 1926, 42.2 percent of the population of the city of Kiev were ethnic Ukrainians, 24.4 percent and 27.3 percent Russians and Jews respectively, while the surrounding countryside was inhabited mainly by ethnic Ukrainians but dotted with Russian, Polish, German, Jewish and other settlements.)[34] True, ethnic diversity was not peculiar to Kiev. Most other major Soviet cities, including Moscow and Leningrad, had large non-Russian ethnic groups. Yet at a time when the threat of war was mounting, people with ethnic and family ties to the supposed enemy countries (Poland, Germany and Japan) became politically suspect by default. Therefore, Kiev's ethnic Poles, Germans, Koreans and Chinese (by their proximity to Japan) were severely affected by the terror. The head of the Ukrainian secret police even stated in 1938 that 'all Germans and Poles living in Ukraine are spies and saboteurs'.[35] Anyone in contact with foreign countries and foreigners was equally affected: Latvians, Greeks, Bessarabians and others suffered as a result. (There is little evidence that Jews were specially targeted by the Great Terror, even though many Jews, like many Russians, fell victim to it.) After the Great Terror, those 'other' ethnic groups (non-Ukrainian, non-Russian and non-Jewish) accounted for a much-reduced 3.8 percent of the population of Kiev.[36]

Taken together, these matters suggest that foreign connections were the most important and preponderant factor leading to the execution of Kiev citizens in the Great Terror. In this regard, Kiev was not exceptional. Leningrad, by origin and spirit a cosmopolitan city, was even closer to the northern border than Kiev was to the western border. Although Eastern and Western Siberia were very remote, the Japanese consulate in Novosibirsk and the Manchukuo consulate (staffed by Japanese military officers) in Chita closely watched these regions in which they claimed a vital stake. Germany maintained its own consulate in Novosibirsk until the spring of 1938, when it was shut down by the Soviet authorities. In addition, Japan maintained a consulate and a Special Intelligence Organ (*Tokumu kikan*) in Manchu-li, a city just across the border from Eastern Siberia and a railway hub linking Eastern Siberia with northeastern China. These areas suffered similarly in the Great Terror, suggesting that foreign factors were a leitmotiv of the Great Terror almost everywhere.

The execution of the Great Terror in Ukraine and Kiev did not initially satisfy the Kremlin, even though torture was used extensively.[37] The NKVD prison in Kiev was described by one inmate as a 'living grave'.[38] (The torture and humiliation that accompanied interrogation were such that suicide was widespread among the arrested. At a very early stage of the Great Terror, in the spring of 1937, this fact attracted the attention of the highest political authority in Moscow, which instructed the secret police to take the necessary preventive measures.)[39] The Ukrainian authorities appeared to Moscow to be more interested in the numbers of executions than in rooting out true subversives. Thus Ukraine was criticised by Moscow for missing numerous important 'enemies' owing to its poor investigative work regarding 'enemy networks' in Ukraine. Moreover, the ratio of guilty pleas to non-guilty ones was said to be low in Ukraine. Even when they managed to extract confessions, the Ukrainian police were criticised by Moscow for failing to extract sufficiently substantive ones that might lead to the uncovering of further hidden 'enemies'.[40] In February 1938 the chief of the USSR's secret police himself, Nikolai Ezhov, travelled from Moscow to Kiev in an attempt to invigorate the local Ukrainian branch.[41] He noted that Ukraine 'had executed a great deal', but had 'not always seized those' who should have been seized, and he urged Ukraine's secret police to focus its activities on Poles, Germans, Romanians and other suspect national groups.[42] Ezhov's visit appears to have achieved the intended effect in Kiev and Ukraine, thanks in no small part to the fact that it gave rise to a more extensive use of torture than before. The police were exhorted to use force. As one provincial secret-police chief in Ukraine noted, 'We will not joke with enemies. If one or two die, nothing bad will happen, none of you will be made answerable; I will answer with my own head and party card.'[43] (When Stalin ended the Great Terror, numerous police chiefs had indeed to answer with their own heads and party cards.) In 1938 the execution rate in Ukraine increased sharply from 51.8 percent in the previous year to 81.9 percent (in 1937, 67,771 of the 130,951 convictions resulted in death sentences and in 1938 55,650 of the 67,967 did).[44] In the process, four heads of the Ukrainian secret police were themselves killed: V. A. Balitskii was arrested in July 1937, taken to Moscow and executed in November 1937; Balitskii's successor, V. T. Ivanov, was arrested in August 1937 and executed in Moscow; Ivanov's successor, I. M. Leplevskii, was arrested in April 1938 and executed in July 1938 in Moscow; and Leplevskii's successor, A. I. Uspenskii, to save his own skin, vanished in November 1938 from Kiev, but was found ensconced in the Urals, arrested in April 1939 and executed in January 1940 in Moscow.[45]

Individuals

I randomly selected several dozen cases to be examined from the vast lists of victims in Kiev. I had only one selection criterion: when I encountered women's names, I always chose them. Otherwise the process was random. Given that women were affected by the Great Terror to a much lesser degree than men and that women were much less likely to be executed,[46] I assumed that such cases would be extreme ones and therefore potentially very revealing. As a result women are disproportionately represented in this book. I am confident, however, that my assumptions are right. Of course, I was not granted access to all of the files I requested at the archive in Kiev, TsDAHO (Tsentral'nyi derzhavnyi arkhiv hromads'kykh ob'iednan', the former Communist Party Archive to which the security police archive in Kiev released many of the case files of 'repressed' people).

Except in a few cases, the lives discussed here ended in execution: the youngest was Vera Emel'ianovna Goroshko, a twenty-three-year-old ballerina (see Chapter 1), the oldest Nikita Radionovich Kravchenko, a seventy-four-year-old beggar (see Chapter 4). Normally, after their arrests, they were put in large cells with many others. There were three major gaols in Kiev. One was in the NKVD building in the centre of the city, right next to the main square, which is today called Independence Square. (The building, constructed in 1838–42 as a school for noble girls, was completely destroyed during World War II. Rebuilt after the war, it now houses the International Centre of Culture and Arts. Before the war, the secret police moved to another site on Korolenko Street, now Volodymyr Street, on the other side of the main thoroughfare Khreshchatyk, where the NKVD's successor, the SBU, is still located.) Another was the Luk'ianivka Prison, situated near the Luk'ianivka cemetery (see Chapter 4). The third was on Rosa Luxemburg Street, now Lypky Street, not very far from the NKVD building.

The arrested were taken out of their cells, usually at night, to an interrogation room. They were often tortured by uniformed interrogators armed with revolvers, and their cries, groans and screams were deliberately allowed to be heard in the cells. (When it was necessary to conceal torture, rooms with doors insulated with leatherette were used. Some rooms had windows; these were invariably covered with dark material.) Interrogations often lasted all night (sometimes days and nights on end, a torture method called the 'conveyor'), but the arrested were not allowed to sleep during the day. As a method of torture sleep deprivation was replaced by beatings in the summer of 1937 to achieve the desired results more quickly. Verbal abuse and other forms of psychological torture (threats of harm to the families of the arrested in particular) were widely employed along with physical torture. Often police spies and provocateurs were planted in the cells.

2: The record of execution of Anastasiia Stanislavovna King (Kink), 10 December 1937 at midnight, signed by Commandant Shashkov.

3: A monument, with the inscription '1937', to the victims of the Great Terror at the entrance to the Bykivnia mass grave site in Kiev (2006).

These sought to intimidate, frighten or otherwise induce the arrested into self-incrimination. The extra-judiciary tribunal (*troika* or *dvoika*), presided over by the secret police chief and attended by a prosecutor and a Communist Party representative, then met on the NKVD premises and handed down sentences for execution, in the absence of the accused. The procedure was in any case *pro forma*, since the sentences had been predetermined by orders from Moscow. The tribunal neither showed interest in nor examined the evidence, which had been faked; and there were so many cases that the sentencing became mere rubber-stamping, usually taking no more than a few minutes. (It is suspected that the tribunal did not even meet sometimes, with signatures merely being collected from the three persons in charge.)

Normally, those sentenced to be shot were taken, between 11 p.m. and midnight, from their prison cells to the basement or execution chamber of the prisons and executed there by a bullet to the nape of the neck. (In fact, two or three were used to ensure death.) Executioners then signed the forms of each individual. (Six signatures appear most frequently on the forms—those of N. I. Vorobiov, A. G. Shashkov, G. L. Nikel'berg,

M. A. Al'tzitser, I. H. Nagornyi and Shlepchenko.)[47] Then the bodies were immediately taken away on lorries. Many of the men and women discussed here were buried in the mass graves in Bykivnia on the outskirts of Kiev. M. Sh. Musorks'kyi, a driver working for the NKVD's 'Department of Anti-counter-revolution' in Kiev who was interviewed in 1989, more than fifty years after the event, testified:

> Part of my work [for the secret police] was to transport the bodies of executed enemies of the people. I only moved them by night. I took the bodies to the district of the village of Bykivnia. Turning right off the highway, there was a large wooded area which was fenced in and heavily guarded [by armed officers]. The bodies were dumped in piles into pits. The bodies had been shot in the basement of the prison [on Rosa Luxemburg Street] and at night were loaded

4: A mass grave in Bykivnia in the 1980s.

5: One of the many crosses that stand on the mounds of Bykivnia, Kiev (2006).

onto lorries by special pincers. With the pincers, we caught hold of the bodies by the neck and legs and dumped them into the bed of the truck. We filled the lorries with bodies, covered them with a tarpaulin and transported them at night to Bykivnia. Usually we carried the bodies in two or three lorries accompanied by NKVD officials.[48]

It is one of the ironies of history that those buried in Bykivnia in 1937–38 were subsequently joined in their graves by those who had tortured them: the political climate changed in late 1938 and it was the secret police who were next purged. In the Bykivnia mass graves, according to one account, as many as 1,199 secret police functionaries are buried, although that number may also include some who paid with their lives for their reluctance to apply torture.[49]

I have made every effort to collect as much information as possible on each of the people discussed here. Their photographs proved hard to come by. Except in a few cases, the files do not contain the 'mug shots' that must have been taken by the police after the arrests. Kiev fares much worse than Moscow in this respect.[50] It may mean that Kiev's police were less diligent, that they did not have enough photographic equipment at the time, that they somehow lost or disposed of most of the pictures, or that the authorities are still withholding them as 'classified'. The three 'mug shots' I did find in the files are haunting images. I have included them here, although the quality of the images varies (see Illustrations 32 on p. 193, 36 on p. 210 and 39 on p. 242).

Nor has recovering their voices from the available records been a straightforward process. These are not people in their everyday lives, but men and women faced with death—they speak with the anguished voices of the threatened, frightened and broken. Yet even their silences speak to us in subtle ways. Silence itself could be a *cri de cœur*. Some people were not broken by even the most hardened interrogators. Their records speak loudly of their courage and strength.

The Bykivnia Mass Graves

The number of people buried in the Bykivnia mass graves is not known. Many people from outside Kiev were buried there as well. After the Great Terror of 1937–38, 2,563 bodies of 'bourgeois nationalists', 'spies' and 'terrorists' are said to have been added to the graves between 1939 and 18 September 1941. (Probably, many were from Western Ukraine, which in 1939 was incorporated into the Soviet Union from Poland.) In addition, eighty-nine Soviet soldiers executed for desertion were added in the summer of 1941,[51] i.e., shortly after the outbreak of war with Germany. During the war, at least 7,000 people are said to have been shot and buried there by the German occupiers, although some witnesses refute the claim. (During the occupation, many more people were shot in the famous Babyn Iar [Babi Yar] in Kiev.) Official estimates of the Soviet terror victims buried in Bykivnia range from 6,329 to 6,783, but in fact more than 10,000 victims have now been identified by researchers. Some suspect that as many as 50,000–150,000 are buried there.[52] Whatever the case, Bykivnia is merely one of many such mass graves in the former Soviet Union. In the areas near Kiev alone, there are mass graves in Uman', Bila Tserkva, Cherkasy and Zhytomyr. There is also the famous case of the Vinnytsia mass graves discovered by the German occupiers during World War II.[53]

Today the Bykivnia mass graves are a vast park and memorial site.[54] It stands aloof from the majority of Kiev's residents: one has to travel quite a distance from the city centre to reach it. It is maintained by local volunteers who care deeply for it. Crosses are ubiquitous among the numerous pine trees that thickly cover the site. Here and there one can descry pine trees on which papers with names and inscriptions have been pasted by survivors in order to commemorate their dear ones. The papers have become stained over time despite being protected by transparent plastic.

Occasionally commemorative events take place on the site. Rehabilitation and commemoration represent a collective act of repentance and courage, the courage to confront the past. Deep in the psyche of the nation, rehabilitation may embody an inchoate belief in the resurrection of the dead. Yet the mass graves of Bykivnia have ineluctably also become embroiled in contemporary politics: the dead are claimed by all sides in political battles. Under the crosses lie Christians, non-Christians and Communists side by side. Eternal peace is hard to come by in Bykivnia.

Except on commemorative occasions, however, the graves are deserted – dark, serene and eerie. History weighs on visitors here. True, one cannot live in the past alone and forgetting is a part of life. Yet, visiting the Bykivnia graves after reading the gruesome case files of the executed, one cannot escape history's heavy burden.

Mikhail Bulgakov once wrote, 'Manuscripts don't burn.'[55] Indeed, some of his manuscripts, long regarded as lost in the midst of Stalin's terror, have resurfaced and been published posthumously. Following Bulgakov, one might say, 'The voices of the people don't die.' However faint they may be, when one cares enough to listen, the voices of the dead can be heard.

The main source for this book is the archival collection 'fond 263' in the TsDAHO, which consists of the files of repressed individuals transferred from the former KGB (now SBU) archive in Kiev. The book offers a close analysis of these files, which contain arrest and search warrants, arrest records, search records (including inventories of confiscated belongings), interrogation records (including records of personal information [*anketa*] taken from the arrested), depositions of witnesses, bills of indictment, sentences, records of execution, documents concerning rehabilitation and many other related items (such as identity cards, personal letters and photographs). They range widely in size, from a few dozen sheets to more than a thousand, depending on the complexity of the case, the number of people involved, the process of rehabilitation and other factors. The vast bulk of the documents are written in longhand. The documents in each file also vary widely in size. They have been read by very few people; most likely once or twice by people charged with the rehabilitation of the executed. They are dusty. Many have turned brown and brittle. (A photograph of the cover of a case file is reproduced on p. 67.)[56] Yet these files provide virtually the only contact with the executed. The present book refers to them so frequently that references are bracketed in the main text. (References are to the folio [*arkush*] number of each file. The verso is designated by 'zv.' (*zvorot*), as in 23zv.) The reading of these files, as discussed earlier, requires the utmost caution. My reading has been enhanced by days and weeks spent working with similar case files in the SBU archives in Kiev, Donet'sk and Luhans'k. The research for this book took me to other archives in Moscow, Warsaw, Tokyo, Berlin and Washington, D.C. However, references to these and other sources, both published and unpublished, are by and large of secondary significance and therefore are made in the endnotes of the book. In each chapter, books and essays are cited in full at the first appearance and in abbreviated form thereafter.

The transliteration of proper names from Cyrillic alphabets always poses difficulties. By and large I have used the US Library of Congress transliteration rules. As far as geographical names are concerned, contemporary local names are used. Hence: L'viv instead of L'vov or Lwów, and Odesa instead of Odessa. Exceptions are made for familiar names such as Kiev, Moscow and St Petersburg. Personal names pose a more vexing difficulty. Should we use, for example, a Polish name or a Russian name for a Russified Pole? Should we use a Russian name (for instance, Nikolai) for the Ukrainian name (Mykola)? Some ethnic Ukrainians discussed here were Russian-speakers, and they and the Soviet officials who dealt with them consistently used the Russian versions of their Ukrainian names. When it comes to non-Slavic (such as Korean or Greek) names, the question becomes even more complicated. To be fair, or to be equally unfair, to all non-Russians, I have used their Russian names as they appear in the archival files. (Russian was the *lingua franca* of the Soviet Union.) Some familiar names such as those of tsars (Nicholas, Alexander) are given in their Anglicised forms. In the case of foreign citizens, I have used the German, Polish and other spellings.

I have tried to use abbreviations as little as possible. However, in the text as in the endnotes, I have used a few repeatedly: GPU (OPGU, NKVD from 1934 and KGB from 1954) refers to the Soviet secret police; TsDAHO has already been mentioned twice (Tsentral'nyi derzhavnyi arkhiv hromads'kykh ob'iednan', the former Communist Party Archive in Kiev); RGASPI (Rossiiskii gosudarstvennyi arkhiv sotsial'no-politicheskoi istorii) is the former Soviet Communist Party Archive in Moscow; RGVA (Rossiiskii gosudarstvennyi voennyi arkhiv) is a Russian military archive in Moscow; and CAW (Centralne Archiwum Wojskowe) is a Polish military archive in Warsaw.

The sources of illustrations are identified in the list of illustrations. Those without such identifications belong to the author.

First of all I should like to express my gratitude to the Ukrainian archives that granted me access to their holdings. While working on a previous book, I became acquainted with the case files of the executed in Donets'k and Luhans'k, Ukraine. After the publication of that book, without a clear goal in mind I began to read the case files of individuals repressed in Kiev. I frequented the TsDAHO to such an extent that its staff began to call me their 'honoured guest'. Without access to those files, I could not have written the present book.

Reading the case files proved time-consuming. Sometimes it took many hours to decipher just one or two sentences or even words. In most cases, however, after a lunch break or a night's respite, what had earlier appeared indecipherable suddenly and miraculously began to decode itself before my eyes. Sometimes, however, I had to throw up my hands in despair. On such occasions friends and archivists in the reading room came to my rescue. I thank them all.

Heather McCallum deserves special gratitude. She encouraged me to believe that I could write a book on the executed. Without her enthusiasm, encouragement and support, I would not have written this book.

In Kiev, Roman Podkur, Yuri Shapoval and Valerii Vasil'ev have always provided good company. So have George Liber, Tanja Penter, Serhy Yekelchyk and my former graduate students Martin Blackwell and Matt Pauly. In Moscow (and wherever else we happened to be together), Oleg Khlevniuk never failed to stimulate my thinking in our numerous conversations. My *senpai* Takeshi Tomita has always welcomed me back to Tokyo.

The Polonists Andrzej Pepłoński (of Słupsk), Marci Shore and Timothy Snyder have rekindled my interest in Polish history. Without their influence, encouragement and help, the scope of this book would have been much more limited. As always, Jeffrey Burds, Lars Lih, Norman Naimark and Amir Weiner have been excellent companions whose inspiration has been indispensable. I have also benefited from discussions with Orlando Figes, who is completing a book on private lives under Stalin that focuses on survivors in Russia.

I owe much gratitude to those who have read the manuscript at various stages. Several press readers have provided me with penetrating criticisms and invaluable suggestions. Lars Lih and Wook-jin Cheun have read parts of the manuscript and given me helpful feedback. My father-in-law, James W. Morley, has read the entire manuscript and alerted me to broader issues. Astra Irmeja-Šēfere kindly translated a Latvian document used in Chapter 8. At Yale University Press, Robert Shore edited the manuscript with great care. Candida Brazil, Hannah Godfrey and Stephen Kent facilitated the publication of the book. I thank them all.

For research in various archives, I have received grants from the Humanities Initiative, the Graduate School, the Department of History and the Russian and East European Institute of Indiana University and the International Research and Exchanges Board (IREX). In addition, Harvard University's Davis Center and Ukrainian Research Institute have assisted me in various ways. I am grateful to them for all the support I have received.

Last but not least, as always I thank my family, Carol, Naomi and Jun, who have had to put up with a difficult fellow member while I worked on this book.

CHAPTER I

Love with Foreign Diplomats
The Lives of Goroshko and Vasil'eva

Love is often destructive: people have killed others and themselves for love. The ancient Chinese called beautiful women 'nation destroyers' and 'castle destroyers' because they could lead an emperor to sacrifice both for love. Stalin did not sacrifice himself for love; rather, he understood that love could be manipulated for political ends. It is with good reason that love and espionage have been intricately linked throughout history.

In ordinary parlance the terms 'diplomacy' and 'diplomats' are benign, connoting skill, tact, subtlety and other qualities necessary to interhuman and international relations. Yet for Stalin 'diplomacy' and 'diplomats' always signified something more sinister. He knew well how to conduct international diplomacy to advance the interests of his own regime, as many foreign leaders have attested.[1] Yet Stalin always regarded foreign diplomats in the Soviet Union with suspicion. During the Civil War that followed the October Revolution, foreign forces intervened to assist the anti-Bolsheviks. Soon after the Bolshevik victory, diplomatic relations resumed (although the United States did not open diplomatic relations with the Soviet Union until 1933–34). To Stalin, foreign diplomats were agents of the international bourgeoisie bent on destroying the first socialist state. Stalin interpreted even the normal gathering of information on the Soviet Union as spying. In 1940 he noted that 'intelligence starts with acquiring semi-official literature' from other countries. He emphasised that 'intelligence consists not only of maintaining a secret agent masked somewhere in France or England', it also consists of such mundane tasks as the clipping of newspapers.[2] Accordingly, anyone gathering information from published sources was in fact a spy. When the Cold War began after World War II, Stalin marked down American diplomats as 'spies' and noted, 'The American diplomatic service is in its totality an intelligence organization.'[3]

Stalin insisted that a spy must of necessity 'be steeped in poison and gall and should not believe in anyone'.[4] International espionage was fierce and ruthless everywhere, although how fierce it was in Kiev is difficult to determine for one obvious reason: much of it still remains secret. Without doubt, Soviet spies used love ('sexpionage'), as did foreign spies in the Soviet Union. Nevertheless, there was sometimes real love too: spies fell in love with citizens of target countries, and vice versa. In the 1930s, when falling in love with a foreign diplomat meant almost certain death, anyone who had contact with foreign diplomats, or any foreigner for that matter, risked great danger. Diplomats and foreigners were followed everywhere by the Soviet secret police. At some point in the 1930s, the Soviet secret police began to monitor all visitors to foreign embassies and consulates. Some of them were pressed into the service of the Soviet secret police. Many were subsequently repressed as foreign spies.[5] There is no doubt that by the mid-1930s the Soviet secret police had succeeded in severely limiting foreign espionage in Kiev and elsewhere. Given the danger of association with foreigners and the small size of foreign diplomatic services in Kiev in the mid-1930s (only Germany, Poland and Italy had consular offices in Kiev),[6] love affairs with foreign diplomats could not have been common. Nevertheless, such affairs did take place.

Vera Emel'ianovna Goroshko

The story of Vera Emel'ianovna Goroshko (Horoshko), who fell in love with a Polish diplomat and was executed in 1937, is a telling example. Goroshko was born on 14 September 1914 in Kiev and finished seven years of schooling. Her father, Emel'ian Grigor'evich, was a railway engineer, her mother, Evdokiia Aleksandrovna, a homemaker, her brother Petr (eighteen years old in 1937) a metalworker. At the time of her arrest on 22 September 1937, Goroshko, a Ukrainian and a non-party member, lived at 7 Danilivs'ka Street, Flat 7, in Kiev and worked as a ballerina at the Kiev Opera Theatre. She was accused of having been an agent of the Polish intelligence since 1934, conducting 'counter-revolutionary intelligence work' and repeatedly receiving money and gifts for her work. On 7 October 1937 she was sentenced to be shot and three days later the execution was carried out. She was one of eighteen people executed in Kiev on that date. Her records show that she was executed in accordance with Secret Order No. 00485 of the NKVD dated 11 August 1937: the so-called 'Polish Operation', which targeted people connected with Poland.[7] All her personal property was confiscated, including those items impounded at the time of her arrest: an overcoat valued at 700 roubles and female attire valued at 500 roubles, as well as a foreign journal, *Mode* (1:4, 17–18, 2:3–5).

According to the bill of indictment, which, unlike most other documents in the Goroshko file which are written longhand, is neatly typed, the investigators established that from 1934 to the day of her arrest she was 'connected' (*sviazana*) to the Polish consulate in Kiev. In 1934 and 1935 she met repeatedly with the consulate secretary Zaleski, who was 'the intelligence officer [*rezident*] of the Second Department [Military Intelligence] of the Polish General Staff', performed the espionage tasks assigned by him, and received money and gifts in return. After Zaleski's departure from Kiev in 1935, Goroshko maintained contacts with Spiczyński, Karszo and other officers of the Second Department Section of the Polish General Staff. Through the 'diplomatic bag' Goroshko received letters, money and gifts from Zaleski. Goroshko was accused of intending to leave for Poland (1:14).

The Goroshko case is interesting, because Wiktor Zaleski was indeed an officer of the intelligence agency (*placówka*) of the Second Department Section of the Polish General Staff, codenamed 'B–41', using the pseudonym 'Nal Niger', and based in Kiev from October 1933 to May 1935.[8] Likewise Spiczyński, or Captain Aleksander Stpiczyński, was an officer from the same intelligence department, codenamed 'F–8', who worked in Kiev from June 1934 to August 1936. Karszo was Consul Jan Karszo-Siedlewski, codenamed 'Karsz', who worked in Kiev from 1933 or 1934 to November 1937 for the Second Department in his capacity as consul. (Karszo-Siedlewski, according to the then German consul in Kiev, Andor Hencke, was a pleasant and helpful man. He thus went out of his way to help his own country's military intelligence. Hencke stated that Karszo-Siedlewski was well informed politically and that it was always worth one's while to have a discussion with him.)[9] Before he worked in Kiev, Zaleski was stationed in Tbilisi, Georgia, under the

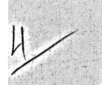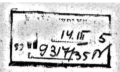

6.III.35 **50**

Sprawozdanie ze spotkania z N-1.

Dnia 5.LLL. miałem spotkanie z N - 1. Spotkałem go o umówionej godzinie na umówionem miejscu. Zabrałem go jak zwykle do samochodu i rozmowa odbywała się podczas jazdy. Na spotkaniu tem był także kolega Napieralski.

Podał on kilka informacyj o charakterze ogólnym i dwie książki wojskowe: jedną swego brata - rezerwisty i jedną czystą, dostarczoną mu przez jego żonę, pracującę w jednym ze składów wojskowych w Kijowi

Nawiązywanie kontaktów idzie mu dość opornie. Nie nagliłem go zbytnio, zalecając raczej maximum ostrożności.

W ostatnich czasach spotkał się on ze swym bratem stryjecznym, który jako technik pracował przy budowie fortyfikacyj na Ukrainie. Sądząc z charakterystyki tego brata, można będzie próbować pozyskać go do pracy. Lubi on wypić i wogóle lubi pieniądzę. Otrzymał on w tym kierunku polecenie.

Poleciłem mu szukać kontaktu na 45 dyw., gdzie ma on też pewne możliwości.

Następne spotkanie wyznaczyłem na 25.III.

Wypłaciłem mu 300 rb.

Nal Niger.

6: On 6 March 1935 'Nal Niger', or Wiktor Zaleski, wrote to Warsaw about his meeting with an informer 'N-1' on the previous day. Zaleski took him to his car where they talked. Zaleski's colleague Napieralski was present, too. N-1 had acquired two military books, one from his brother (a reservist) and another from his wife who worked at a military storehouse in Kiev. N-1 had recently seen his cousin working as a technician at a fortification building site in Kiev. Judging by N-1's characterisation of him, he liked drinking and, generally, money. Zaleski noted that it would be possible to try to recruit him. An appropriate instruction was given to N-1. Zaleski directed him to seek contact with the 45 army command as well, as this would offer further possibilities. Their next appointment was set for 25 March. Zaleski paid N-1 300 roubles.

code name of 'A–14' with the pseudonym 'Anton Sozhko', and after his
stint in Kiev worked in Istanbul as the chief of intelligence with the
code name of 'Gazi/Ghazi II'.[10] Almost certainly Zaleski was a very
important spy, because he was posted to key intelligence posts (Tbilisi,
Kiev and Istanbul). It was from these posts, among others, that Poland
operated the 'Promethean Movement', an 'anticommunist international,
designed to destroy the Soviet Union and to create independent states
from its republics' in the 1920s and 1930s. 'It brought together grand
strategists of Warsaw and exiled patriots [Ukrainians, Georgians, Azeris
and others] whose attempts to found independent states had been
thwarted by the Bolsheviks.' It was 'supported by European powers
hostile to the Soviet Union, morally by Britain and France, politically
and financially by Poland'.[11]

Zaleski's files in the Central Military Archive in Warsaw contain a
large number of reports filed by him from Kiev. Like all good spies, he
reported on anything of potential value. He travelled widely in Ukraine
and sent Warsaw reports on railways, airports, telecommunications,
industry, agriculture, military exercises, the movements of officers and
soldiers and many other subjects, with press clippings, photographs and
hand-drawn diagrams of airports and bridges attached to some reports.
At one point he even bought a Japanese dictionary in Kiev and sent it
to Warsaw, presumably believing that it would be useful for intelligence.
Naturally, as he acknowledges in his reports to Warsaw, he was followed
and watched by the Soviet secret police.[12] In Istanbul Zaleski succeeded
in creating a special intelligence cell called 'Hussein' and worked hard
both to establish closer contact with the agents already working inside
the Soviet Union and to send new ones there too. As he acknowledged
in one of his reports to Warsaw, his participation in the Promethean
Movement was quickly detected by the Soviet intelligence.[13]

It is this Polish intelligence officer with whom Goroshko had a
love affair. Possibly this love affair was genuine on both sides. It is also
conceivable that Zaleski used the Goroshko in the hope of reaching the
Ukrainian political higher-ups. Even had Goroshko proved less useful,
her relations and acquaintances might have provided useful information:
as Illustration 6 shows, informers' family members and acquaintances
were targeted for recruitment. The absence of any information in
Zaleski's massive official files suggesting his connection to Goroshko
is puzzling. Had she been a useful source, she would surely have been

noted in official documents. On the other hand, if the relationship was strictly or primarily a personal one, then the absence of official documentation makes eminent sense.

The handwritten records of Goroshko's interrogation by the NKVD strongly suggest that her association with Zaleski was not an ordinary or business one, but a matter of love, at least on her part. The records are of much interest, because Goroshko, unlike many others in similar circumstances, was never broken by the interrogators and denied all charges against her. Her raw voice comes through clearly in her records. Three days after her arrest she was first interrogated by the NKVD's Lieutenant Iakovlev (who conducted all her interrogations) (1:10–11):

Q: The investigator possesses information that you are an agent of the Polish intelligence. Tell me under what circumstances you were drawn to espionage activity.

A: No. I have never been drawn to espionage activity by anyone.

Q: Whom do you know among the officials of the Polish consulate in the city of Kiev?

A: Among the officials of the Polish consulate I know: Albert Spiczyński,[14] Jan and Piotr (I don't know their surnames). I also know Wiktor Zaleski, a former secretary at the consulate, who left Kiev in 1935.

Q: With whom from among those consular officials you have mentioned did you meet?

A: I met with all of them, because I was very often at the consulate. Wiktor Zaleski courted me and I saw him more often than other officials.

Q: When did you last see him?

A: After Zaleski's departure for Poland, I saw him on 30 March 1936, when he came to Kiev for several days. Zaleski also came to Kiev in March 1937, but I did not see him, because he was in Kiev for just a day. I knew about it from Jan, whom I saw specifically to find out about Zaleski's visit to Kiev.

Протокол допроса обвиняемой—
Горошко Веры Емельяновны
от 25/IX 37г.

Вопрос: Следствие располагает данными, что Вы являетесь агентом польской разведки. Расскажите при каких обстоятельствах Вы привлечены были к шпионской деятельности.

Ответ: Нет. Я к шпионской деятельности не была никем привлечена.

Вопрос: Кого Вы знаете из сотрудников польского консульства в г. Киеве.

Ответ: Из сотрудников польского консульства я знала: Сошинского Альберта, Яна и Петра (фамилии их не знаю). Знала также Виктора Залесского 2-го секретаря консульства, уехавшего в 1935г. из Киева.

Вопрос: С кем из упоминаемых сотрудников консульства Вы встречались.

Ответ: Встречалась со всеми, так как очень часто бывала в консульстве. Ухаживал за мной Залесский Виктор и с ним я встречалась больше, чем с остальными сотрудниками.

Вопрос: Когда Вы последний раз виделись с Залесским.

Ответ: После отъезда Залесского в Польшу, я его видел 30 марта 1936г., когда он приезжал в Киев на несколько дней. Залесский в марте 1937г. также был в Киеве, но я ... как он был в Киеве всего ...

7: Goroshko's 25 September 1937 interrogation record.

Q: When and under what circumstances did you begin to visit the Polish consulate?

A: In 1934 at the Continental restaurant several ballerinas and I got acquainted with those consular officials I have mentioned. Someone called Duperama, a visitor to the restaurant, introduced us to them. Who he is and what he does I don't know. After that I began to visit the consulate. Because Zaleski courted me, I visited the consulate very often. This continued until Zaleski's departure from Kiev. After his departure, I never went to the consulate.

Q: Did you maintain contact with Zaleski after his departure from Kiev and how?

A: I received letters from Zaleski. These letters were handed to me by the consular official Albert. I wrote back to Zaleski through him.

Q: Whom among the consular officials did you see after Zaleski's departure?

A: I saw them all and Spiczyński most often.

Q: Name those ballerinas who visited the consulate with you.

A: Zhenia Gofman, Nadia Kotlova, Valia Iakub, Ol'ga Kop [Kopp].

Q: Did you receive money and gifts from the consular officials?

A: I received gifts and money from the former secretary of the consulate, Zaleski.

Q: How many times did you receive money and how much?

A: I received money several times, but I don't remember how much. I received 100, 200, 300 and 400 roubles and one time more than 400 roubles.

Q: Did you happen to go to Moscow and Leningrad with Zaleski? With whom among the consular officials in Moscow and Leningrad did you get acquainted?

A: I went to Moscow and Leningrad with Zaleski to have a good time before his departure for Poland in March 1935. In Leningrad he acquainted me with no one from the consulate, but in Moscow when I was at a station he introduced me to a consular official whose name I don't recall.

Q: Did you intend to leave for Poland?

A: Yes. I wanted to go with Zaleski, but he said that it was impossible, because he'd lose his job.

Q: You are telling a lie. You were drawn to espionage activity and are an agent of the Polish intelligence. I demand frank confessions on this matter.

A: I was not drawn to espionage activity.

The interrogation ended here, and Goroshko signed the interrogation minutes (1:11zv.). She appears frank and honest, hiding nothing. No physical pressure seems to have been applied at this stage. In light of the fact that any association with a spy was fatal in the political climate of the 1930s, her apparent naïveté is stunning.

The following day, on 26 September 1937, the interrogation resumed (1:12–13):

Q: Name your acquaintances whom you saw.

A: I saw Doctor Kholar [Cholar?] recently. I visited him at his home by myself and also in company. I strolled with my friends Tamara Levinskaia and Zina Akimova. Apart from Kholar, his friend Leva also came to see us. I don't know anything more about him. The night they came to arrest me, I was at Kholar's home where I was spending the night.

Q: Among the things impounded from you was a photograph of Dmitriev. Who is he?

A: Dmitriev is a police chauffeur. I met him in 1935. Recently I haven't seen him.

The interrogation ended here, and Goroshko signed the minutes. According to the police file, Dmitriev was a chauffeur working for the

NKVD (1:9). It may be that he had been assigned to monitor Goroshko. Why did she have a photograph of Dmitriev and why was it impounded? Quite likely Goroshko had an affair with him.

A few days later, on 1 October 1937, the last interrogation took place (1:13–13zv.):

Q: Clarify your meetings with the Polish consular officials in Kiev.

A: As I have already told you, I began seeing them in 1934. At first, in 1934 and 1935, I saw the consular secretary Wiktor Zaleski. I continued to see him until his departure from Kiev. I last saw him on 30 March 1936 when he came to Kiev for a few days. I saw him very often at his home or at the home of the consular official Spiczyński, in the Mayday Garden, in the square off the Franko Theatre, near the State Bank, in Prorizna Square, near the opera theatre, and in other places. At the beginning of 1936 I saw Albert Spiczyński in the square off the Franko Theatre or at my flat. In 1936 I also saw (two or three times) a consular chauffeur, Krzanowek. I saw him in the square near the Franko Theatre, at a cinema, in the Red May café. In 1937 I saw the consul (whose surname I don't know, only that he is called Jan) twice in the Mayday Garden.

Q: From whom among the consular officials you met did you receive money and gifts?

A: I received money and gifts only from Zaleski. When he left Kiev, I received money and gifts from him through Spiczyński.

Q: Who among the consular officials drew you into espionage activity?

A: No one.

Q: You are telling a lie. I demand a frank confession.

A: I was not drawn into espionage activity.

The interrogation ended here, and Goroshko signed the minutes.

The records probably do not show every word uttered by the interrogator and Goroshko, but Goroshko's voice comes through clearly all the same. Perhaps too naïve to understand the sinister politics of the time, she found foreign diplomatic life infinitely more attractive than the drab Soviet life of the 1930s. It seems likely that she felt betrayed by Zaleski and had not recovered from his treatment of her. Whether Zaleski was in love with Goroshko as well, or used her merely for professional purposes, or both, in the end he chose his career (and his country) over her.[15]

In any event, Goroshko, standing her ground to the end, never admitted that she was a Polish spy. She may have been frightened by her arrest. She was a dancer and, quite possibly, had little understanding of the gravity of the charges against her. It is also possible that she understood all too well but was willing to face death. Or, possibly, she had faith in Soviet justice and believed that no innocent person would be punished. Most likely, she was not tortured. Even if her interrogation records were manipulated, as was often the case, they do not reveal that she gave in to the NKVD. Nevertheless, the typed bill of indictment against Goroshko does not mention that she denied the charges of espionage. Instead, it maintains that Goroshko confessed to her 'crimes'.

Her close connection to those whom the NKVD knew as Polish spies was so evident that the NKVD apparently found it unnecessary to extract an actual confession. Goroshko's denial of the charges meant little, because she, like the vast majority of those indicted in 1937–38, was executed in extra-judiciary fashion—*without* trial. Goroshko was not an exception.[16]

Goroshko was arrested in the middle of the so-called 'Polish Operation'. She was one of some 111,091 people sentenced to be shot as part of it.[17] She was executed on 10 October 1937 at the age of twenty-three. Nine days *after* she was executed, the military tribunal in Kiev signed its approval of her bill of indictment. More than fifty years later, in 1988, at the time of *perestroika* and *glasnost'*, the Ukrainian KGB enquired of the Special Archive in Moscow (which possessed information on foreign intelligence personnel who worked in the Soviet Union) whether there was any information linking Goroshko to the 'special services of bourgeois Poland' (i.e., the Second Polish Republic before World War II). Within a week, the Special Archive reported that it had found no such information (1:21–21zv.). In 1989 Goroshko was finally rehabilitated. No surviving relations were found at the time.

More than fifty years after her death, it became known that, like so many others executed in Kiev, Goroshko's remains were buried in what became the mass graves in Bykivnia in Kiev.[18]

There is no evidence to suggest that Goroshko was ever a Polish agent. However, a perusal of her file suggests a striking alternative possibility. Could she have been used by the NKVD to monitor Zaleski and other Polish diplomats and spies? Was Dmitriev, the NKVD driver, there to assist rather than monitor her?

Unlike in many other cases (for instance, that of Vasil'eva which follows the Goroshko case in the present chapter), the bill of indictment against Goroshko is short, with no depositions of witnesses and no references from anyone such as her superiors, colleagues, neighbours and others concerning her character, life or work. This may explain why the bill noted wrongly that Goroshko had confessed to her crimes. The bill does not even mention that there was no material evidence in the case. Furthermore, an extensive investigation of her dancing career (for example, the roles she played) in archives and museums has so far revealed nothing, even though the colleagues she mentions—Gofman, Kotlova, Iakub, Kopp and Akimova—all appear in the programmes of the mid-1930s at the Kiev Opera Theatre.[19]

All this is odd. It is possible that Goroshko was a largely unknown junior ballerina, but almost all the colleagues mentioned in her file were established ballerinas. It seems far more likely, then, that her career had all but ended by the mid-1930s because of her connection to Zaleski. Her encounter with Zaleski may have been accidental on her part (although perhaps not on that of Zaleski, who was always looking for reliable informers), but once the NKVD detected the affair, it may well have forced her to spy on Zaleski and other Poles. Goroshko probably did not provide much information to the NKVD or, as was often alleged with regard to other informers, perhaps misinformed the NKVD,[20] which in turn feared that Goroshko had been recruited by the Poles. This would have led to her subsequent arrest on espionage charges.

Zaleski may have been aware of the Soviet intrigue. The Central Military Archive in Warsaw contains a report written by him to his superior Jerzy Niezbrzycki on 24 March 1935. In it he discusses a 'social conversation' he had with the ballet master 'Zhokov' (probably Leonid A. Zhukov), a 'degenerate drunkard', who told him that the Ukrainian

8: The Kiev Opera Theatre in 2006. Goroshko probably danced there in the 1930s. Completed in 1901, the theatre is known also for the fact that in 1911 the Russian prime minister Petr Stolypin was assassinated there.

secret police chief Vsevolod Balyts'kyi had told him that 'his little girls could meet with foreigners whenever they wanted'.[21] So Goroshko may have been one of Balyts'kyi's 'little girls'. Formerly a Polish intelligence officer stationed in Ukraine, Niezbrzycki encouraged his subordinates to cultivate Ukrainian women, thus playing the 'delicate role of long-distance national security pimp'.[22] This may mean that Zaleski courted Goroshko, fully aware of her possible connections with the Soviet secret police. Probably both the Soviet and the Polish sides sought to use Goroshko.

The bill of indictment against Goroshko may well be accurate in recording that she confessed to her 'crime'. The police accused her of misinformation or disinformation while she was working for them; that is, she did not betray her Polish lover. She understood the implications of the accusations and was broken in the end. Yet the secret police chose not to include documents about their operations in her case file. This is merely one of a number of possible scenarios, none of which disproves that Goroshko was killed for love.

Ol'ga Semenovna Vasil'eva

Like Goroshko, Ol'ga Semenovna Vasil'eva fell in love with a foreign diplomat. Unlike Goroshko, Vasil'eva incriminated herself, if only indirectly. The result was the same: execution.

Vasil'eva was born in 1896, in Rawa (or Rava Rus'ka), Galicia (a part of Austria till 1918, then of Poland, and after World War II of Soviet Ukraine), into the family of a border guard. An ethnic Russian, she was a Soviet citizen, non-party member, literate but with only an elementary education, and worked as a seamstress in Kiev's military workshops. Vasil'eva was arrested on 4 February 1938 and executed on 7 October 1938. She was one of twenty-eight people executed in Kiev on that date. At the time of her arrest, she was living at 78 Zhylians'ka, Flat 2, in Kiev.[23]

According to the typed bill of indictment, Vasil'eva became acquainted with the German citizen Franz F. Gut, who from 1924 worked as an official at the German consulate in Kharkiv (then the capital of Soviet Ukraine). However, Gut may well have been Franz Huth. Huth was born in 1894 in the German settlement of Altnassau in the Crimea. In 1922 Huth was hired to work at the German consulate in Kharkiv as a carpenter and cleaner, and security guard on the night shift. His citizenship, according to the German consul Siegfried Hey, was not fully established, because as a 'civilian prisoner' (during World War I) he had had his 'paper' (passport) confiscated by the Russian authorities. Huth spoke both German and Russian.[24] Hence, if 'Gut' was Huth, he was not a diplomat, as the bill of indictment claimed, but merely a worker at the consulate. At any rate, in 1926 Vasil'eva was allegedly recruited by Gut to conduct espionage work in the interests of German intelligence. Under the guise of being his wife, Vasil'eva accompanied him to Kharkiv and, over many years, allegedly gave him the information she collected at the request of German intelligence. In the period 1926–29, for example, she provided information on housing construction, workers' living space and political mood, and the factories in Kiev. In 1928 she took a holiday with him at the expense of the German consulate. In 1929 Gut left for Germany, thence to Canada and later to Alaska.[25] Vasil'eva continued to correspond with him until the day of her arrest (23–24).

For whatever reason Vasil'eva seems to have been left in limbo for more than four months after her arrest. In what appears to have been her first interrogation on 21 June 1938, she was asked whether she knew Gut (7–8):

> Yes, I know him well. I first met him in 1923 in the Crimea. At the time he was in the wine-making business, but he left for where I don't know, and I lost contact with him until 1925. In 1925 Gut came to see me in Kiev, and told me that he was working as an official at the German consulate in the city of Kharkiv.
>
> Then he left for Kharkiv, but I stayed in Kiev and kept corresponding with him until 1928.
>
> I correct myself: Gut came to see me in Kiev every year for a few days or a few hours. But in 1928 Gut came to me in Kiev and we began to live together because by then we were already lovers. We went to Alushta in the Crimea and lived together for two weeks as husband and wife, but I did not register my marriage with the ZAGS [civilian registry office].
>
> After two weeks in the Crimea, we went to Kharkiv where I spent a day and came back to Kiev.
>
> In Kharkiv I stayed at a hotel, but Gut had a flat in the consulate and I did not go there. In 1928 [someone marked here '1929?'] I received letters from Gut that he was to leave for Canada from where I received letters until 1934. I also wrote to him in Canada until 1933, but after that I lost contact with him.

It was quite common in the 1920s for couples not to bother to register their marriages. Was Gut actually a German spy? Was his wine-making business a front for espionage? Where was he between 1923 and 1925? (It is possible that Vasil'eva met him not in 1923 but in 1922, before he was hired by the German consulate.) Why did he leave for Canada? These questions remain unanswered. Asked whether she had ever visited the German consulate, Vasil'eva answered that she had not. Asked whether she had ever received money from Gut, she likewise responded negatively. She never received any material help from him: even though he offered money, she did not take it because she already had money. The interrogator told her that he had evidence that Vasil'eva was an agent of the German intelligence and had conducted espionage work on Soviet territory. When asked whether she would confirm the allegation, she responded, 'No, I don't confirm the charge. I was never an agent

I

Вопрос: Вы знаете Губа Франца Фридеховича довича и какие были у Вас с ним взаимоотношения.

Ответ: Да, знаю. Я его хорошо с ним и первый раз познакомилась. В 1923году в Крыму. он тогда занимался воен делом, после он выехал неизвестно куда, и я с ним связь потеряла до 1925года. В 1925году Губ приехал в город Киев ко мне, и мне рассказал что он работал в городе Харькове в германском консульстве сотрудником.

После этого он Губ поехал в Харьков я же осталась в Киеве и вела с ним переписку до 1928. Оговорилась. Губ ко мне каждой год приезжал гор. Киев на несколько дней или часов Но в 1928году Губ приехал ко мне в Киев, мы с ним уже сошлись. Я с ним стала жить. Поехали в Крым город Алушта где я с Губом прожила 2 недели как муж и жена, но я в заксе не регистрирована. Пробыли две недели в Крым

В. Васильева

9: Vasil'eva's 21 June 1938 interrogation record, from her file.

of the German intelligence and never engaged in espionage' (9). There the interrogation ended.

Three weeks later, on 15 July 1938, when she was interrogated a second time, Vasil'eva changed her story. Now she confessed to being a 'German spy'. After renewing contact with Gut in 1925, 'I understood that Gut got involved with me for espionage purposes'. What had changed between interrogations? Was she tortured physically or psychologically? Vasil'eva continued: 'Yes, I helped him in his espionage work, as I was in love with him' (11). She added (13–14):

> [In 1926 when Gut came to Kiev] he told me that in Germany people lived better, food and goods were plentiful and cheap, the workers had bicycles and on days off went to resorts for holiday-making. He said further, we'd get married and leave for Germany, and asked whether I'd agree to go to Germany. I said, yes, as your wife I'll go wherever you go. After that he said that we'd need to work for a while in the Soviet Union in the interests of the German people, because the German people are interested in what is happening in the Soviet Union. By my silence I gave him my consent that as his future wife I would agree to everything. From that time I became his informer.

The following day Vasil'eva was interrogated again and confirmed what she had said the day before. Yet when the interrogator asked her whether in her letters to Gut she informed on and slandered the Soviet Union, she responded: 'In my letters I never informed on anything, because I understood that letters were being monitored [by the secret police] and that I could be exposed by the Soviet organs' (17).

Vasil'eva confessed to no concrete crimes. She merely said that as a 'wife' she was ready to do anything for her 'husband'. What her carefully worded statement suggests is that she confessed to being guilty by default: as the wife of a German 'spy', she was by definition an informer. Most likely this was the logic the interrogator had pounded into her. Vasil'eva seems to have been broken by this false logic regarding spousal loyalty and treachery. She confessed to the minimum in order to survive the interrogation. Unlike Goroshko, Vasil'eva was probably aware of the danger of her foreign connections and knew that her correspondence with her German lover would be read by the Soviet secret police.

Unable to find any evidence of espionage, the interrogators seem to have reasoned that Vasil'eva was an experienced operative who had carefully avoided leaving traces of her activities in her correspondence with her German 'spy master', Gut.

On the day Vasil'eva confessed to 'espionage activity', three witnesses were interrogated. One said that Vasil'eva lived very modestly and did not participate in politics. Another, her neighbour, testified that Vasil'eva considered Gut her future husband, but when he left for Canada, Vasil'eva had said that he had turned out to be a 'scoundrel'. All the same, she continued to correspond with him. Clearly she still loved him. Yet another witness gave testimony that Vasil'eva had no acquaintances, did not go out, and led a very modest life as a hard-working dressmaker (19–22). No incriminating testimonies were gathered from the witnesses. The bill of indictment notes that there was no 'material evidence' in the case (24). Yet on 1 October 1938 Vasil'eva was sentenced, like Goroshko without trial, to be shot, and was executed six days later at the age of forty-two. Her execution took place in accordance with NKVD's Special Order No. 00606 of 17 September 1937 (24), which was issued to expedite the Polish Operation as well as other similar terror operations.[26]

In 1989, when Vasil'eva's case was reconsidered in the general rehabilitation campaign of the *glasnost'* era, the Soviet authorities found no evidence against her apart from her own confessions. The authorities tried to locate her mother, the sole known relative, Emiliia Matveevna Vasil'eva, in vain (28). Had she been alive, she would have been 119 years old. Only in the 1990s, more than half a century after her death, did it become known that, like Goroshko, Vasil'eva's remains were buried in a mass grave in Bykivnia.[27]

The Soviet Union of the 1930s was a country under siege. Not without reason did Stalin believe that the capitalist countries were bent on destroying it. Some nations were more suspect than others. In the 1930s, three were perceived as particularly dangerous, Germany, Poland and Japan, all of which were suspected of planning serious campaigns against the Soviet Union.[28] Contact with foreigners from these countries, particularly diplomats, was to be avoided by Soviet citizens on pain of death. Clearly, falling in love with German or Polish consular employees was a fatal mistake. Goroshko's and Vasil'eva's were probably genuine love affairs. Both were straightforward about their relations with their lovers. Ultimately, the affairs were ended by the men. Although both Polish and Soviet authorities may have tried to use Goroshko for espionage purposes, it is doubtful that she helped either side, for it was love, not politics, that mattered to her.

CHAPTER 2

Informers

The Story of Moshinskaia and Others

Like other dictatorships, the Soviet Union deployed a wide network of secret police functionaries and their collaborators and informers. Because of the nature of such operations, it is not easy to grasp the full extent of Soviet secret police activities. According to one comparative study of the Soviet secret police under Stalin and the Gestapo under Hitler, there were

> 7,500 persons employed in the Gestapo against 366,000 working for the NKVD (including gulag personnel). That implies a saturation rate of one secret policeman per ten thousand population in the German case and one per *five hundred* of population (twenty times as great!) in the second. Even if later research requires some adjustment of these figures, it is not likely to change the difference in their order of magnitude.[1]

What is certain is that the network was extensive. In 1937 the NKVD chief boasted that unlike the tsarist police the Soviet secret police were an organ of the people: among the people there were 'millions of informers'—'our eyes and ears'.[2] This did not mean that the NKVD was omniscient. Far from it. Therefore there was a perceived need for secret informers and collaborators, or *seksoty* (*sekretnye sotrudniki*). The extent of this secret network of informers is difficult to establish. When a regime that relies for its legitimacy on its secret police collapses, the extent of its use of informers often comes to light. Thus after the collapse of East European Communism, it became known that numerous individual citizens voluntarily informed or were coerced to inform on their neighbours, colleagues, friends, relations and sometimes even spouses.[3] It is now known that in the 1930s the hero of the 1956 Hungarian Revolution, Imre Nagy, had worked in Moscow for the Soviet secret police, under the code name 'Volodia'. His work contributed to the downfall of many Hungarian Communists in Moscow.[4] Unfortunately for historians (but perhaps fortunately for many citizens of the former Soviet Union), in Ukraine as in Russia the collapse of the Soviet regime has not yet led to a full disclosure of the secret police's informer network.

Becoming an informer is a choice with moral implications, but it is sometimes one made without any real alternatives. Taking advantage of politically, morally and otherwise compromised people and targeting them for recruitment is a practice that is not limited to dictatorships. Though not publicly discussed, it is practised in democracies as well, as is sometimes revealed in sensational fashion. Rumour persists that Stalin himself had been a secret police agent under the tsar. It is unlikely, but he did help Roman Malinovskii, a Bolshevik leader, to get elected to the Russian Duma in 1912, apparently unaware that he was a police agent. It is known that Lenin was deeply shaken by the revelation, made after the October Revolution, that Malinovksii, his trusted colleague, had been a tsarist police agent. Malinovksii, a Pole born in tsarist Russia, was executed by Lenin in 1918.[5]

Just like its tsarist predecessor, the Soviet secret police's informer network extended far beyond the borders of the Soviet Union. The Soviet secret police managed to recruit unknown numbers of émigrés abroad, using threats, nostalgia, blackmail or whatever other means were available. One example is that of the husband of the poet Marina Tsvetaeva, Sergei Efron, who was recruited in Paris around 1930. Efron was executed as a foreign spy in Moscow in October 1941 even though he refused to confess to his 'crime'. Shortly before his execution, Tsvetaeva hanged herself. (Some believe that she had been under pressure to act as an informer.)[6]

Clearly some people believed that becoming a police informer would protect them or at least give them a better chance of survival. Although there is no evidence that the police actually promised protection, all assumed it to be the case. Some volunteered, others were coerced. Some informers survived the Great Terror, others did not. Some were paid, others were not. Some were proud of working to uncover 'enemies', others ashamed. This business was the most secretive aspect of life under Stalin: even the spouses and families of informers did not normally know of their secret life. In numerous cases, the lives of informers were ruined as a result of their activities.

Iadviga Feliksovna Moshinskaia

The story of Iadviga Feliksovna Moshinskaia is complex, but at the same time it is representative of the NKVD's convoluted interrogations of its own informers. Moshinskaia became a police informer in 1934, was arrested on 26 August 1937, sentenced to be shot on 26 November 1937, and executed on 7 December 1937 in Kiev, at the age of twenty-six. (She was one of forty people executed in Kiev on that day.) At the time of her arrest she was living at 5 Mala Zhytomyrs'ka, Flat 16, in Kiev. She was born in 1911 to the family of a Polish clergyman in Bila Tserkva, not far from Kiev. Until she was arrested she worked as a translator and literary editor at *Głos Radziecki* ('Soviet Voice'), a Polish-language newspaper of the Central Committee of the Communist Party of Ukraine. She held this post even though she was not a party member.[7] At the time of her arrest she had two brothers, agronomist Karl, 29, and livestock specialist Kazimir, 27, as well as three sisters, seamstress Anel', 39, housewife Sof'ia, 31, and teacher Mariia, 23, but when she was rehabilitated in 1989, the Soviet authorities could find no surviving relatives. At the time of her arrest, her mother, Balbina Pavlovna, was apparently still alive and in her sixties, but her father's fate is not known.[8]

Moshinskaia was originally accused of conducting anti-Soviet agitation and counter-revolutionary activities against the Soviet regime, but on 11 November 1937 the gravamen of her case was changed to espionage activity in the interests of 'a foreign country' (obviously Poland). Later, the espionage charges were dropped and the original accusations reinstated (1–4).

Her case file suggests that Moshinskaia was not interrogated until 14 November 1937, two and half months after her arrest. She confirmed that her father was a 'servant of the Catholic Church' and had a house and half a hectare of land, and that many of her acquaintances from her student years had been arrested as participants in a 'Polish Fascist organisation'. When the interrogator asked, 'By whom of those [Polish Fascists] were

10: Moshinskaia's 1937 trade union membership card, from her file.

you involved in the Polish nationalist counter-revolutionary organisation that existed at the Polish Pedagogical Institute [in Kiev from which she had graduated three years earlier]?' she answered:

> By no one. I was not recruited into the counter-revolutionary organisation and I didn't know about the existence of such an

organisation at the Polish Pedagogical Institute when I studied there. As a result when the 'Polish Military Organisation' [POW, 'Polish nationalist counter-revolutionary organisation']⁹ was uncovered [in 1933], I went to student meetings and learnt that the teachers of the pedagogical institute were members of this counter-revolutionary organisation.

Although the interrogator retorted that Moshinskaia was lying and that he knew her to be a member of the POW and that she had engaged in espionage for Poland, she maintained her innocence: 'I categorically deny this accusation. I was not a member of the POW and did not engage in espionage activity on the territory of the Soviet Union' (10–12).

Moshinskaia worked at the office of *Głos Radziecki* from 1 November 1935 to 26 August 1937. As at the institute, many colleagues at the newspaper had been arrested as members of the POW. She insisted that their counter-revolutionary activities were unknown to her and that they had not drawn her into their organisation. When the interrogator then tried to induce her to admit that she had conducted counter-revolutionary agitation and had slandered the Soviet Union, she categorically denied that charge as well. The interrogator next presented the testimony of a witness, Elena Al'binova Rybinskaia (a teacher, and also a proofreader at the newspaper), that Moshinskaia conducted agitation concerning the oppression of the Poles in the USSR and that she was connected with 'enemies of the people'. Moshinskaia replied:

> I know Elena Rybinskaia well, but I have no personal score to settle with her. I confirm her testimony that concerns my contact with the enemies of the people Ianuteskii [?], Perlin [?] and others, but with regard to the anti-Soviet agitation about the oppression of the Poles in the USSR and [the superiority of] Polish culture I deny her testimony.

When the interrogator, Dobryk, demanded an explanation of her 'clandestine' (and 'counter-revolutionary') manipulation of text, Moshinskaia admitted that she was guilty. In an essay discussing 'enemy activity' within a party organisation, she translated 'the party should learn a lesson' as 'the party has to be an example', and had dropped an entire paragraph. This made the article read like counter-revolutionary agitation. Her records at this point seem to suggest that she intentionally mistranslated what thus became a 'counter-revolutionary' article (15). Yet the tone of this particular section is at odds with the rest of her records, suggesting that a war of wills may have gone on between Dobryk and Moshinskaia, who most probably insisted that the mistake was not intentional. Such accusations against writers, translators, interpreters and radio newsreaders working in non-Russian languages, suggesting that they intentionally distorted the message of the Communist Party and the Soviet government for 'counter-revolutionary' purposes, were quite common at the time. It is not known what Moshinskaia's mother tongue was. It was probably Polish, but it is likely that her command of Ukrainian and Russian was nonetheless better than her Polish.[10] (In 1926, 48.4 percent of the Poles in Ukraine listed Ukrainian, and 44.2 percent Polish, as their mother tongue.)[11] The interrogations were conducted in Russian, and the records, also in Russian, suggest that Moshinskaia's Russian was fluent. In any case, according to a report by the Polish consul Piotr Kurnicki that appears to date from the mid-1930s, the state of affairs at the Polish Pedagogical Institute (PIP) was dismal:

> The level of knowledge of the students is awfully low. The majority of students are mobilised to work in the field and do not have a command of written or even spoken Polish. The majority of instructors, even of the Polish language, Polish history and Polish literature, are of foreign nationality. Even the most elementary textbooks are lacking.[12]

So Moshinskaia's knowledge of the Polish language was probably less than perfect.

In the wake of the POW affair (see Chapter 12), Polish culture was under attack. By 1934 all the Polish Catholic churches were closed in Kiev.[13] Educational institutions fared slightly better, though many Polish professors and instructors were arrested or expelled and, as Kurnicki notes, their positions were often taken by people of non-Polish origin (such as Russians and Ukrainians). Still, the PIP and other Polish-language higher education establishments continued to expand in Kiev and elsewhere. The PIP reached its high point of enrolment in 1935, only to be abolished in the same year.[14]

Dobryk introduced another witness, Regina Kogan, a literary editor at *Głos Radziecki*, who alleged that Moshinskaia had said that the Soviet peasants were starving, an obvious reference to the Great Famine and its aftermath, and that she had spread provocative rumours about people having better standards of life in capitalist countries. Moshinskaia denied this charge as well: 'I have known Regina Kogan since my time at the Polish Pedagogical Institute. I have no personal score to settle with her. I don't confirm her testimony' (13–16). These denials were not even recorded in the official typed bill of indictment against her.

At this stage Moshinskaia's work for the NKVD was not even referred to by either side. Moshinskaia almost certainly hoped that her status as a secret informer would protect her. Why did she not mention that she was an NKVD informer? Did she fear that the secret police suspected that her work for them had in fact been clandestinely subversive? The NKVD interrogator may have had a hidden agenda to try to implicate her in some grave 'crime'. At any event, the tone of her answers to his questions is confident and firm except in admitting her mistranslation (or 'manipulation').

The testimonies of Rybinskaia and Kogan were in fact more detailed than is apparent from the interrogation records. Rybinskaia, an ethnic Pole, quoted Moshinskaia as saying: 'The Polish nation [in the Soviet Union] as such is oppressed, they [the Soviet regime] don't give any opportunity for the development of Polish literature and Polish arts.' Rybinskaia also tried to present Moshinskaia as an anti-Semite. (This made sense, because in the 1930s, unlike in the later Stalin years, anti-Semitism was still considered a serious offence.) According to Rybinskaia, rumour persisted at the PIP that Moshinskaia was known for recounting anecdotes in which Jewish people always turned out to be 'unworthy', while Poles were always elevated in behaviour. Moshinskaia was 'very furtive by character'. At the institute, Rybinskaia added, Moshinskaia was friendly only with Poles and ignored Jews, Russians and others. 'From all of this,' said Rybinskaia, 'it is clear that she is nationalistically minded' (20zv.). On the face of it, Rybinskaia's testimony may have been damaging, but it was as formulaic as the official press attacks on alleged Polish nationalists at the time. Rybinskaia was probably able to cite such damaging phrases by heart because she proofread anti-Polish nationalist articles almost every day. She may have been forced to give false testimony, or it is also possible, as was often the case, that the interrogator simply wrote the testimony himself and Rybinskaia was obliged to sign it out of fear of arrest. (Conceivably, Rybinskaia, a proofreader, had been accused of failing to detect Moshinskaia's alleged counter-revolutionary agitation.)

Kogan's testimony was equally incriminating. Interestingly, Kogan, a native of Warsaw and probably Jewish (judging from her surname), does not appear to have accused Moshinskaia of anti-Semitism, even though her testimony would have carried weight. This probably implies that Moshinskaia was not really known as an anti-Semite. Instead, Kogan reported Moshinskaia as saying that the people of the USSR, particularly those in the countryside, were starving and that the Soviet regime had ruined agriculture, a clear reference to the sorry state of affairs on the collective farms. She had allegedly praised 'Fascist Poland', contending that the Soviet Union would be defeated in a forthcoming war because the Soviet regime had ruined the country and caused suffering owing to all kinds of deprivations and that things could not go on in that way any longer (26–27). These accusations are as formulaic as Rybinskaia's and cannot be taken at face value. Kogan, too, probably felt pressured to testify against her colleague out of fear of being arrested herself.

Moshinskaia denied the accusations. As in many other cases, the NKVD could have indicted her and had her shot without obtaining a confession. Yet on 15 November 1937 the interrogator Dobryk used a different tactic, and the case shifted dramatically. The change was not precipitated by the two testimonies used against her the day before. Rather, Dobryk abruptly asked Moshinskaia when she had been drawn into secret work for the NKVD. She responded (17): 'On 7 March 1934, while a student at the Polish Pedagogical Institute in Kiev, I voluntarily gave a commitment to the NKVD that I would assist it in discovering the enemies of the people mainly among my acquaintances, the students of the Pedagogical Institute and the instructors.' When asked whether she had fulfilled her commitment to the NKVD, Moshinskaia said (17–18):

No, because I gave the NKVD absolutely no material about my circle which contained enemies of the people whom I could have unmasked but did not. These people were unmasked not by me, but by other people. I plead guilty to the fact that, having the possibility of helping the NKVD in unmasking enemies, I did not do so.

Dobryk suggested that Moshinskaia's crime was more egregious, noting that, while working as a secret collaborator for the NKVD, she 'encumbered' it with insignificant material, thereby distracting the NKVD's attention from her circle. When Dobryk asked her whether she would plead guilty to this crime, she said, 'Yes, I plead guilty' (18). Was her 'crime' simply fabricated by the police? Almost certainly it was, as will be discussed shortly. In any case, she was broken.

As it turns out, Moshinskaia had been working for the secret police under the pseudonym of 'Raia' (30). The printed official bill of indictment refers to pages 17–18 of her file for this information, but the pages are missing. Either some of her interrogation records were withdrawn at some point by the police, or they were never put in the file in the first place, being deemed too sensitive in nature.

The question arises whether Moshinskaia actually volunteered, as she testified, to work secretly for the NKVD; it is possible, but not likely. According to one witness, Moshinskaia always hid her background (the fact that she was a daughter of a Catholic clergyman) and 'in particular hid the fact that she had a mother, living in Bila Tserkva— why, I don't know' (28–29). Obviously Moshinskaia was afraid that her background might prove a liability. Simply being of Polish descent was becoming increasingly dangerous by the mid-1930s, but being the daughter of a priest, let alone a Polish Catholic priest, had always been dangerous. Nevertheless, she had managed to enter the PIP. This suggests two possibilities: she did indeed volunteer to become a secret informer to protect herself, possibly even be fore she entered the PIP; or she somehow managed to get a place at the Institute but, when her background was later discovered, she came under threat from the NKVD and so began to work for it. Her identity as an NKVD informer almost certainly helped her to gain employment at *Głos Radziecki*, an organ of the Central Committee of the Communist Party of Ukraine, while remaining a non-party member. Perhaps she was even assigned to the newspaper as an informer.

If Moshinskaia was an informer, was she a provocateur as well? This seems unlikely, as she could easily have used that to explain any 'counter-revolutionary' remarks attributed to her by her accusers. What, then, was Moshinskaia's situation with regard to the NKVD? Did she actually do very little for it, hence the NKVD felt betrayed by her? Or did she deliberately protect her colleagues, using her status to create a smokescreen to distract the NKVD from those she knew to be genuinely disposed against the Soviet regime? If the latter was the case, it would mean that she had surreptitiously fought against the regime. Yet this story was almost certainly made up by the NKVD. After all, the police did not know what crimes Moshinskaia might have committed and, as noted above, they changed the charges against her twice between August 1937, when she was arrested, and November 1937, when she was indicted.

In the end she was indicted on a charge of anti-Soviet agitation. She was accused of disinforming the NKVD while working as its secret agent by concealing the 'counter-revolutionary' activities of those around her. There is a note in the official indictment, however, that states that there was no 'material evidence' in the case (31). Like the vast majority of those executed in 1937–38, she was sentenced, without trial, to be shot in accordance with the Polish Operation (34). Moshinskaia was executed at midnight on 7 December 1937 (32). More than half a century later, her remains, like those of so many others, were found in a mass grave in Bykivnia in Kiev.[15]

Selling his Soul

Moshinskaia was not unique in ending up executed after becoming an informer. A similar case, that of Cheslava Nikolaevna Angel'chik, a professor of Polish, is discussed in Chapter 12.

As has recently become known in other former Communist countries such as Poland, priests, regarded as the most virulent opponents of the atheist regime, became targets of intensive police recruitment efforts. Sigizmund Karlovich Kvasnevskii (Kwaśniewski), a sixty-year-old Polish Catholic clergyman, was arrested on 3 June 1937 and executed on 25 September 1937 in Kiev. He was born near Kiev in 1877 and completed his studies at a classical gymnasium in Nemyriv near Vinnytsya, Ukraine. Then, while a medical student in Kiev, he joined a circle of Socialist Revolutionaries. Expelled from university, he went on to graduate from a Roman Catholic seminary in Zhytomiyr and worked in various cities in Ukraine as a priest. In June 1920, during the Polish–Soviet war, he fled to Poland; then in the autumn of the same year he returned to Ukraine, becoming a dean of a Proskuriv (present-day Khmel'nyts'kyi) parish. Arrested repeatedly in 1920, 1923, 1924

11: A typical scene in Bykivnia commemorating the executed with a cross, a photograph, name plates and ribbons, one in blue and yellow for Ukraine and one in red and white for Poland (2006).

and 1926, by 1927 Kvasnevskii had begun to cooperate with the Soviet government. This did not prevent him from being arrested again in 1930 for espionage on behalf of Poland and anti-Soviet activity. He was exiled in Russia.[16] During his 1930 arrest, he is said to have become a secret police informer. (In 1930, at the time of collectivisation and de-kulakisation, there was a concerted effort to destroy village churches everywhere as the centres of old village life. Simultaneously, the secret police arrested priests en masse and made informers of some of them. As a result, almost all religious organisations were infiltrated by the police.)[17] Later Kvasnevskii was bailed out of his exile in Russia and returned to Ukraine with the help of the Polish consul in Kiev. When he was arrested in 1937, he was accused of using his collaboration with the police to conceal and increase his counter-revolutionary activities. He was accused of having maintained contacts with Polish spies since 1921 and of helping anti-Soviet Poles and Catholics. Kvasnevskii incriminated himself as a Polish spy and was executed. Like many others executed in Kiev, he was buried in a mass grave in Bykivnia. He was posthumously rehabilitated in 1989.[18]

Many priests were forced to work for the Soviet secret police. One of the archbishops of the Russian Orthodox Church and the last president of the Moscow Theological Seminary, Varfolomei (Nikolai F. Remov), turned out to have worked for the police. Varfolomei's case is all the more surprising because he clandestinely converted to Catholicism in 1932. (This caused a sensation in the post-Soviet Russian Orthodox community.) Born in 1888 in Moscow, Varfolomei became a learned theologian. He was arrested in 1920 for counter-revolutionary agitation and sentenced to five years of correctional labour. Released early owing to poor health, he was arrested again in Moscow in 1928 for 'hiding a spy'. The spy in question may have been a Frenchman and a secret representative of the Vatican, Bishop Pius Neveu, a long-time resident of Russia and the Soviet Union, whom Varfolomei met in 1928.[19] Varfolomei was only released when he agreed to work for the Soviet secret police: his tasks included reporting on the bishop. Later Varfolomei was accused by the secret police of working with Neveu instead of 'working Neveu'. In the atmosphere of the Soviet all-out attack on all religious authorities, Varfolomei, like some other Orthodox leaders, may have seen a union with the Catholic Church as the only means of survival. The Catholic Church, in turn, saw a golden opportunity to make inroads into the

12: Sigizmund Karlovich
Kvasnevskii.

bastion of the Orthodox Church even though it was under harsh attack. In 1932 Varfolomei seems to have secretly converted to Catholicism under the influence of Neveu, although his conversion may have been a cover for his police-promoted provocation.

Whether Varfolomei sold his soul and became a police provocateur or used his police cover to preserve and advance faith in untoward circumstances is not entirely clear. However, the available evidence appears to support the latter possibility. In early 1935, shortly after the assassination of Sergei Kirov, the party chief in Leningrad, Varfolomei was arrested. He was accused of handing secret information (on conditions in the Russian church, the mood of the believers, the closure of churches, the arrest of priests, popular reactions to the Kirov murder and other matters) to Neveu and of *not* providing the necessary information on Neveu to the secret police. (Varfolomei told Neveu, for instance, that it was impossible to approach the Russian Orthodox Church metropolitan Sergei because he was surrounded by secret police agents and that, in connection with the Kirov murder, 'the Russian people will be happy if they [the Bolsheviks] shoot each other'.)[20] Varfolomei accepted the accusations, noting that he did not pursue any particular goal in providing information to Neveu. Pressed to answer why he had rendered service to Neveu and *not* to the police, Varfolomei responded that he had sought to find 'appropriate material' but could not find any.

The Soviet secret police, however, did not believe Varfolomei's confession. They insisted that he was a double-dealer, a Janus, who had worked with Neveu against the Soviet government. Varfolomei apparently responded that regrettably it was true and then asked for pardon.[21] Is this statement credible? Did the police invent it to present Varfolomei as a crafty double-dealer? If so, why was it necessary, when the records were not meant for publication? Antoine Wenger, who has studied Neveu and Varfolomei in depth, argues that Varfolomei did not collaborate with the police.[22]

Whatever the case, Varfolomei was accused of espionage and terrorist intentions against the leaders of the Soviet government. On 17 June 1935 he was sentenced to be shot. Whether he was actually executed is not known. According to one account, he died in the infirmary of the Butyrki prison on 1 August 1935. When his sisters asked for his body, they were refused. Their request for his ashes was denied as well.[23]

It is likely that the police never trusted Kvasnevskii, Varfolomei and other such secret informers. It would be odd if they had fully trusted the information supplied by those whose political loyalty they suspected to begin with. The police used priests and later destroyed them when they were deemed no longer useful or necessary. Informers of this sort had to act in a duplicitous fashion; as such their behaviour is often puzzling. Such was the case with Nikolai (Nikolai F. Rozanov), archbishop of the Russian (Renovationist) Orthodox Church in Tver' (then in Iaroslavl'). In connection with the Varfolomei affair, Nikolai, along with more than twenty others, was arrested and implicated in a 'Russian Catholic counter-revolutionary organisation of priests'. A secret monastic order, to which Nikolai was accused of belonging, may indeed have existed under the leadership of Varfolomei within the Orthodox Church hierarchy. Nikolai was born in 1873 and was married.[24] He sought out Neveu several times between 1929 and 1933, expressing his interest in a union with Rome. (Like Varfolomei, he saw this as the only way out of the Church's crisis.) Initially Neveu was not sure whether Nikolai was a police provocateur or a sincere but sick person.[25]

Nikolai, like Varfolomei, was indeed a secret informer for the Soviet secret police. As with Varfolomei, however, it is not entirely clear whether Nikolai actually helped the police or simply acted to preserve and advance his faith by using his police cover. The police records suggest that Varfolomei—himself a secret informer for the police, of course—warned Neveu that Nikolai and other acquaintances were working for the police. Neveu was aware of this (although he was not aware of Varfolomei's own police connections).[26] In his interrogations after his arrest, Nikolai categorically denied the charge of harbouring pro-Catholic views as well as of having contact with Neveu.[27] This is odd, because his contact with Neveu must have been sanctioned by the police or, if not, Nikolai could have justified it in those terms anyway. Did he try to prove to the police that he did not meet Neveu of his own volition? Or did the police fabricate his interrogation records to cover the trail of provocation against Neveu or the fact of Nikolai's having been recruited as an informer? No clear answer exists. In this case, as in so many others, recovering the voice of the dead turns out to be a formidable task.

Unlike Varfolomei, Nikolai was given a relatively mild sentence: five years of correctional labour. Yet in 1937 Nikolai was executed in the infamous Gulag on the Solovki Islands in the White Sea.[28]

Nikolai A. Tolstoi may be a more clear-cut case, having apparently sold his soul to the NKVD. He was born in 1867 into a noble family with ties to the tsars, and converted from Orthodoxy to Catholicism in the 1890s.[29] In 1919 he moved to Kiev and became the leader of the Uniates (Greek Catholics) in Ukraine. At some point in the 1920s Tolstoi became (voluntarily or otherwise) a police agent, testifying against his colleagues and writing for Soviet newspapers. One of his sons also worked (most likely was coerced to work) for the police. In 1935–36 Tolstoi served as a prosecution witness in the fabricated 'case of the counter-revolutionary Fascist organisation of Roman Catholic and Uniate priests in right-bank Ukraine'. Arrested in December 1937 on charges of spying for Poland and involvement in counter-revolutionary activities aimed at the separation of Ukraine from the Soviet Union, Tolstoi was executed on 4 February 1938.[30] His two sons were also executed.[31]

Another, somewhat different case is that of Aleksandr Petrovich Zubovskii, born in 1895 in Mahiliou (Mogilev) into the family of a member of the Russian clergy. A medical doctor in the city of Voroshylovhrad in the Donbas in eastern Ukraine, he was arrested in February 1931 and accused of being a member of a counter-revolutionary, insurgent organisation of doctors. During his five-month detention, he was recruited by the secret police to inform on his fellow doctors. Unlike Moshinskaia and Kvasnevskii, Zubovskii survived the Great Terror. During World War II, after Voroshylovhrad was occupied by Nazi soldiers, he collaborated with the occupying forces, believing that the Soviet regime had been destroyed for good. He became mayor of the city. But towards the end of the war he was arrested by the Soviet forces in Odesa, tried in Voroshylovhrad in October 1944 and executed in January 1945 as a traitor. Zubovskii testified that, even though he was an informer for the Soviet secret police in 1931, he had done very little for them. He claimed that he had even protected fellow doctors who were true 'enemies' of the Soviet regime. According to his interrogation records, even though he worked for the police as a secret informer, he himself was an enemy of the Soviet regime. He had considered his 1931 arrest 'unjust', but that had not been solely responsible for convincing him to become an 'enemy of the Soviet regime'. What convinced him was his wife's suicide while he was held in detention.[32]

Clearly, collaborating with the police, whether by choice or not, offered little or no protection during the Great Terror. Those who were politically suspect and therefore vulnerable to police repression, such as ministers of the cloth and ethnic minorities (Poles in particular), were targeted for recruitment. Under constant threat, they were given no choice but to agree if they wanted to survive. Whether they actually compromised themselves and actually assisted the police is sometimes difficult to know. Tolstoi was probably completely broken by the police, but Kvasnevskii, Varfolomei, Nikolai and Zubovskii were probably not. Moshinkaia's interrogation records suggest that, however frightened she may have been, she initially stood her ground, declaring her innocence. What, then, was the crime for which she was executed? She appears to have been a reluctant informer and kept her activities as a secret police agent to a minimum. Such reluctance did not please the NKVD. Although this alone would probably have been enough to doom her in 1937–38, the fact that Moshinskaia also was the daughter of a Polish Catholic priest had probably predetermined her fate anyway. Certainly Moshinskaia's alleged 'crimes', like those of so many others, were fabricated by the NKVD. The police were not even sure what charges to bring against her. Her only verifiable 'crime' was being born into the wrong family at the wrong time in the wrong place.

The police knew the kinds of people who were most vulnerable politically and targeted them for recruitment. Priests were one such group, and more cases will be discussed in Chapter 4. Yet the use of the politically suspect as informers by definition was inherently dangerous, because the police often could not trust the information supplied by them. This was a self-defeating game. Indeed, many informers were executed in the end as traitors.

The ubiquitous presence of informers strained individual lives and relations between ordinary people to the extreme. Mutual distrust and fear became the order of the day. The case files of Moshinskaia and other informers show the dire circumstances in which ordinary people found themselves.

CHAPTER 3

A Monarchist's Swan Song?

'Monarchist' was probably the most serious political accusation that could be made in Stalin's Soviet Union. 'Bourgeois', 'kulak', 'Trotskyite' and the like were widely used condemnations, but the term 'monarchist', implying a desire for the restoration of the old regime with the tsar as its head, was the ultimate anathema, signifying the antithesis of the Soviet regime. Indeed, the monarchists were so damned that they had been almost completely exterminated or banished abroad by the time 'Trotskii', 'Trotskyism' or 'Trotskyite' became curses in the 1930s.

Nevertheless, suspicion died hard that some monarchists were still hiding in the Soviet Union, waiting for an opportunity to restore the old regime. The Soviet secret police regarded them as foreign spies willing to support any (even a Fascist) regime against the Soviet Union. In the official discourse of the 1930s 'Trotskyites', 'spies', 'anti-Soviet elements' and other 'enemies of the people' were equated with 'monarchists', because they were portrayed by the Soviet regime as scheming with the 'international bourgeoisie' and Russian 'monarchists' abroad to restore the old, capitalist regime to the country.

In practical terms, anyone closely associated with the old regime was suspected of being a crypto-monarchist and 'restorationist'. Thus, former policemen, government officials, military officers and even industrial engineers and technicians were held to be politically suspect. Popular enmity towards policemen was such that in 1917, even before the Bolsheviks took power, many were lynched as emblems of tsarist political repression. According to a resident of Petrograd, then the capital of Russia:

The only people who remained loyal to the Tsarist government, I recollect, were the police. I do not think that there is much about this in the literature. The police in the streets were called Pharaohs— oppressors of the people. Some of them sniped at the revolutionaries from rooftops and attics. I remember seeing a policeman being dragged off, pale and struggling, by a mob, obviously to his death— that was a terrible sight that I have never forgotten; it gave me a lifelong horror of physical violence.[1]

Once the Russian 'bourgeoisie' had been liquidated or banished abroad as a result of the Revolution and Civil War, those regarded as its former representatives or spokesmen became targets for popular resentment. Thus, industrial engineers and technicians were very often harassed and terrorised by workers on the shop floor. (This phenomenon acquired its own name: 'specialist-baiting'.)

The old (tsarist) military officers comprised a special case. During the Civil War the employment of some of them in the Red Army became a bone of contention among the Bolshevik leaders, with Stalin taking issue with the practice. The end of the Civil War softened the party's position in relation to the employment of old specialists in all spheres of life, alleviating the tension. Yet the party remained suspicious of the tsarist officers. When Stalin embarked on his 'revolution from above' (rapid industrialisation and wholesale collectivisation), using the rhetoric of 'class war', the position of former tsarist officers appeared tenuous indeed. In 1930–31 more than 10,000 of them (the 'All-Union Counter-revolutionary Organisation of Military Officers') were arrested on fabricated charges (Operation 'Spring') and at least 110 were executed.[2] M. N. Tukhachevskii and other prominent Red Army officers and commanders escaped, but in 1937–38 fate caught up with them, and many were arrested and executed.

Their wives and other family members suffered in their wake. Tukhachevskii's spouse, Nina E. Grinevich, was exiled as the wife of an 'enemy of the people' and in 1941 was executed. So were his brothers Aleksandr and Nikolai. His four sisters were sent to the Gulag. His two daughters, when they reached adult age, were arrested. His mother and one sister, Sof'ia, died in the Gulag. What political beliefs they maintained is not known, but it is hard to imagine that they, as family members of a Soviet marshal, entertained monarchist or 'restorationist' thoughts. Yet suspicion persisted, and many Soviet citizens died as a result.

Antonina Zhelikhovskaia's Ordeal

Antonina Ivanovna Zhelikhovskaia was the wife of a former tsarist army officer. In fact her husband, Iosif, whose last name, 'K____', is not easily decipherable from the Zhelikhovskaia file, was long dead: an army officer (captain) who at some point became a police official, he died in 1921. (Under what circumstances is not known.) Born into an army officer's (major's) family in 1871 in Chernihiv (in today's northern Ukraine), Zhelikhovskaia, an ethnic Russian of noble origin, graduated from a gymnasium in Mahilioŭ (Mogilev, in today's Belarus) and married in 1889. After her husband's death, she lived as her son's dependant. On 3 March 1938 Zhelikhovskaia was arrested at her house, 30 Artem Street, Flat 3, in Kiev, and accused of engaging in anti-Soviet activity as a member of a counter-revolutionary organisation.[3]

Being the wife of a tsarist army officer and a policeman was damning enough. To complicate the matter further for Zhelikhovskaia, two of her sons, Arkadii and Ivan, during the Civil War, had emigrated to Yugoslavia, where they were still living at the time of her arrest. From 1929, Zhelikhovskaia was said to have been receiving money from her sons abroad sent to secret addresses (18–19).

The police contended later that at the time of her arrest the 'latest monarchist literature' had been confiscated from her flat (18–19). Yet the record of her arrest and the search of her flat listed only two items taken by the police: her passport and correspondence consisting of sixty-seven items (4). It is conceivable, however, that such literature was contained in the seized correspondence records.

In the end, Zhelikhovskaia was accused of engaging in anti-Soviet agitation, using the economic difficulties of the country for this purpose, and propagating monarchist ideas (18–19). Her alleged membership of a counter-revolutionary organisation was not brought up again. On 8 May 1938 Zhelikhovskaia, classified as belonging to 'category one' (the category to which those who were to be executed were assigned), was sentenced to be shot and two days later was executed (2, 21–22). Oddly, Zhelikhovskaia was indicted in accordance with the Polish Operation, even though she had no connection with Poland (19).[4] Like so many

УССР

Комитет государственной безопасности при Совете Министров УССР

АРХИВ

КГБ при Сов. Министров УССР

СЛЕД. ФОНД

УГОЛОВНОЕ ДЕЛО № 101954

по обвинению _Желиховской_

Антонины Ивановны

Начато „3" III 1938 г.   в _Одном_ томах

Окончено „ " V 1938 г.   Том № 1

После судебного рассмотрения и вступления приговора в силу, настоящее дело подлежит немедленному возвращению в_____	Передача находящихся в производстве уголовных дел, а также взятых из архива дел в другие отделы или органы КГБ, хотя бы и временно, производится исключительно через
(указать название органа КГБ)	
К делу должна быть приобщена копия приговора.	(название учетного аппарата)

Архив №_____

60228

Сдано в архив „ " 19

_63605 фп_

13: The cover of Zhelikhovskaia's case file.

others repressed in Kiev at the time, Zhelikhovskaia was buried in an anonymous mass grave in Bykivnia in Kiev.[5]

Was Zhelikhovskaia a monarchist as accused? The secret police did provide *prima facie* evidence, because, like so many others, Zhelikhovskaia confessed to her alleged crime. A little more than a fortnight after her arrest, on 20 March 1938, she was interrogated by Mushkin of the NKVD:

Q: Do the notes, excerpts and fragments of monarchist literature seized from you at the time of the search belong to you?

A: Yes, they do. I was brought up by military parents in a monarchist spirit. I received the same kind of education in a gymnasium. Later, I married my husband, who was at first an army officer and then became a police officer—he remained a monarchist. I am no longer a young woman. I am sixty-seven years old. All my adult life I believed in monarchy and now in my old age I cannot be re-educated. That's why I kept these notes.

Q: The investigator possesses data proving you guilty of conducting counter-revolutionary agitation. Do you plead guilty to this crime?

A: I have made some remarks of a counter-revolutionary nature, and I plead guilty to them. I have not engaged in organised agitation, because to have done so would have exposed me to the risk of being detained. It would have been all the more dangerous to do so because of my past.

Q: Why did you receive [material] help sent to secret addresses and not to your address?

A: Because I feared the consequences [of using my own address].

Q: Did you ever receive help from a [foreign] consulate?

A: No, never. I received packages and money from abroad, from my sons, by way of banks and Torgsin.[6]

Here the interrogation ended, and Zhelikhovskaia signed the interrogation records (10–10zv.).

In the meantime, several witnesses were deposed to ensure her incrimination. On 2 April 1938 Petr Ivanovich Dzhuzha, 24, who lived at the same address as Zhelikhovskaia, was interviewed. (It is possible that Zhelikhovskaia, unable to afford her own flat, rented just a corner of a room, as was widely practised at the time.) Dzhuzha testified that Zhelikhovskaia was 'monarchistically minded'. He quoted her as saying that life was worse under the Soviet regime than under the tsar; that the Soviet government had impoverished her; and that she was starving (12–13). On the same day, another witness, Nikolai Nikolaevich Grigor'ev, 31, who lived next door to Zhelikhovskaia, also testified that she was 'monarchistically minded'. At the time of some domestic difficulties, she purportedly said, 'See where the Soviet government has led us!' and she praised Fascism, which she regarded as the only correct politics of 'civilisation' (14–15). Like so many similar testimonies, these are so formulaic and stylised that one has to question their authenticity.

Three days after these testimonies and a fortnight after her first interrogation, on 5 April 1938, Zhelikhovskaia was subjected to another session of interrogation by the same Mushkin (11):

Q: Do you plead guilty to the crime presented to you?

A: Yes, I plead guilty to this: having been educated in the old
   spirit, I have expressed discontent with the Soviet system.
   Experiencing material privation and discontented with
   the policies of the Soviet government concerning class
   discrimination, [obligatory government] bonds, elections
   and other issues, I led anti-Soviet agitation to show that
   these measures of the government were wrong—the poem
   'Motherland' you seized from me, composed in a monarchist
   and émigré spirit, belongs to me.

This poem had not been mentioned before. Did Zhelikhovskaia actually write some compromising verse, or did she copy it from a publication?

Her case file contains an envelope which the archivists labelled as 'Poems' (30–32). The contents seem to be random compositions, dated midnight, 10 November 1925 (noted 'New Style') and sharply critical of the Soviet government. The first section, handwritten in pencil, starts with a lament:

> Every nation has its motherland and something dear, but only we—once a great fatherland—have an unfortunate country in ruins, having lost our glorious name. The best people of our motherland have been trampled in the dirt, others are forced to wander through foreign lands and still others have paid with their lives for being Russian and for loving our unfortunate motherland. We don't have a fatherland now, our government is the Council of Old Siberian Robbers [*Sovet Starykh Sibirskikh Razboinkiov* or SSSR] and mobs of Jews [*tolpy Iudeev*] bent on sowing strife and discord abroad as well.[7]

The 'poems' go on to criticise the Soviet government for its inability to create 'anything great' and therefore 'riding on the back of the peasants' while uttering 'only eloquent and loud phrases on the bright future of Communism'. But 'a time will come', the poems continue, 'when the world will see Russia, tormented and distressed, rise to its feet and over Russia the tricolour flag will flutter again'; 'Our motherland will rise again on the pedestal of greatness and power.' The writings refer to the government as the 'Bolshevik horde' and at one point use the past tense to describe a dream: 'Evil triumphed at home but Nemesis was already nearby and the punishing sword cut off the head of the leader whose name is L[enin]' (32zv.). The sentiments are indeed monarchistic and anti-Semitic. Yet did Zhelikhovskaia actually write them? Perhaps, but there is something odd here. The use of the 'New Style' calendar introduced by the Bolshevik government was a small compromise necessitated by daily life. Yet the 'poems' were also generally compliant with the new Russian orthography introduced by the Bolshevik government. This is curious given that monarchists and anti-Bolsheviks abroad refused to accept the new orthography. Would a monarchist use the simplified Soviet orthography in private writings of this sort? Clearly, questions remain regarding the authorship of these 'poems'.

At any rate, the reference to the 'motherland' in Zhelikhovskaia's interrogation record suggests that she was interrogated before the 20 March session. What she may have said in earlier sessions is of course

10/XI 1921 года
К. 51.
25?

T   30

У каждаго народа есть родина
есть что то дорогое, и только
у нас отъ великаго когда-то
Отечества осталась
несчастная разоренная
страна даже потерявшая
свое славное имя. Лучшие
люди нашей родины втоптаны
в грязь многие принуждены
скитаются по чужимъ
государствамъ а другие
заплатили своей жизнью за
то что быть русскими
любили и любимъ свою
несчастную Родину.
И теперь у нас отечества
нету а ~~svoe~~ правительство
представляет собой
Совет Старыхъ Сибирскихъ
разбойниковъ и толпы
иудеевъ стремящихся и
в других государствах

14: The first page of a 'poem' allegedly composed by Zhelikhovskaia.

unknown. What is clear is that her case file as it stands is not complete: documents recorded *before* she was broken are missing from her file. This is supported by an odd document in her file, 'the protocol of an interrogation', dated 15 March 1938, five days before she confessed, which takes the form of a statement by Zhelikhovskaia. She said in it that her sons, Arkadii and Ivan, were students who had emigrated abroad when Denikin (an anti-Bolshevik White officer) occupied Ukraine in 1919. Neither had served in any army, nor had Georgii, another of her sons. She and her husband owned no property. From 1923 or 1924 she corresponded with her sons abroad. In 1924 she began to receive help from them through banks and Torgsin. What they did for a living she did not know. She never received money through foreign consulates. From 1929–30 she began to receive 30–50 roubles regularly from some woman whom she did not know personally. From the postal transfer records, she knew her identity, however: Ol'ga Nikolaevna Kulibina from Kharkiv, then the capital of Ukraine (7–9). (Her file contains letters from this stranger [24–28]). There is no mention of the poems in this odd document.

Zhelikhovskaia was interrogated before 20 March 1938 (the day on which she admitted to her alleged crime). In these sessions, she denied the charges of anti-Soviet agitation, while admitting that two of her sons lived abroad and that she received money from them. This was documented on paper (the protocol of the 15 March interrogation), but she refused to admit to the other accusations. That she refused to sign any compromising statement while the interrogator refused to record her denial explains the unusual protocol of the 15 March interrogation.

Four days before she was sentenced to death and six days before her execution, Zhelikhovskaia was interrogated again (17). This session seems to have been an attempt to implicate her son, Georgii (22). It does not seem to have succeeded:

Q: Is it known to your son Georgii Iosifovich Zhelikhovskii that you, in a counter-revolutionary disposition, conducted anti-Soviet agitation systematically by praising a Fascist regime and discrediting the measures taken by the party and [Soviet] government?

A: In spite of the fact that I lived with my son in the same place, I hid it [my counter-revolutionary convictions and actions] from him. More accurately, when I engaged in anti-Soviet agitation, I tried to do so in a way not to affect his career.

Clearly, Zhelikhovskaia marshalled what little strength she still had to protect her son.

Rehabilitation

Because Zhelikhovskaia was the widow of a former tsarist army officer and policeman, the Soviet secret police suspected that she was a monarchist. The emigration of her sons made her even more suspect politically. The confessions recorded in her case file may indeed have been genuine. She herself allegedly said that she was too old to change her political views. Her confessions will appear to uncritical readers as a monarchist's swan song. But it is more likely that the secret police made them appear that way: Zhelikhovskaia's swan song or, at least, her parting shot before death.

There is an interesting twist to Zhelikhovskaia's story. She had managed, at least in an immediate sense, to protect her son Georgii. According to a 26 March 1955 KGB document, Georgii was suspected of collaborating with the Nazi occupying forces during World War II. The KGB hunted Georgii as a former member of the German 'punitive organs'. In this connection, Zhelikhovskaia's file was re-examined (41). Whether the KGB found Georgii is not known. They probably suspected that, like his mother, he was a monarchist or at least had become anti-Soviet because of her execution.

Even if Georgii did betray his country, one could argue that he did so because his mother was unfairly executed by the Soviet regime. (It should be noted, however, that numerous sons and daughters of executed parents later fought bravely in the Red Army during World War II.) It is also possible, of course, that Georgii did not serve the German forces, but simply disappeared or was killed in the war.

The Zhelikhovskaia file contains no proof of her alleged crime. Her apparent monarchist 'poems' come closest to providing 'material evidence' of political 'crime' discussed in the present book. Yet the authorship and authenticity of these 'poems' is suspect. The testimonies of her neighbours are not reliable at all. They may have lied, or their accounts may have been falsified by the secret police. The records of her interrogation appear to be incomplete, casting doubt on the authenticity of her confessions, which turns out in the final analysis to be virtually the only evidence against her. No swan song, no parting shot, her confession, like that of so many others, was likely coerced by force and threat. It was not her alleged monarchism that doomed her but her foreign connections: she was actually executed as part of the Polish Operation.

Zhelikhovskaia's file shows that, after the Bolshevik Revolution, those who were politically disenfranchised and materially impoverished developed private networks of assistance for survival. Such networks were supported at least partially by funds from abroad. The police saw in them clandestine political activity under the guise of private charity. The foreign links were the critical factor, for the police suspected that the formerly privileged such as the nobility would turn to any regime for support in their endeavour to overthrow the new Soviet government. Germany, where many former Russian nobles sought refuge, was the most prominent among the suspect foreign countries. Therefore the police found it politically expedient to link the former nobles and 'monarchists' and their private networks to Fascist (Nazi) Germany.

Even when such links were missing, the existence of private charity and foreign funds aroused often fatal suspicions. This can be observed in the file of another Kiev woman, Zinaida Mitrofanovna Levina, a midwife who was thirty-nine years of age in 1937. Levina was arrested on 14 December 1937. Like Zhelikhovskaia, Levina received money from abroad and distributed it among several people in Kiev. It was alleged that the money was sent by 'Fascist organisations', although no evidence was found. In fact, the money she received came from her sister in Zurich, Switzerland, who, with her husband, formerly the owner of a confectionery factory in Kiev, had left Ukraine in late 1918 when the Skoropads'kyi regime, which was supported by the Germans and which promoted the resurrection of the former regime, collapsed as a result of the defeat of Germany in World War I). Although her interrogator pressed her to admit that her private philanthropy amounted to 'anti-Soviet agitation', Levina refused. All the same she was accused of conducting 'anti-Soviet agitation', sentenced to be shot on 19 January 1938 and executed on 29 January 1938. Levina, like Zhelikhovskaia, was executed as part of the Polish Operation, even though neither had anything to do with Poland. (Levina was an ethnic Ukrainian and the money came from Switzerland.) In 1957 Levina was rehabilitated, for lack of *corpus delicti*. Her surviving relations helped her rehabilitation.[8]

Zhelikhovskaia's rehabilitation only came later, probably because there was no one left in the country who cared about her fate: her sons Arkadii and Ivan could not have done much for her from abroad, and Georgii had probably himself been repressed. In 1989, towards the end of the Soviet regime, the government, finding no evidence of her crime, rehabilitated Zhelikhovskaia. No relatives were found at this time (43).

By recording her testimonies selectively, the secret police appear to have almost completely extinguished Zhelikhovskaia's voice. Yet, paradoxically, this very absence speaks volumes for her: she was silenced by force.

CHAPTER 4

'The NKVD is Satan'

Priests and a Beggar

Marxism is antithetical to religion. It turns religion upside down by presenting a materialist view of world history. The Soviet Union, the first socialist state, was an explicitly atheist and anti-religious body politic. However, like other modern states, it sought to capture the hearts and minds of the people as well as to have its version of Marxism accepted. Not content with simple submission, the regime wanted citizens actively to embrace its world view. Religion may have been seen as 'the opium of the masses' (as Marx said), but the Soviet leaders seized upon the religious paradigm as a means of propagating Marxism. As Stalin said, 'Marxism is the religion of the [working] class, its symbol of faith.'[1] He even maintained that the country needed 'Soviet priests'.[2]

In the event, substituting Marxism for religion proved difficult. The 1937 population census, the only one in the history of the Soviet Union to survey citizens' religious convictions, showed that as many as 84 percent of the 'illiterate population' (25,139,192 out of 29,937,843 people) and 44 percent of the 'literate population' (30,137,857 out of 68,473,289 people) responded as believers, even though revealing their religious convictions was dangerous. A number of factors may have skewed these figures in one direction or the other. Fear of repression may have caused an underrepresentation of believers. However, other factors may have contributed to the opposite effect and inflated the figures: some religious people

used the census to encourage massive registrations, even of those who wavered or did not even believe: 'Once Hitler comes to Ukraine, he will destroy all those who did not register as believers.' Such agitation was effective: 'In some villages, almost the entire population (to the last person) registered as believers'.[3]

Whatever the case, excluding the slightly fewer than one million who did not respond, approximately 56 percent of the Soviet adult population (sixteen years and older) declared themselves to be believers.[4] The result prompted one Ukrainian party leader to declare, 'This was a complete surprise to all of us ... we have overestimated our success in the fight against religious prejudices.'[5]

In the eyes of the Bolsheviks, the priests were a form of bourgeoisie who spiritually exploited the proletariat. By default they were therefore politically suspect. Under the circumstances, aside from a complete submission to the atheist regime, two forms of response suggested themselves for the clergy: fighting actively against the Soviet regime or ignoring it altogether. Neither was really possible under Stalin. The Soviet government coopted some religious leaders (the 'Living Church', a splinter group from the Russian Orthodox Church, some Baptists, followers of Lev Tolstoi, a Christian pacifist, and others),[6] but there was no rapprochement in any fundamental sense. The priesthood as a whole remained suspected of being an enemy of the Soviet regime. Consequently, the latter infiltrated the ecclesiastical organisations[7] and terrorised priests more consistently than it did any other group (including the kulaks, who were tolerated under the NEP).

Anti-religious and anticlerical campaigns reduced the number of clergy significantly. The 1937 census counted 'a total of 31,298 "servants of cults" in the Soviet Union out of a total population of just over 160 million, not including Red Army soldiers and border guards'. Still, these data, which included the dependants of 'servants of cults' as well as retired clergy, clearly undercounted the actual number of clergy.[8] Shortly after the census, members of the clergy, like many other Soviet citizens, were targeted for execution. Many were arrested and executed as part of Secret Order No. 00447 of the NKVD, the so-called 'Kulak Operation'.[9] According to the data of the Federal Service of Security (FSB) in Moscow, the successor to the NKVD and the KGB, 33,382 'servants of religious cults' were arrested in 1937 in the Soviet Union,[10] over 2,000 more than the census records. Of them, approximately 80 percent are believed to have been executed.

The Case of Nademskii

Andrei Grigor'evich Nademskii was among those executed in 1937–38. A Ukrainian, he was born into a church deacon's family in 1869, completed an ecclesiastical education and married Liubov' Evgen'evna. He was an Orthodox priest at the Heorhii church, built in the seventeenth century on the site of the Vydubychi monastery. On 20 December 1937 he was arrested, charged with conducting anti-Soviet agitation and executed less than three weeks later, on 8 January 1938.[11]

Nine days after his arrest, Nademskii was indicted. The bill of indictment charged that as a priest he had stated that the Soviet regime was the rule of atheism and that it destroyed churches and religion. He allegedly called the Communists 'barbarians' and 'atheists' who, when the Soviet regime fell, would be severely punished. Nademskii supposedly deplored the uncovering of such 'enemies of the people' as M. N. Tukhachevskii and I. E. Iakir and called the NKVD 'Satan' (17).[12]

Did Nademskii actually make these allegations against the Soviet regime? Coming from a priest, they may appear credible at first. However, considering the tenor of the times, the NKVD charges should not be accepted at face value.

Six days after his arrest, Nademskii was interrogated. Because he had been arrested twice before, in 1922 and 1930, the interrogator began by asking him why he had been arrested by the secret police (Cheka) in 1922. Nademskii responded that he had been arrested for leading a procession of the people of the Heorhii church on a pilgrimage. He sat in gaol for a week and was released. The year, 1922, had been difficult for all churches. The Soviet government had confiscated church property, especially gold and silver artifacts, using the widespread famine as its excuse. Many priests and believers protested and were arrested, and unknown numbers were executed. Nademskii and his followers escaped harsher repression, probably because their 'pilgrimage' was peaceful. Next asked about his arrest in 1930, Nademskii said that he had been arrested by the Kiev OGPU (successor of the Cheka and predecessor of the NKVD) and sat in gaol for five months. On this occasion he was accused of conducting anti-Soviet agitation. The reason, according to his own testimony, was that his parishioners (Nademskii was later to learn that a parishioner, Ivan

15: The Vydubychi-Heorhii church in Kiev in 2006. The church was built in the seventeenth century.

Vasil'evich Kapshuk,[13] had denounced him) had submitted a statement to the effect that when bandits were active around the parish he had taken part in a secret meeting in preparation for an uprising against the Soviet regime. Moreover, when church land was confiscated at the onset of the Revolution, he had resisted the peasants. Lastly, before the Revolution he had allegedly maintained contact with the tsarist police and betrayed revolutionary-minded peasants to the police. When the interrogator stated that Nademskii had been arrested this time for spreading provocative anti-Soviet rumours directed against the Soviet regime and asked him whether he would plead guilty, Nademskii answered: 'No, I don't plead guilty to spreading provocative rumours and anti-Soviet agitation.' When the interrogator retorted that he was lying and demanded his confession, Nademskii responded (10):

> No, I state again that I never conducted any anti-Soviet activity directed against the existing regime. I personally adhere to the tactic of not going against any regime and therefore consider it superfluous to conduct any activity against any regime. I am an apolitical person and never discuss political subjects with any of my acquaintances.

As in so many other cases, Nademskii's denial of his alleged crime, recorded longhand, did not make it into the typed bill of indictment.

At this point, Nademskii's interrogation records take a sudden turn. A new sheet of paper is started and the handwriting appears suddenly animated. The reason appears clear: the interrogator had begun to extract the confessions he wanted from Nademskii. The new page starts with Nademskii's denial of accusations that he organised women and believers, and worked to collect their signatures for the reopening of churches that had been closed. The interrogator then interjects that he has obtained the testimony of Antonii Skliaruk, Nademskii's acquaintance, and reads him an excerpt (11):

> In a conversation with me, Nademskii said: Look, Antonii, how terribly you live now, this is because of the Soviet regime, which persecutes believers and religion. It is destroying Orthodoxy, but the people lived well under the tsar. Never mind, Antonii, an end to the Soviet regime as the rule of atheism will come, it will be overthrown and the old regime which always was the defender of

religion and churches will be restored. All these barbarians and atheist Communists will be severely punished.

When the interrogator asked Nademskii whether he would confirm the testimony of Skliaruk regarding his anti-Soviet sentiments, he answered (11–12):

> Yes, I am forced to confess that, being oppressed by the Soviet regime, I told some individual priests and clergy about my anti-Soviet sentiments. But I have to say that I did not conduct open agitation or actively attack the Soviet regime. I am old, and for this reason I did not have an understanding of the essence of my [anti-Soviet] sentiments. I expressed my view [only] among individuals. Now I want to ask the organs of the Soviet government to consider my old age [Nademskii was sixty-eight or sixty-nine then] and not to punish me severely.

Was this an honest confession? Already arrested twice, Nademskii could hardly have favoured the atheist political regime. However, he stated initially that he stood above politics, considering it meaningless to fight against secular authorities. It is likely that as a priest who had opposed the seizure of church land by peasants in 1917 or 1918 he was disliked by the peasants (as Kapshuk had reported to the police in 1930). Nevertheless, his sudden confession of anti-Soviet sentiments was almost certainly coerced and fabricated.

Whether Nademskii was tortured is not known. In his statement he requested mercy, which prompted the interrogator to humiliate him further by asking whether during the Soviet period he had engaged in socially useful work for the construction of socialism. Nademskii responded, 'No, because of my religious convictions, I did not abandon church activity until I was arrested and so I did not engage in socially useful labour.' The interrogator's rejoinder was: 'So, you lived a parasitic way of life.' Marshalling his courage, Nademskii corrected him: 'No, I personally consider my work to be honest work, but under the conditions of the Soviet regime my work is parasitic, affording no use to society' (12). Did Nademskii in fact qualify his confession? Or did the interrogator insert this qualification to show that Nademskii never fully submitted to the Soviet regime? In any case, this is all that was said by Nademskii before he was indicted by the special NKVD *troika* three days later and executed ten days thereafter.

Nademskii's file contains the testimonies of two witnesses. One, cited above, is Anton Isakovich Skliaruk, a Ukrainian, seventy-four years of age, formerly a monk at the Bohoiavlens'k monastery. Skliaruk worked at the Vydubychi-Heorhii church as a guard and conversed with Nademskii often. In addition to his other allegations, Skliaruk contended that Nademskii had said that believers and the clergy would support him, especially in the event of a war against the Soviet regime by other states, and help to overthrow the Soviet regime more successfully and more quickly (26).

A second witness, Ivan Semenovich Pustotin, a Russian, forty-three years of age and a deacon at the Vydubychi-Heorhii church, made an equally harsh condemnation. According to Pustotin, Nademskii was a fervent monarchist, always asking what was new, what was happening in Spain: Hadn't the Fascists there destroyed the Republican scoundrels yet? Perhaps the Fascists would come here next and go after the Communists. Pustotin said that Nademskii kept in close touch with monks and nuns and said that thanks to them Orthodoxy would stand firm. When the 'anti-Soviet conspiracy' of Tukhachevskii, Iakir and others was uncovered, Nademskii was beside himself that such great people had failed. Their scheme was exposed by the NKVD which was Satan from whom nothing could be hidden. When the elections to the Supreme Soviet took place, Nademskii called the Soviets a 'quartet' (after I. A. Krylov's famous fable in which a quartet made up of a monkey, a donkey, a goat and a bear think that they can play music better simply by rearranging their seating, not realising that in fact they have tin ears). Pustotin quoted Nademskii as having declared that the people did not really elect the Soviet. The deputies elected themselves. The Supreme Soviet was an impostor, not recognised by the people—it was a bunch of Communists (13–14).

Nademskii may in fact have made all of these 'anti-Soviet' statements (including the reference to the NKVD as 'Satan'), but it is also possible that Skliaruk and Pustotin were forced to make false statements, or that they had some personal score to settle with Nademskii. The comparison of the elections to the Krylov fable was an ingenious one, but one that may have been circulating underground or may have been made up by Pustotin or the interrogators. Nademskii's alleged 'anti-Soviet' remarks appear credible only if he was actively disposed against the Soviet regime. Even then, Nademskii may not have expressed his thoughts to Skliaruk or Pustotin.

No one asked for his rehabilitation after Stalin's death, which suggests that his wife, too, may have been executed as the spouse of an 'enemy of the people'. As a result there was no re-examination of his case in, say, 1961, when at least Pustotin may still have been alive. As in most other cases, one is hard-pressed to uncover Nademskii's true voice from his interrogation records. What is certain is that he was fully rehabilitated in 1989. No relatives were found. It was only in the 1990s that it became known that his remains, like those of so many others, were buried in a mass grave in Bykivnia.[14]

No doubt, critical thought never died in the Soviet Union, and one is tempted to believe that Nademskii was an example of this. If one believes uncritically what the records examined here tell us, however, one is falling into the trap set by his interrogators to convict him. The truth is elusive. Nademskii may have privately suspected that the NKVD was Satan, but it is unlikely that he said so in public.

Guardians of a Beggar

Like Nademskii, Vladimir Andreevich Zakharevich, Aleksandr Kapitonovich Polishchuk and Nikita Radionovich Kravchenko, all priests, were executed in Kiev in 1938 as religious counter-revolutionaries. Their cases appear somewhat simpler, because the evidence presented against them meant they were unable to withstand interrogation from the beginning and confessed to everything. Yet a perusal of their file reveals a more complex case as well as a striking fact about Soviet life on the margins.

All three were arrested on 3 May 1938. Zakharevich was fifty-five years of age and Ukrainian, had a secondary education, lived with his wife, Evgeniia Fedorovna, 50, and his daughter, Margarita, 30, on the premises of the Mykola Prytyska church in Kiev, and worked as a priest at the Luk'ianivka cemetery in Kiev. (Until the mid-1930s, unbeknown to the people of Kiev—although the priests at the cemetery must have known—many of those executed for political crimes in Kiev were buried in the Luk'ianivka cemetery.)[15] Polishchuk was fifty-six and Ukrainian, had a secondary education, lived, like Zakharevich, on the premises of the Mykola Prytyska church, worked as a priest at the Luk'ianivka cemetery, and had been arrested in 1932 for 'anti-Soviet' agitation. Kravchenko was seventy-four and Ukrainian, had an elementary education, and carried no internal passport. (This meant that he was illegally residing in the city.)[16] Polishchuk and Kravchenko were single and had no family. According to the bill of indictment, Zakharevich was accused of being closely associated with Petr Petrovich Vorob'ev, allegedly a member of a 'counter-revolutionary insurgency organisation', of conducting active counter-revolutionary agitation, of forming a group of church officials and various vagrants, of spreading slanderous rumours about the defeat of the Soviet Union in a forthcoming war and of extolling Fascism. (Priests were particularly vulnerable to charges of 'anti-Soviet counter-revolutionary agitation', because every sermon and every service they conducted could be perceived as inherently hostile to the atheist regime.) Zakharevich was also accused of having ties to Polishchuk and Kravchenko, who in turn were accused of spreading counter-revolutionary rumours about the defeat of the Soviet Union and extolling Fascism. Just five days after their arrest, on 8 May 1938, they were sentenced, without trial, to be shot by the NKVD *troika* and two days later, on 10 May at 11 p.m., were executed, with all their personal possessions confiscated by the state. It took a mere week for them to travel from freedom to execution.[17]

The arrest of the three priests was prompted by the earlier arrest and confessions of one Vorob'ev, a forty-five-year-old native of Tver' in Russia who worked as the manager of a cemetery in Kiev. He was interrogated on 29 April 1938 and the arrest warrants for the three priests were issued on the same day. Here again, as in numerous other cases, foreign connections were a factor. Vorob'ev turned out to have been a soldier during World War I and had been interned in Austria as a prisoner of war, returning home in 1918. His interrogator told him to confirm information in the hands of the secret police to the effect that while in Austria he had established contact with the commandant of his internment camp and informed on his fellow prisoners of war. Vorob'ev confirmed that he had been against the Bolshevik Revolution and had informed the Austrian commandant of the revolutionary ferment among the Russian prisoners of war. Treachery of this kind remained a serious crime in the eyes of the secret police's interrogators. When Vorob'ev returned to Russia in late 1918, the Soviet regime was already established

16: A crypt being used as a chapel in the Luk'ianivka cemetery (2006). The wooden church was built in 1911 and torn down in 1972. The construction of a new church began in 2005.

and he allegedly entertained hostility towards the new government. In 1919 he began to work at a cemetery in Kiev where he stayed until he was arrested. He remained hostile towards the Soviet regime, but did not engage in any active work against it until 1936. When asked what had happened in 1936, Vorob'ev said that at the beginning of that year he had employed several new people to work at the cemetery. Some of them, in particular ones named Iaremchuk, Krivenko and Pustovoi, turned out to be former kulaks. They were, according to Vorob'ev, openly against the Soviet regime. After observing them carefully, Vorob'ev is said to have decided to recruit the named trio plus Boiko, Forostovets, Pis'mok, Petrov-Zhidlovskii, Seratskii and others to anti-Soviet activity. He set them the task of conducting anti-Soviet agitation, spreading rumours about the defeat of the Soviet Union in a forthcoming war with Fascist countries and recruiting other members. According to Vorob'ev, Zakharevich said, in conversations with him in 1937–38, that it would not be a bad idea to infiltrate certain sections of the population to discredit the Soviet government and arouse popular discontent. Vorob'ev, however, testified that Zakharevich was not a member of his group and appeared to belong to some other 'counter-revolutionary organisation' (16–20).

Almost certainly, Vorob'ev's confessions were coerced. His status as a former prisoner of war and his association with priests and possibly other politically suspect elements (such as de-kulakised people, who, because of their backgrounds, could not find employment in the city) probably doomed him. Indeed, former soldiers of the Russian Imperial Army, like Vorob'ev, who were held prisoners of war in Germany were systematically targeted by the 'German Operation' of the Great Terror.[18] Vorob'ev may have been arrested in connection with other 'members' of his 'organisation' such as Iaremchuk and Krivenko, but it is also possible that he was a police agent. Unfortunately no further information on Vorob'ev's fate is available. He cannot be found in the extensive index of victims of the Stalinist terror in Kiev.[19]

On the day he was arrested, Zakharevich was interrogated. Whether willingly or under coercion, the records show that he confessed to his alleged crime from the beginning. (It is likely that he initially denied the charges but that records of this were discarded or simply not taken.) He said that, being hostile towards the Soviet regime, he engaged systematically in 'anti-Soviet' agitation until the day of his arrest. Before he moved to Kiev, he worked in Novohorod-Volyns'kyi to the west of Kiev, near the border with Poland, where, as a 'convinced enemy of the Soviet regime', he constantly laboured to create popular discontent with the Soviet system. Particularly successful were his activities at the time of collectivisation in 1930, when his extensive anti-Soviet agitation inspired a number of organised kulak uprisings and strikes against the Soviet regime. He personally travelled around villages and prepared strikes. Women were easy prey for agitation, according to Zakharevich, and he was successful in organising them. In 1932–33, as a result of his anti-collective farm agitation, a mass exodus of peasants from collective farms took place in a number of villages in Novohorod-Volyns'kyi. He took advantage of the 'food shortages' (i.e., famine) for his agitation and was helped by local kulaks.

After his move to Kiev in 1935, Zakharevich and his colleague Polishchuk conducted political agitation with Vorob'ev concerning war with Germany and the defeat of the Soviet Union: 'I agitated the believers to dislike the Soviet regime'; 'I propagated rumours that war would start soon with Germany and the Soviet Union would collapse'; 'I used the church for my anti-Soviet activity'; and so on (22–23). Zakharevich added that he was not a member of an insurgent organisation even though he was a convinced enemy of the Soviet regime. All the same he said that he had supported insurgency unconditionally, thinking that the overthrow of the Soviet regime would be easier to achieve by way of an uprising. He told his interrogator that in the event of an uprising he would definitely join the insurgents (21–25, 26–28).

Unlike Nademskii's, Zakharevich's confessions are completely formulaic ('the Soviet Union would collapse in a war with Germany' and the like), with facts about the disorder in the countryside at the time of collectivisation and de-kulakisation in 1930 and the famine in 1932–33 mixed in. Evidently he had witnessed the disorder, but it is not at all clear whether he helped to organise it or took any part in it. He was almost certainly not a friend of the Soviet regime, and therefore is likely privately and spiritually to have supported the desperate peasant actions.

Like Zakahrevich's records, Polishchuk's contain simple formulaic repetitions of police conceptions of 'counter-revolutionary crimes'. Polishchuk was interrogated on 4 May 1938, the day after his arrest. From the beginning, he pleaded guilty to 'anti-Soviet agitation directed at undermining the Soviet system'. (Even though the printed indictment alleged that he was arrested in 1932, his other records indicate no previous arrests.) He confessed that as a priest he did not and could not come to terms with the Soviet regime and constantly conducted anti-Soviet agitation among believers ('I propagated rumours that war would start soon with Germany and the Soviet Union would fall' and the like). Like Zakharevich, he detested the Soviet regime. Like Zakharevich, Polishchuk stated that he was not a member of a counter-revolutionary organisation, but worked against the Soviet system as someone who detested it, spreading rumours about a forthcoming war against Germany, the defeat of the Soviet Union in that war and the 'restoration of a Fascist regime in Russia' (29–30). The following day, Polishchuk was interrogated again. He stated that he had had Kravchenko disguise himself as a beggar and conduct agitation among the population (40).

Like Zakharevich, Polishchuk denied being part of a counter-revolutionary organisation. That this assertion was included in the records and not expunged is curious. It may be evidence of a final act of resistance: his interrogators probably thought that membership of a 'counter-revolutionary organisation' constituted a more serious political crime than 'anti-Soviet agitation'. It may also be that they simply could not fabricate an organisation from the priests' cases. Either way, the police probably failed to break the priests completely.

It is likely that both Zakharevich and Polishchuk, like the priests discussed in Chapter 2, had been police informers employed to spy on groups of peasants and former kulaks. Both had been arrested before and probably coerced to work for the secret police. They were released on this condition. (Vorob'ev, too, may have been working for the police.) They were given the task of spying on those working on the margins of Soviet society (such as former kulaks, many of whom were living in Kiev illegally). Before the Great Terror the priests working at Luk'ianivka cemetery, whether they approved or not, accepted bodies for burial from police commissioners. It is quite likely that instead of helping the police, Zakharevich and Polishchuk protected those living on the margins. The curious records of their insistence that they did not belong to any 'counter-revolutionary organisation' imply that they may have stated at this point that they were assigned to spy on the people working in the cemetery by the police. The latter chose not to note in the interrogation records that the two priests were police agents or informers. They wanted to extract confessions from Zakharevich and Polishchuk, who refused to give them because they had worked for the police, if only reluctantly, and were indeed not members of any such 'counter-revolutionary organisation'.

As one reads the records, one encounters curious passages that reveal an interesting aspect of Soviet life in the 1930s. On the day that Polishchuk was questioned, 4 May 1938, Kravchenko was also interrogated. On the face of it, it appears that, like Zakharevich and Polishchuk, he pleaded guilty to counter-revolutionary agitation against the Soviet regime from the beginning. With the permission of Zakharevich and Polishchuk, he had visited the church of the Luk'ianivka cemetery and spread among the believers 'provocative rumours about a forthcoming war and the toppling of the Soviet system'. He added, like Zakharevich and Polishchuk, that he was not a member of any organisation and that no one had recruited him into any organisation: it was simply 'their common hatred of the Soviet system' that had kept them in contact with one another. However, he added an interesting and important piece of information: he told the interrogator that he had had the permission of Zakharevich and Polishchuk to 'beg for crumbs of bread at the church porticos'. According to Kravchenko, they gave him permission to beg because they knew his anti-Soviet sentiments. The crumbs were his 'salary' (34–37). This suggests that Kravchenko was not a priest, as alleged in the indictment, but a mere beggar patronised by Zakharevich and Polishchuk.

In his confession on the following day, 5 May 1938, Kravchenko repeated his gratitude to the priests and their parishioners: he had conducted anti-Soviet activity in Luk'ianivka for which he received 'support and sympathy'. Kravchenko stated further that Zakharevich and Polishchuk spoke with him often and urged him to continue his anti-Soviet activities, which would have a positive outcome. Kravchenko added that he also spoke with many parishioners, including workers from the 'Bolshevik' factory whose surnames he did not remember. He told them that they were being 'deceived by the Soviet regime', forced to use their 'last bits of wages to buy government bonds'.[20] 'Instead of resisting, they worked only harder.' He reportedly said these things to them in order to arouse anti-Soviet sentiment among them and arm them against the Soviet regime (41–43).

All this suggests that Kravchenko was merely a beggar who talked too much and too openly at church porticos about his misery and possibly criticised the government or its officials. The interrogators seem to have trumped up counter-revolutionary crimes out of a beggar's ranting in order to implicate the priests who had patronised the poor man. Accordingly, Zakharevich and Polishchuk were said to have used Kravchenko as a beggar to conduct 'counter-revolutionary agitation'. Somehow Kravchenko's gratitude to the two priests who allowed him to beg at their church slipped into his interrogation records, revealing his true status as a beggar.

This is important in two respects. First, official propaganda notwithstanding, in 1937–38 there were indeed beggars in the Soviet Union, which in 1936 had claimed to have achieved socialism. Begging was a form of social parasitism, according to Soviet ideology, and was not permitted. Even though the country was supposed to have achieved an important (socialist) stage in economic development, beggars did still exist. Second, even though it is likely that the priests had been coerced into police service, they did not betray their consciences completely. Kravchenko the beggar probably had no means of survival. Begging in public was dangerous. Zakharevich and Polishchuk took pity on him and let him beg on church premises. It was an act of underground charity.

If Zakharevich and Polishchuk were police agents, all the matters discussed here, including their 'anti-Soviet agitation' (for instance, saying that 'war would start soon with Germany and the Soviet Union would fall') and use of Kravchenko, may have been true. If so, there are two further possibilities. First, the two priests had sold their souls but in the interrogations protested their innocence because they had merely been following police directions. Second, they had made a strategic compromise with the police by which they, following police directions, engaged in and encouraged others to engage in 'anti-Soviet agitation', fully aware that it was a calculated compromise, a subversive one that allowed them to express their true sentiments under police cover. This was a dangerous game. Whatever the case, once their utility expired or their provocative actions grew out of control, they were doomed. This may explain why they were despatched so expeditiously, with a mere week between arrest and execution.

Almost certainly, Kravchenko knew nothing about the police connections of Zakharevich and Polishchuk. This explains why he remained grateful to them.

In 1989 Zakharevich, Polishchuk and Kravchenko were all rehabilitated. No relatives were located for any of them (51–53). Only in the 1990s did it become known that their remains, like those of Nademskii, were buried in a mass grave in Bykivnia in Kiev.[21]

On the face of it, the case of Zakharevich, Polishchuk and Kravchenko was simple: they were accused of political crimes, they confessed, at least partially, and they were executed. The police intended it to be straightforward. Yet the case file contains subtle hints that there was something more to it. The question is not whether their interrogation records reflected their authentic voices or falsified ones, or whether they were guilty or innocent of the crimes, but what information was hidden by the police. The police appear to have concealed their earlier recruitment of Zakharevich and Polishchuk. Withdrawing such information was the norm: rarely were the connections of the arrested with the police divulged in the case files. (For exceptions, see Moshinskaia in Chapter 2 and Angel'chik in Chapter 12.) Because the file was not meant to be published or studied by historians, the police did not take the greatest care to expunge any hint of the secret collaboration of the priests, so odd fragments of information were left in the handwritten records of interrogation to which no one paid any attention. Thus a perusal of their file today reveals the existence of an elaborate piece of provocation by the police which trapped the three accused. Although it is difficult to know whether Zakharevich and Polishchuk had genuinely sold their souls to the police, it is clear that they compromised themselves by working with them. Almost certainly they had no alternative in order to survive.

Did they in fact actively seek to undermine the atheist state under police protection? It is possible. Were they and Nademskii in their private thoughts unfavourable towards this violently atheist regime? No doubt. Did they reveal such sentiments to their confidants? It is possible, but it is no more than a possibility.

Kravchenko the beggar and other 'marginal people' (such as the homeless, the unemployed, prostitutes, hooligans and criminals) constituted a special yet sizeable category of people targeted by the Great Terror for extinction.[22] They were deemed undesirable elements to be purged from society. Yet there was a more serious political calculation at work: they were deemed socially parasitic and politically unstable and therefore dangerous. In 1935 secret police chief Genrih G. Iagoda excoriated his subordinates for failing to see the political significance of hooliganism: there was 'merely one step' in the transition 'from hooligan to terrorist', and 'hooliganism' was 'an element leading to the emergence of sabotage groups'.[23]

The case of the priests discussed in this chapter raises a matter of particular significance. Priests in general were an ideal target for recruitment as police agents. They interacted with people, especially believers and church-goers. The police assumed, quite reasonably, that those politically disposed against the Soviet government saw in them the spiritual fulcrum of opposition. The police exiled or executed those priests who refused to work clandestinely as their agents. Those who consented compromised themselves by collaborating with the atheist Soviet regime. No doubt they depraved themselves by their choice—a pact with the devil. Whatever they did helped the police.

This, however, proved a dangerous and self-defeating game for the police too: they could not fully trust information provided by people whose political loyalty they distrusted in the first place. They could not be confident that the priests were in fact working for them. Suspicions persisted that priests used police-approved provocations to promote their own religious and political beliefs. Provocations could backfire. The danger of 'blowback' to the police was constant. In the eyes of the police, at some point, the actions of priests began to appear too risky, and the information supplied by them too suspect.

Whatever choice they made, the priests were doomed from the beginning. Like Nademskii, Zakharevich and Polishchuk, many were executed in the Great Terror.

CHAPTER 5

Ukrainian Peasants and Kulaks
Ubiquitous 'Enemies'

'Kulaks', roughly defined as rich peasants, were for the Bolsheviks the rural equivalent of the urban 'bourgeoisie'. During the 1920s, they were tolerated by the government because of their critical importance to the restoration of an economy ruined by war, revolution and civil war. Once this had been achieved, however, the kulaks began to appear in the eyes of Stalin and his supporters as the embodiment of the danger of a capitalist restoration. The collectivisation drive and the de-kulakisation campaign, begun in late 1929, resulted in the dispossession and arrest, deportation and even execution of numerous kulaks. In fact, any peasant who was opposed to collectivisation and de-kulakisation (there were numerous peasant uprisings) was branded a kulak. Thus, the kulaks represented the largest group of explicitly declared 'enemies' of the Soviet regime.

Indeed, de-kulakised peasants constituted a very large group. An unknown number of peasants de-kulakised themselves and left for the cities and construction sites where they became workers. Probably more than 3 million people were directly affected by de-kulakisation. Many of them were deported to the remote northern regions, Central Asia and Siberia. The de-kulakised also made up the core of the Gulag population in the 1930s.

The problem for the Soviet government was that former kulaks appeared to be hiding everywhere. Numerous kulaks entered the wage- and salary-earning workforce. Unknown numbers of kulaks were dispersed throughout the country. The Ukrainian kulaks were considered particularly dangerous. The memory of the Ukrainian peasants' bitter fight against the Bolshevik forces in 1918–20 was still fresh in 1937–38. Land in Ukraine tended to be much more fertile than in central Russia, and the kulaks in Ukraine were generally believed to be richer than those in Russia. Therefore the Soviet government suspected that the enmity of the Ukrainian kulaks towards it must be all the stronger. (Indeed, Ukraine accounted for a very large percentage of the peasant uprisings against collectivisation.) The 1932–33 famine, which took several million lives in Ukraine, left bitter memories among the population. Moscow insisted that it had been caused by a grain strike by Ukrainian kulaks and peasants (although many scholars contend that it was actually caused by Moscow's excessive grain procurements). Whatever the case, the famine made Moscow ever more suspicious of the Ukrainian peasantry. Moreover, the Ukrainian peasants in general and the Ukrainian kulaks in particular were suspected by the Bolsheviks of being the most ardent supporters of Ukrainian nationalism and separatism, which were anathema to Stalin. Unlike Moscow or Petrograd (from 1924 Leningrad), which had never been occupied by enemy forces during the Civil War, Kiev fell repeatedly into enemy hands (various Ukrainian forces such as those led by Pavlo Skoropads'kyi and Symon Petliura, as well as German and Polish forces that supported the separation of Ukraine from Russia).

Furthermore, many Ukrainian peasants who had ended up abroad wished to come back to Soviet Ukraine should an opportunity arise. In 1930, for instance, 'tens of thousands' of Ukrainian peasants crossed the borders into Poland and Romania to avoid collectivisation and de-kulakisation, in the same way that Belarusan peasants fled to Poland, Lithuania and Latvia and in the east Kazakhs went to China and Bur'iats to Mongolia.[1] Although the Soviet borders were tightly guarded, many managed to cross them. Ukrainian peasants and others often moved back and forth across the Polish–Soviet borders. When caught, they were likely to be executed if there was any suggestion that they had a tainted political past.[2] The borders in the Far East were also dangerous areas, with numerous illegal transgressors who provided a fertile ground for international intelligence and counter-intelligence (see Chapter 7); so were the southern Caucasian borders, which Turkey, Poland, Japan, Germany and other countries interested in Soviet affairs carefully monitored. Polish intelligence reported, for example, a massive border crossing in Adjara (in today's Georgia) in 1937 as a result of rebellions caused by intensifying political repression. In turn, the Soviet Union was said to have sent its own agents to Kurdistan to incite anti-Turkish rebellions. Two Soviet agents were caught and executed by Turkey in 1937.[3]

In Ukraine, the border with Poland provided the most serious problem. Poland sent its agents across it, and Polish intelligence made efforts to recruit informers among those Soviet citizens (such as de-kulakised peasants) who appeared embittered or who were in dire need. Reports by Polish intelligence officers in the 1930s provide vivid accounts of such efforts (see the commentary in the caption to Illustration 17).

Transgressors

Ul'ian Petrovich Gorodovenko (Horodovenko) was one of those border transgressors who fled abroad from the Soviet Union in 1930. He was born in 1892 into a peasant family in the village of Skvyr, to the south of Kiev. Ul'ian Gorodovenko, along with his brother Fedor, was said to have served in the army of Symon Petliura who had led an independent Ukraine (the Ukrainian Directory) in 1919–20. Ul'ian was later accused of selling Communists and Jews to the Petliura and other anti-Soviet forces when the Reds retreated during the Civil War. After the Polish army had come and gone in 1920, he was said to have engaged in pro-Polish agitation. He was pursued by the Soviet secret police but managed to hide. Apparently amnestied, he worked as a 'speculator' (probably a small-time pedlar) in 1921–24. He was described in his case file as a 'swindler' capable of anything. He was always treated badly by village party activists. According to Ul'ian Gorodovenko, some of the activists themselves had dark political histories (i.e., anti-Soviet political pasts), but when he wrote to the local newspaper about them, he was ignored. This only increased the activists' hostility towards him. His brother Fedor fared no better. He fled to Poland in 1920 with the Polish army, but in the autumn of 1921 returned to Ukraine with the anti-Soviet Tiutiunnyk Ukrainian army, only to be repelled back to Poland.[4] Fedor was interned in a Polish camp in Kalisz, from which he illegally returned to Ukraine in 1925. Deprived of voting rights because of his service in the Petliura army, he was not treated as a Soviet citizen and was rejected by society. He began to drink, and in 1930 was sent to

Zgłosił się w amcie niejaki Witalij Budzko, ur.1904 r.
mieszkaniec wsi Prozoroki,pow.Dzisna i zameldował,że w 1930 r,
został on wysłany przez plac.Głębokie na wywiad do Rosji.

Po przekroczeniu granicy wpadł i siedział w więzieniu
przez 4 lata. Po zwolnieniu z więzienia pracował jakiś czas
w Dniepropietrowsku. Obecnie zgłasza się z chęcią wyjazdu do
Polski.

O powyższem melduję i proszę o ewentualną odpowiedź,
bym wiedział jak się do niego mam ustosunkować.

Na mnie zrobił on wrażenie ujemne.

Nal Niger.

17: A note by the Polish intelligence officer 'Nal Niger' (real name: Wiktor
Zaleski; see Chapter 1), dated 3 November 1934. Someone called Witalij Budzko
had presented himself at his office. Budzko, born in 1904, lived in the village
of Prozoroka in Dzisna. He reported that in 1930 he was sent to spy on Russia
(i.e., the Soviet Union). After crossing the border, however, he was arrested
and sat in gaol for four years. After his release he worked in Dnipropetrovs'k,
an industrial city in eastern Ukraine, for a while. Now he wanted to return
to Poland. Budzko did not make a good impression on Zaleski. Zaleski asked
Warsaw what to do. Narbut Nering, Zaleski's boss, responded on 21 December
1934. Witalij Budzko, son of Antoni and Marja Czyszkiewicz, was indeed a
Polish intelligence agent in 1929–30. He did not perform the tasks entrusted
to him, exposed himself through his own fault and was useless, Nering wrote.
According to available information, he was lured into Soviet territory allegedly
by one of the Polish agents who was working for the OGPU (Soviet secret
police), and to whom he reported. Nering added that Warsaw would not hinder
Budzko's possible return to Poland. From CAW, I:303.4.1929, 168/137.

a local labour camp for two years. (Ul'ian, too, seemed to have been imprisoned there for 'hooliganism', although in one section of his case file it is said that he had never been charged with a criminal offence.) In July 1930 Fedor fled from the camp to Poland, saying that he could not work in the Soviet Union. Ul'ian followed suit.[5]

In Poland, the brothers worked as masons and plasterers. Ul'ian apparently left behind in Skvyr a wife, Luker'ia, with whom he corresponded frequently and from whom he received contact addresses in Poland (38). His mother and sister as well as two other brothers also lived in Skvyr. A relative on his mother's side, Kozłowski, lived in Łomża, Poland, and many acquaintances were said to live in various parts of Poland (86).

On 31 July 1932, at a time when Ukraine had begun to suffer severe famine conditions, the two brothers crossed from the Polish side of the Soviet border near Olevs'k in the northwest of Zhytomyr. They were shot at by Soviet border guards. Fedor was killed, while Ul'ian was arrested. Ul'ian may not have been detained immediately, because in his case file he is only said to have been arrested on 2 August 1932 (85, 91).

Formally charged with espionage on 17 February 1933, Ul'ian was sentenced to be shot on the same day. Even though no records of his execution have been found, a reference in his case file to Document No. 4749/367vv suggests that he was executed soon thereafter (85–90, 91, 93, 123). Like so many other victims of terror in Kiev, he was buried in the mass graves in Bykivnia on the edge of the city.[6]

In this case as in so many others, there was little concrete evidence of Ul'ian's espionage. It is reported that the police found a stack of counter-revolutionary, Petliurite leaflets on his brother's body as well as a forged passport. Ul'ian himself was said to have been carrying a forged passport bearing the name of Anton Iakovlevich Davidenko, a resident of a village near Olevs'k, 200 Soviet roubles and a suitcase of counter-revolutionary, Petliurite leaflets which he was alleged to have dumped in a swamp when he was chased by the border guards (85). The Gorodovenko brothers were said to have been instructed by the former Petliurite Colonel Litvinenko-Morozenko to cross the border with the explicit purpose of conducting espionage. Ul'ian pleaded guilty to the charge. Yet not a single one of the leaflets allegedly carried by the brothers was produced as evidence to indict Ul'ian.

In 1989, Ul'ian Gorodovenko was rehabilitated on the grounds that the only evidence against him was his own confession. No relatives were found at the time (91).

Were the Gorodovenkos in fact Ukrainian nationalists? There is simply too little evidence available to support such a view. Of course, it is possible that they were (the Ukrainian nationalists must have thought that the famine provided a good opportunity to explore intervention in Soviet Ukraine), but it is equally possible that they simply wanted to return home. Also possible is that the Gorodovenkos were smugglers or that they were being used for provocation by Soviet agents who had penetrated the Ukrainian nationalist groups. The Soviet secret police used people like the Gorodovenkos to entrap the anti-Soviet émigré forces in elaborate counter-intelligence operations, in which case the Gorodovenkos may not have been aware of being used by the Soviet police. In any case, the Soviet authorities, keen to control the flow of people and information in the severe famine conditions, guarded the borders with extraordinary care.

Of course, the Gorodovenkos, whether secret Ukrainian nationalists or smugglers, may also have been used previously by the Polish authorities who perhaps now wanted to be rid of them. The Polish authorities may not have wanted potential troublemakers on Polish soil. (Indeed, Fedor was interned in Poland for some time in the 1920s.) The surest way to have them taken care of by the Soviet regime was to send them back to the Soviet Union carrying subversive literature. If caught, they would be arrested and incarcerated, freeing Poland of troublesome elements.

The Gorodovenkos' case was not an isolated one. A glance at Soviet records reveals numerous incidents of border transgressions in the west. From 1922 to 1936, the Ukrainian border authorities arrested 1,763 'spies' (the Gorodovenkos no doubt among them), 66 'diversionary elements', 5,326 'smugglers' (of whom 479 were armed). There were also 144 cases of armed conflict with border transgressors, as a result of which 60 'bandit groups' were 'liquidated'. Similarly, from 1921 to 1935 the Belarusan authorities apprehended 4,902 'spies', 550 saboteurs and 13,656 'smugglers'. In addition there were 282 cases of armed conflict.[7]

Like these thousands of 'spies' and 'saboteurs', Ul'ian Gorodovenko was despatched expeditiously.

The Fugitive Stashchenko

People fled not only abroad but within the Soviet Union too. Those exiled to remote regions often absconded to places closer to home or to new locations altogether. With the vast expansion of industry, people were constantly on the move in search of new work and new opportunities. It was not difficult even for the de-kulakised to find employment and refuge in cities and on construction sites.

Stepan Prokhorovich Stashchenko was born in 1893 into a Ukrainian kulak family in the village of Rulikiv to the south of Kiev. He served in the Red Army during the Civil War as an engine driver on the Murmansk railway line. Nevertheless, in 1930, Stashchenko fled to Moscow from Rulikiv when he was de-kulakised. He returned to Kiev at some point and worked as a mechanic at the 'Kiev Fiber' factory, living with his wife, Aleksandra Andreevna (born in 1896), also from the village of Rulikiv, in the company dormitory in Room 6, Barracks 10, Darnytsa, Kiev. He was arrested on 10 November 1937. Accused of anti-Soviet agitation, he was sentenced to be shot on 27 November 1937 by the NKVD *troika* and on 9 December 1937, at midnight, the execution took place.[8] Like Gorodovenko, Stashchenko was buried in a mass grave in Bykivnia.[9]

Interrogated on 13 November 1937, Stashchenko stated that when he had been de-kulakised in 1930, he owned 5 hectares of land, a house, a shed, a cow, a horse and agricultural equipment. (It is possible that his family was indeed relatively well off: his father was said to have owned 32 hectares of land, 2 cows, 4 horses and a thresher.) When the investigator told him that he had information that in 1929–30 Stashchenko had engaged in anti-Soviet and anti-*kolkhoz* (or collective farm) agitation, Stashchenko categorically denied the charge (7).

Testimonies were collected. Already, the day before he was first interrogated on 13 November 1937, several people were deposed. They gave damning evidence: Stashchenko stood against collectivisation, saying:

> The collective farms won't last in any case, because the Soviet government is unstable, war is inevitable, the government will be smashed, and Germany will come to power [in the Soviet Union]. Then people will begin to live well as they did under the tsar, and those who entered the collective farms will be shot.

Stashchenko's 'agitation' was said to have had an impact on many peasants, who began to take their property back from the collective farms. In 1936 Stashchenko began to reappear in Rulikiv, and on the adoption in December 1936 of the new, 'Stalin' constitution, he returned to the village but soon found work in the city of Kiev and moved there. Around the time of his arrest, he was necessarily accused of taking revenge on the village party activists, particularly those who had taken part in his de-kulakisation in 1930. With the reappearance of Stashchenko in the village, rumours began to circulate about the arrest of party and government leaders such as Molotov and Kaganovich. According to one witness, these rumours must have originated with Stashchenko (10–17).

It is possible that Stashchenko, encouraged by the adoption of the new constitution, which granted civil rights to many disenfranchised kulaks, wanted to recover some of his former property or else that he merely wanted to see what had happened to it. The reappearance in Rulikiv of a former kulak whom the Soviet authorities had deprived of everything must have alarmed the villagers who had known him before. It is not certain but it is entirely possible that his wife, Aleksandra, in fact still lived in the village: two of Stashchenko's brothers were said to be living in the village at the time (5zv.).

On the day Stashchenko was interrogated, he was allowed to question the witnesses. He challenged them and categorically denied all the charges, including his alleged anti-*kolkhoz* and anti-Soviet agitation and circulation of rumours about the arrest of Molotov and Kaganovich (18–19).

Nevertheless, Stashchenko was declared guilty and executed. His bill of indictment noted that there was no 'material evidence' in his case (20). Stashchenko may have been well off in 1930, but by 1937 he appears to have been utterly impoverished. When he was arrested, the police found absolutely nothing to confiscate from his residence, not even an internal passport. (As a former kulak, Stashchenko had not been issued with one.) This meant that he had been living illegally in the city of Kiev. Even though he owned nothing, the NKVD solemnly resolved on 27 November 1937 that he was to be executed and all his personal property confiscated (21).

Like so many others, Stashchenko was buried in a mass grave in Bykivnia and was rehabilitated in 1989 (26–26zv.).

The Fugitive Bigotskii

Nikolai Vasil'evich Bigotskii (Bihots'kyi), like Stashchenko, was a former kulak and a fugitive from exile. He was arrested and executed in 1938.

Bigotskii was born in 1878 (so he was sixty in 1938) in the village of Kano-Brid near Volodarka to the south of Kiev. He was de-kulakised in 1930 and exiled to the northern region in 1930, whence he fled in the same year. At the time of his arrest on 2 August 1938 he lived in the village of Katerynivka in Sviatoshyne, just outside the city of Kiev, and worked at the Sviatoshyne rope-making factory as an unskilled labourer. He was suspected of being a member of a 'Ukrainian insurgent organisation', for which he was said to be 'conducting counter-revolutionary agitation', such as threatening his neighbours with remarks like 'A moment will come when I'll hang these cursed Komsomols on a bayonet' (Komsomol was the youth wing of the Communist Party). In one document he is listed as single, elsewhere he is said to have been married (his wife, like Bigotskii himself, was illiterate). His daughter, Mariia Nikoaevna, born in 1914, worked on a collective farm.[10]

Oddly, his first interrogation appears to have begun on 29 July 1938, i.e., before he was arrested. When interrogated, Bigotskii stated that two months after he was exiled to Arkhangel'sk in the wake of his de-kulakisation, he escaped back to Ukraine, taking up residence near the railway station in Teteriv, about 75 km from the city of Kiev and about 50 km from where he had lived before he was dispossessed by the de-kulakisation campaign. When asked whether he belonged to any counter-revolutionary organisations or knew anything about such organisations, Bigotskii stated that he had never belonged to any organisation inclined against the Soviet government. However, he volunteered to tell his interrogators about other members of anti-Soviet groups. Timofei Evstafievich Lomatkin, for example, now living in Building No. 23 on the main thoroughfare in Sviatoshyne, was a member of the 'Efremov band' which in 1932–33 had had contacts across the Polish borders. (This was probably one of the peasant or criminal groups that mushroomed at the time of the Great Famine to fight against outside forces sent to the Ukrainian countryside to procure grain.) He often visited someone called Smolich, a Pole. In 1934 Lomatkin bought a house in Sviatoshyne where he lived now. Bigotskii helped Lomatkin to move to his new house from a flat near the railway station. While carryng his belongings, Bigotskii had felt some metal objects wrapped in a blanket. When asked what they were, Lomatkin said that they were parts of a machine gun and might turn out to be useful some day. Bigotskii noted that Lomatkin probably still had the gun. Lomatkin had worked at a railway station in Kiev, but had been dismissed for theft. Lomatkin, according to Bigotskii, was married to the daughter of a kulak (10–10zv.).

Bigotskii continued that Lomatkin was in contact with Petr Zhidnitskii (?), now living in Or ... (indecipherable). He had been convicted of being a member of the Efremov band and sentenced to three years of forced labour. According to Bigotskii, Lomatkin was inclined against the Soviet regime and was connected to the Pole Smolich. Zhodetskii or Zhidnitskii was a signaller for the Efremov insurgent band (10zv.).

Bigotskii then added that in 1934 when he carried the machine-gun parts, Lomatkin had said that he had once belonged to a big organisation but that it had been destroyed by the Soviet government. Bigotskii further stated that in 1937 several secret meetings took place in Lomatkin's house. He went on to implicate another person, Gavriil Grigor'evich Vasilenko, then living in Sviatoshyne but originally from Austria (i.e., Galicia), who had lived in Poland and, while there, had served in the Petliura army. (He had wanted to fight 'for the independence of Ukraine'.) When Vasilenko caught a wild boar, he had reportedly said, 'We should carve up not a boar but them—the Soviet regime' (11–11zv., 16zv.).

Bigotskii signed the interrogation records, but his signature betrays that he was illiterate, unable even to spell his own name properly. However, his skills were somewhat superior to those who used their fingerprint to sign, because he was at least able to write a few characters (i, g, k and ts).

It is possible that Bigotskii was merely deposed and not interrogated on 29 July 1938, even though the document is marked as the 'record of interrogation'. One cannot know for certain that these statements were really those of Bigotskii, because, like so many others examined in this book, they are standardised and formulaic in character. Vasilenko appears to have lived in the same house as Bigotskii. It may be that Vasilenko was arrested and that Bigotskii, sensing his own arrest was imminent, tried to protect himself by quickly denouncing others living

16. Каким репрессиям подвергался при Соввласти: судимость, арест и др. (когда, каким органо

и за что) _осужден был как кулак, на тч ... года домаш. высылки._

17. Состав семьи _дочь Мария Николаевна 1914г. рожд_
(близкие родственники, их имена, фамилии, адреса и род занятий)
работает в колхозе.

Подпись арестованного _Дуюшки._

18: Bigotskii's signature (the handwritten word on the bottom line).

around him. Equally likely, these statements may have simply been made up by Bigotskii's interrogator.

After his arrest Bigotskii was interrogated on 8 August 1938. He sought to defend his legal status as a citizen and to refute the allegation that he was a fugitive by explaining how he, as a former kulak, had managed to obtain an internal passport: when he was working on a giant construction site in eastern Ukraine, the Dnieper dam construction, he had presented his birth certificate and a certificate from the village soviet and had been issued with one. Such cases were common: at a time of acute labour shortages, factories and construction sites hired whoever was available and helped them to acquire a passport so that they had the right to travel outside their village. (Of course forgeries were also prevalent.) When Bigotskii came to the Kiev region in 1934 with his new passport, Lomatkin told him that Pavel Zhidnitskii (Petr's brother?) had been sentenced to ten years of forced labour for his participation in Efremov's SVU.[11] Lomatkin boasted to Bigotskii that his organisation was a big one—there were SVU members everywhere, from the border with Poland to Kiev. In the spring of 1938, according to Bigotskii, someone 'from the SVU' whom he knew was arrested carrying a rifle and a revolver (12–16). These statements were almost certainly fabricated by the interrogator: the SVU did not really exist.

A fortnight later, Bigotskii was interrogated again. He vigorously denounced Lomatkin and his wife. Lomatkin, according to Bigotskii, said, 'We'll soon begin to live as in the old days. Our troops are gathering in Poland, and will soon begin an offensive to throw out the Soviet government.' Bigotskii tried to show that Lomatkin's wife was even more inclined against the Soviet government than Lomatkin. She said, 'How is it that they sent my brothers into exile for nothing? What did my brother Fedor die there for? Why are another brother of mine and his wife still in exile? ... Maybe they have died of hunger by now.' She insisted that her father had died because of the Soviet government which simply 'suffocates the people and won't let them live'. Bigotskii even embellished his account by quoting a joke allegedly told by her: 'Soviet power! It's just an owl, such a foul owl, what a foul power, what a foul name they thought of' (19–20). Using the similarity between 'Soviet' and *sova* ('owl'), she referred to 'Soviet power' as 'owl power'.

Bigotskii's denunciations did not help him. The interrogator became impatient and asked why he had not spoken of his own anti-Soviet activities. Bigotskii was not easily broken. He pleaded guilty to having fled from exile and to having 'anti-Soviet conversations' with Lomatkin and his wife. Though fully aware that Lomatkin possessed a machine gun, he had not informed the appropriate Soviet organs. But apart from these talks with the Lomatkins, Bigotskii insisted that he had never had any other anti-Soviet conversations with anyone (22–23).

Meanwhile three testimonies were collected against Bigotskii. As mentioned earlier, one quoted him as saying, 'A moment will come when I'll hang these cursed Komsomols on a bayonet.' According to another, Bigotskii said, 'A time will come when I'll thread these Komsomols by five on a bayonet.' Bigotskii allegedly made these remarks in the spring of 1938 when local children organised a play in the yard of his residence and he became angry. To prevent the play, he collected human excrement from the cesspool and littered the yard with it. Some other minor neighbourhood conflicts were also cited against him (24–29).

These testimonies suggest that Bigotskii was an angry man who could not easily tolerate children and terrorised them. His remarks about threading or hanging Komsomols 'on a bayonet' may not have had any political connotations. They probably merely reflected his irritation (albeit extreme) with his neighbours and the children, who, however, saw political meaning in his anger.

In any case, on 29 August 1938 Bigotskii was sentenced to be shot by the NKVD *troika*. His execution was carried out two days later (32–33). Like Stashchenko and others, he was buried in the mass graves in Bykivnia.[12] Also like Stashchenko, he was rehabilitated in 1989. No relatives were found at the time (39–39zv.).

Ul'ian Gorodovenko, Stashchenko and Bigotskii were merely three of the numerous Ukrainians who were executed as Ukrainian nationalists and kulaks in the 1930s. There are cases in which dozens of suspected Ukrainian peasants were summarily executed.[13] Unlike the more prominent cases of writers and party activists, these people lived on the margins of society, often as fugitives. Their lives rarely attract the attention of historians except in generalities. Leaving few or no records of their own, they were despatched summarily.

Many, like Ul'ian Gorodovenko, had been rejected by Soviet society, and some had fled abroad but later sought to return to their homeland, only to face death. Like Stashchenko, many lived in utter poverty. To Stalin and the secret police they appeared security risks because they could potentially be recruited by foreign agents (indeed, Poland managed to recruit at least a few).

As was the case with Bigotskii, there were ways for them to sneak back into society by way of employment in factories and on construction sites where labour was in short supply. Even fugitives could find employment of this kind. Nevertheless, their existence remained extremely precarious. As it turned out, the adoption of the Stalin constitution in 1936 encouraged some formerly disenfranchised kulaks, such as Stashchenko, to assert their civil rights as supposedly guaranteed by the new constitution. This in turn made them more visible to the security organs.

Stalin deemed such people security risks (and destroyed them) at a time when the clouds of war were gathering rapidly.[14] It was precisely those who illegally or clandestinely found their way back that the Soviet regime targeted for physical destruction in 1937. This brutal terror operation was enacted by the NKVD's infamous July 1937 Secret Order 00447 (the so-called 'Kulak Operation'). In accordance with this operation, approximately 380,000 'kulaks' were executed in the Soviet Union in 1937–38.[15]

Sprawozdanie ze spotkania z N - I.

Spotkanie z agentem wyznaczone zostało jeszcze przed otrzymaniem zakazu utrzymywania kontaktów wogóle. Nie miałem więc możności uprzedzić go i wyznaczyć mu inny termin. Spotkałem się z nim dn.3.I. o oznaczonej godzinie i miejscu. Rozmawiałem z nim przeszło godzinę w samochodzie, pojechaliśmy za miasto, bez szofera.

Dostarczył on szeregu informacyj o garn.Kijów, o ploteczkach w mieście i zakupił na moje polecenie maskę gazową w sklepie "Dynamo". Zachowanie się jego nie budzi i nadal żadnych zastrzeżeń. Informacje podawane są szczupłe, jednak przeważnie dobre. Otrzymał dalsze zadanie obserwacyjne na garn.Kijów i następne spotkanie wyznaczone zostało na 25.I.

19: This note by Wiktor Zaleski, written in January 1935, reported on his meeting on 3 January 1935 with an informer, 'N-1', working in Kiev for the Polish intelligence (see Illustration 6, p. 31). N-1, a disenfranchised man (*lishenets*, probably a former kulak and possibly an ethnic Pole), lived in Kiev illegally and changed his place of residence almost daily. He had a family in Kiev, a wife and two children, and was hoping to leave for the provinces. He had a brother, a reservist, who lived in the suburbs of Kiev. Shortly before the meeting, apparently, Warsaw issued an order to prohibit the maintenance of contact with Soviet citizens working for Poland, probably because of the sharp change in the Soviet political climate in the wake of the 1 December 1934 assassination of the Leningrad party boss, Kirov. Zaleski stated that the appointment with N-1 was made before the order and it was impossible to get in touch with him and warn him. So Zaleski met him, drove him out of the city and they spoke for more than an hour without a driver present. N-1 delivered much good information on the Kiev garrison and on rumours and, by Zaleski's order, had bought a gas mask at the 'Dynamo' store. Zaleski gave him 300 roubles. Oddly, Zaleski noted that he made another appointment with N-1 for 25 January and gave him the further assignment of observing the Kiev garrison. In the meeting N-1 expressed a desire to emigrate to Poland where he had relations in Kalisz, but Zaleski could not promise him anything on that matter.

It is not entirely clear, however, that every suspected kulak who was executed was condemned as part of this operation. Stashchenko's case, for example, has no notation that the resolution of the *troika* was in accordance with Order 00447. Likewise, many others who had little to do with kulaks, for instance, criminals and 'servants of religious cults', were executed under the terms of this secret order.[16]

Without doubt many former kulaks survived the terror by going into exile or by living quietly on the margins of Soviet society. Bigotskii, having acquired a passport, might have survived the terror of 1937–38 had his neighbours not reported him when he was heard shouting 'anti-Soviet' sentiments at the children in his neighbourhood. His confessions regarding the SVU and other insurgent groups were almost certainly concocted by the police. The SVU existed only in the fantasies of the police; whether actual criminal gangs pursued any political goals is not certain. It is difficult to believe that popular complaints about life in general and about the Soviet government (which had failed to prevent the famine, resulting in millions of deaths in 1932–33) did not exist. Lomatkin, whom Bigotskii denounced, may have been inclined against the Soviet regime. As in so many such cases, almost no proof existed, however. The remark 'A moment will come when I'll hang these cursed Komsomols on a bayonet' may well really have been made by Bigotskii, but they seem the words of a man angry with the neighbourhood kids.

Of course, one inevitably wonders whether Bigotskii's outburst might also have been a genuine expression of political bitterness. One does not know for sure, but what is certain is that that was how the police understood it. His careless remark probably did not have any political connotations and someone with a spotless background might not have attracted the attention of the neighbours and the police for making it. But Bigotskii had a tainted political past. He was thus deemed a hidden enemy, a grave security risk in the event of war, and put to death.

Ukrainian Bandurists
Singers of 'National Ballads'

Bandurists play the bandura, a string instrument which is a hybrid of the lute and the harp. The bandura, which appears to have evolved from an old Cossack instrument called a *kobza*, is widely acknowledged as the Ukrainian national instrument, just as the hopak is the Ukrainian national dance. The bandura is used to accompany *dumy* (epic ballads) and folk songs. The bandurists, many of whom were travelling musicians, also served the Cossack fighters in their campaigns.[1] In the modern era, after the destruction of the Ukrainian (Zaporizzhan) Cossacks in the eighteenth century at the hands of Peter I and Catherine II, the bandurists and their music were appropriated by the Ukrainian national movement as the embodiment of 'Ukrainian-ness'.

Modern nationalists have often turned to folk music and folklore in a quest to establish the emotional underpinnings of a nation state. In Ukraine's case, folk songs and folktales also provided inspiration for 'Russian' literati and musicians (Nikolai Gogol, Nikolai Rimskii-Korsakov, Petr Tschaikovsky and Igor Stravinskii, to name just a few). What distinguishes the Ukrainian nationalist movement from that of Russia is its adoption of Ukrainian Cossack legends about the fight for freedom from foreign (Russian, Polish and Turkish) oppression. Cossack themes were the favourite subject of the bandurists as well as of the nineteenth-century poet Taras Shevchenko, universally regarded as Ukraine's national poet, the equivalent of Aleksandr Pushkin in Russia and Adam Mickiewicz in Poland.

Traditionally, the bandurists enjoyed a degree of freedom as artists and performers in expressing ideas and thoughts not otherwise readily tolerated by political authorities. After the October Revolution, however,

Cossack themes began to pose a problem for the Bolsheviks. While the songs condemned the tsarist oppression of non-Russian nationalities (in this case Ukrainians), they also praised freedom from foreign (Russian) rule. The 1920s were a time of relative tolerance, and the 'off-shoots of the urban national bandura ensembles appeared among sighted youth in both the village and the city'. Aided by the policy of 'Ukrainisation',[2] 'hundreds of urban and village bandura ensembles were formed all over Ukraine in which young men and women performed a secularised and standardised repertory'. The Soviet authorities hoped to appropriate the bandurists and their music in a form suitable to socialism. Yet in the atmosphere of the 1930s, this experiment was largely abandoned.[3]

In June 1930, two ethnographers recorded the following scene in Kremenchuk, a town downriver from Kiev: an old, blind man (probably a minstrel) sang a song at a bazaar critical of the new order in the countryside as represented by the *kolkhoz*:

> Winter asks Frost,
> Whether the *kolkhoz* has boots
> —There are no boots, just sandals,
> The *kolkhoz* will fall into pieces.

When a policeman arrested him, he continued:

> Oh, see, good folks,
> What world has arrived now:
> The policeman has become
> A guide for a blind man.[4]

In the 1930s, many bandurists were indeed arrested and even executed as Ukrainian nationalists and separatists.

The political danger represented by the bandurists was apparent to Moscow, as one concerned Red Army colonel in Kiev commented in the late 1930s:

[W]hy is it that when I listen to a piano concert, a violin concert, or a symphony orchestra, or a choir, I always notice that the audience listens politely. But when they listen to the women's *bandura* choir, and they get to singing the *dumy*, then I see tears welling up in the

eyes of the Red Army soldiers? You know, these *banduras* have a
Petliurist soul.[5]

The colonel's interlocutor, a Ukrainian musician, responded later:

> Do you recall when you asked me why the Ukrainian *bandura* has
> that special tone that makes people cry when they listen to it, and
> you said that this instrument reflects the very soul of Petliura. And I
> answered you that it's simply the embodiment of the national spirit.
> The *bandura* moves people, and especially so if a person misses his
> native land, his father and mother, or if a person has the kind of life
> that is filled with burdens and disappointments, or if there is pain
> and outrage all around him and the person is in tears.[6]

The bandurists were dangerous to Moscow because of their 'spirit'.

Doroshko and Kopan

Fedor Vasilevich Doroshko was one of those bandurists. Doroshko,
born into a poor peasant family in Chernihiv in 1882, acquired only an
elementary education. Before the Revolution he was a metalworker at
the 'Arsenal' factory in Kiev made famous by Oleksandr Dovzhenko's
film of the same name. Doroshko was a good musician, and in 1918 he
became one of the founders of the Kiev bandura chorus.[7] At the time of
his arrest in 1937, he was still working in Kiev as a bandurist. According
to police records, he had been arrested by the Cheka in 1919. He had
a wife, Anna Ivanovna Doroshko, a son, Iurii Nikolaevich Lakhno,
19, and a daughter, Vera Fedorovna, 7. Doroshko was arrested on 15
December 1937 on charges of being a Japanese agent and conducting
espionage in the interests of Japan.[8]

When he was interrogated on 22 December 1937, Doroshko denied
spying for Japan. (What linked him to Japan in fact or in the imagination
of the police is not clear.) He did concede, however, that, being disposed
against the Soviet regime, he had engaged in 'counter-revolutionary
activity', particularly against the collective farms (1:41–43). According
to his later confessions, from 1917 to 1918 Doroshko was an active
member of the Central Rada,[9] a Ukrainian government which was
composed of socialists and social democrats and, in opposition to the

20: Bandurists in 1939.

Bolshevik attempt to take control of Ukraine, declared independence in January 1918. Like other members of the Central Rada, most notably the prominent historian Mykhailo Hrushevskii, who returned to the Soviet Union in the 1920s from abroad,[10] Doroshko may have come to accept the Soviet regime, believing that the more conciliatory policy introduced after the Civil War would gradually soften the Bolsheviks. If this was the case, Doroshko was mistaken. Stalin's 'revolution from above' fundamentally transformed the country through rapid industrialisation and the collectivisation of agriculture. Whatever their private feelings, however, very few people dared to voice them for fear of political persecution. In 1934, Hrushevskii, for example, was implicated in a fictitious anti-Soviet political plot and died in suspicious circumstances while in exile in Russia.[11] While it is possible that Doroshko was against the collectivisation of agriculture, it is unlikely that he would have voiced such concerns.

On the following day, 23 December 1937, Doroshko was interrogated again and confessed that he was guilty of the crimes of which he was accused (44). It is not clear whether his guilty plea included the espionage charge. It appears that he was not interrogated again for more than two months. Then, on 13 March 1938, Doroshko was subjected to a new interrogation. This time he was accused of not fully confessing to his crimes. There was now no discussion of his espionage activity for Japan; rather he was accused of having been a member of an active counter-revolutionary organisation and of conducting counter-revolutionary activity until he was arrested. Doroshko is quoted in the records as fully accepting the new charges (1:45–46):

> Realizing the uselessness of further defiance, I have decided to speak the truth about the counter-revolutionary activity I conducted until recently. I was an enemy of the Soviet regime and waged an active fight against it from the first days of the Revolution. By conviction I am a Ukrainian nationalist and a supporter of Ukrainian independence. In the period 1917–18 I was a member of the Central Rada and took an active part in it. In 1925, while in the village of Uzin in Kiev Oblast', I got in touch with the active Petliurite,[12] Iosif Grigor'evich Snezhnyi, also a member of the Central Rada.

Then he said that in December 1936 he was approached by Mitrofan Lavrent'evich Reshetilo, who had been a prisoner of war in Germany during World War I and joined the Sich Riflemen unit of independent Ukraine. Reshetilo told him that he was a member of a 'counter-revolutionary military insurgency organisation' that existed in Kiev, and asked Doroshko to join. The aim of the organisation was to carry out sabotage and espionage and to disrupt the rear of the Red Army in preparation for war against the Soviet Union. The ultimate goal was to overthrow the Soviet regime, restore capitalism in Ukraine and reorient the country towards 'German Fascism'. The head of the organisation was Afanasii Liubchenko.[13] Liubchenko was arrested on 3 September 1937. In detention, he attempted to seize the weapon of his guard and was killed. In 1956 he was rehabilitated (2:118–20). Doroshko said that he joined the organisation and that subsequently two Ukrainians, Ivan Tarasovich Doroshko, a twenty-seven-year-old metalworker, and Fedor Mikhailovich Koziuba, a thirty-nine-year-old, were also recruited (1:47–51).

Reshetilo, Ivan Doroshko and Koziuba were indicted along with Fedor Doroshko. The arrest warrant for Reshetilo was issued on 1 February 1938 on suspicion that he was conducting espionage for Poland, but for some reason he was not arrested until 20 March. He was fifty-one years of age, an ethnic Ukrainian and an artist, but unemployed at the time of his arrest (1:15). When interrogated on 22 March 1938, Reshetilo noted that he had indeed been a prisoner of war during World War I and that he had joined Ukraine's Sich Riflemen unit. (Former prisoners of war came under suspicion in the 1930s because of their suspected foreign ties. As many as 2.5 million of these former prisoners were said to have been living in Ukraine at the time.)[14] When Hetman Skoropads'kyi overthrew the Central Rada in the spring of 1918 with the help of German forces, Reshetilo had joined him. Then when the Hetman regime was overthrown by the Directorate, headed by the Ukrainian socialist Symon Petliura, a former member of the Central Rada, Reshetilo joined the latter's camp. When the Directorate was defeated by the Bolsheviks, he stayed on in Kiev and joined the Borot'bists, the radical Ukrainian socialist party. According to Reshetilo's confession, which was patently absurd, he was directed by one of its leaders, Oleksandr Shums'kyi, to collect information for the Polish intelligence.[15] When the Borot'bists joined the Ukrainian Bolsheviks in the spring of 1920, he followed suit. When Polish forces occupied Kiev briefly in May 1920, he was ordered to stay in Kiev by the party. However, he secretly helped the Polish intelligence, as a result of which more than a hundred Soviet supporters were arrested. In 1921, when the party conducted a purge, he was expelled. In 1923 or 1924 he re-established contact with the former Borot'bists. In the summer of 1936 Reshetilo said that he was recruited by Andrei Liubchenko, who told them that 'the time has come for us to move to more serious counter-revolutionary activity'. The group counted on support from Poland and Germany. According to Reshetilo, Liubchenko received orders from his brother Panas. He then confessed that he had recruited Fedor Doroshko and Georgii Iakovlevich Kopan among others (68–88, especially 78–79).

This confession was probably responsible for the change in the charges brought against Doroshko. Now the Japanese connection disappeared altogether, and the Doroshko-Reshetilo link to the Ukrainian insurgency organisation was targeted. Yet the confessions of Doroshko and Reshetilo, like many others examined in this book, are plainly formulaic: 'I am a Ukrainian nationalist and a supporter of Ukrainian independence'; 'I was against collectivisation'; 'Our goal was to overthrow the Soviet regime and restore capitalism in Ukraine with the help of Germany and Poland' and the like. Indeed, they are so formulaic as to be devoid of meaning, even if one allows for the fact that Reshetilo and Doroshko had non-Bolshevik political backgrounds.

A warrant for Kopan was issued on 14 March 1938 and he was duly arrested. Like Doroshko and Reshetilo, Kopan belonged to the Kiev artistic circle. Fifty-one years of age, he was born into a Ukrainian peasant family and worked as a metalworker in various factories before the Revolution. Yet he must have been an accomplished musician as well. From 1921 he worked as a leading bandurist and choirmaster (1:23). However, he had a compromising political past: in 1930 he had been arrested for allegedly carrying counter-revolutionary propaganda (to the effect that in spite of Ukrainisation 'Ukrainians do not enjoy any rights and no measures are being taken for the blossoming of Ukrainian culture'). According to a testimony taken in October 1930 by a witness (P. F. Vyshinskii), Kopan said, 'Ukrainisation is promoted only for the sake of appearances, to show foreign countries that everything is fine here.' As choirmaster and artistic director, Kopan was alleged to have sought to instil and arouse in audiences 'narrowly nationalistic sentiments' by giving a 'chauvinistic performance, saturated with nationalistic sentiments'. Kopan more than once said that it was necessary to cultivate in the audience a 'nationalist spirit'. Leading his choir, Kopan consciously sought to achieve this goal (2:90, 92–93). How Kopan defended himself in 1930 is not known. After four months of detention he was released, apparently without indictment (1:23).

Kopan was interrogated again on 1 April 1938. This time he incriminated himself from the beginning: he was a past master of musical subversion. He said that his 'counter-revolutionary activity' began in 1921 when he worked in a Ukrainian bandura chorus. Together with other bandurists, he performed Ukrainian songs that had been removed from the repertory as ideologically unsound. They played other songs in a purely nationalistic spirit so as to deprive them of their 'real' (i.e., Soviet) content and instead reveal their nationalistic character to the audience. By doing so, he sought to kindle nationalism in the audience. He did this particularly when the ensemble went to theatres in the provinces where the control of the Communist Party was weaker than in Kiev (1:149–149zv.).

Ten days later, on 11 April 1938, Fedor Doroshko, Reshetilo, Kopan, Koziuba and Ivan Doroshko were sentenced to be shot. According to

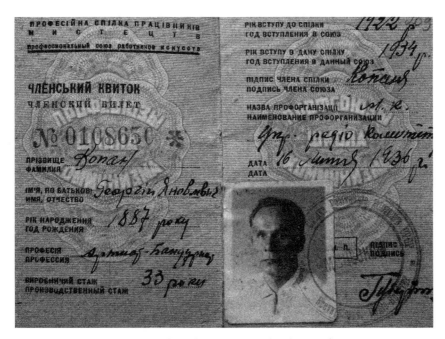

21: Kopan's trade union membership card.

the police medical record, Fedor Doroshko died on 21 April 1938 at 6.25 a.m. from 'paralysis of the respiratory centre'. (It is possible that he died naturally under strain. It is also possible that he was further interrogated to implicate other people and in the process was tortured to death.) The other four were executed a week later, on 28 April 1938 at 11 p.m. (1:203, 204–8).

After Stalin's death, in May 1957, Reshetilo's daughter, Nadezhda Mitrofanovich, wrote to the Gulag authorities in Moscow. In June 1957 the KGB responded that her father had been sentenced to ten years of incarceration in 1938 and on 3 November 1941 had died of nephritis (1:213, 219). This kind of blatant lie was standard practice even at the time of de-Stalinisation. Nevertheless, the KGB investigated the case against the five dead. The 1930 witness against Kopan, P. F. Vyshinksii, could not be located. However, a former colleague of Kopan's in the bandura chorus who also knew Doroshko, Andrei Nikitich Kononenko, testified that Kopan had contributed greatly to its creation and to the preservation of Ukrainian national arts, and that Doroshko enjoyed much popularity among the bandurists, was a good musician and was a master of the bandura. His impression was that Doroshko was an honest Soviet person who liked his work and dedicated all his knowledge and energy to it. In a similar vein, another witness, V. S. Pokhil, testified that both Kopan and Doroshko enjoyed respect and authority among their colleagues (2:243–44, 293).

In October 1958 all five men were rehabilitated (2:231, 257). Their voices, like those of many others, are almost completely buried in their files. Yet their music was not lost. This was their true voice. It is not known which particular repertory was condemned by the secret police. Probably it included something like the 'Duma about Marusia from Bohuslav', the beginning of which runs:

> On the Black Sea,
> On a white rock,
> There stood a dungeon of stone,
> In this dungeon there lived seven hundred Cossacks,
> Poor captives,
> They had languished in captivity for thirty years,
> And they saw neither the Lord's daylight nor the righteous sun.[16]

These Cossacks were in Turkish captivity, but when sung in the context of the 1930s, the *duma* could have easily been interpreted by Ukrainians as referring to Ukrainian kulaks or national heroes in Soviet captivity. Another *duma* about the seventeenth-century Cossack chief Ivan Bohun ends as follows:

> All the Cossacks
> And soldiers
> Stood in ranks,
> And shouted with all their might,
> And as they spoke,
> The kobzars [bandurists] were playing,
> They were plucking their strings,
> And with their songs they were praising
> Bohdan and Bohun.[17]

The police might have considered this a 'nationalistic' song honouring Ukrainian heroes. Doroshko and Kopan liked Ukrainian music and lived by it. It was inherently 'national', but not necessarily 'nationalistic'. Almost certainly they felt constrained in their activities in one way or another by Soviet ideology, but there is absolutely no verifiable evidence that they were inclined, even surreptitiously, to fight against the Soviet regime. Surely they were not spies for Japan, Poland or Germany.

Balatskii

The voice of Dmitrii Ievmenovich Balatskii, a better-known bandurist than either Kopan or Doroshko, is easier to make out today because Balatskii survived the terror. He was born in 1901 into a Ukrainian peasant family in Haisyn, near Uman', to the south of Kiev. He graduated from the Lysenko Music and Drama Institute in Kiev in 1929. When he was arrested on 2 February 1938 on suspicion of participating in a counter-revolutionary nationalist organisation and conducting counter-revolutionary agitation among his colleagues, he was working as the director of the State Model Bandura Chorus in Kiev. He was married to Agnesa Anatol'evna Rozanova-Balatskaia, his junior by five years and a graduate student at Kiev State University.[18]

For unknown reasons, Balatskii was left in limbo for several months after his arrest. He later said that he was indicted only on 7 July 1938 (1:46–47). The first available record of his interrogation dates to 26 August 1938. The interrogator asked him about his brother Konstantin who lived in Poland (yet another Polish connection). This apparently came as a surprise to Balatskii, who believed that his brother had died in the Civil War. Balatskii admitted that he knew that his brother had been mobilised by the Petliura army even though Konstantin was ill at the time. Subsequently Balatskii had been informed by people who knew Konstantin that he had died not far from his own home in Haisyn. So it was news to him that Konstantin had left for Poland. Balatskii categorically denied the charges presented against him: 'I never belonged to a counter-revolutionary organisation and don't know about its existence at all, nor did I carry out anti-Soviet agitation in my work' (1:14–16). Then the interrogator pressed Balatskii about his relations with 'enemies of the people' already arrested. He responded (1:16):

Yes, indeed, in my practical work I had close contact with Al'tshulir and Shevchuk [a composer] and less close contact with [Andrii]

Khvilia [a former Borot'bist and deputy education commissar in Ukraine], who promoted me to be leader and conductor of the Kiev State Model Bandura Chorus. Al'tshulir was the director of the music department in the Arts Administration of Ukraine, and he, in cahoots with Khvilia, forced me to become the artistic director of the Kiev State Model Bandura Chorus under threat of arrest. He and the former director of the Arts Administration of Ukraine, Khvilia, assigned me to adopt and I indeed adopted almost exclusively Ukrainian songs for the repertory of the Bandura Chorus. There were almost no songs of other nations of the Soviet Union.

Balatskii tried to defend himself by passing the blame onto his superiors, who had already been arrested. (Khvilia was executed in February 1938 as one of the organisers and leaders of an 'anti-Soviet, nationalist, Fascist, diversionary-terrorist organisation in Ukraine'.) It is possible that it is true that his superiors decided the repertory, although whether this was actually nationalistic is a completely different matter.

On 18 September 1938 Balatskii's colleague and fellow bandurist, Aleksei Teret'evich Dziubenko, who was also under arrest, was interrogated about Balatskii. Dziubenko testified that Balatskii was clearly anti-Soviet and nationalistically minded and that he slandered the leaders of the party and the government, sympathised with enemies of the people like Khvilia and gave preference to Ukrainian songs in his selection of material (1:24–25). The following day Zakhar Abramovich Aronskii, a party member and the director of the State Ensemble, also testified that Balatskii preferred old Ukrainian songs and nationalistic songs from Western Ukraine (Galicia), then under Polish control, ignoring contemporary Soviet revolutionary songs. Aronskii also alleged that Balatskii played a song about Ezhov, then the chief of the Soviet secret police, which sounded like a Ukrainian nationalist song and was therefore later removed from the repertory. Aronskii and another witness, Vasil'ii Iosifovich Lutaenko, conductor of the Kiev City Dumka Chorus,[19] gave almost identical testimonies that Balatskii said that the Soviet regime had forbidden many good Ukrainian songs and suppressed Ukrainian culture (1:30–31).

The police let Lutaenko and Balatskii question each other to resolve their contradictory accounts. Lutaenko repeated his testimony against Balatskii, adding that Balatskii also included songs by the composer

Kashits (who had emigrated abroad)[20] and that Balatskii also told anti-Soviet anecdotes (1:36–37). Interrogated by the police again on 19 September 1938, Balatskii repeated his earlier testimony that he had not initially agreed to become leader of the chorus, that he was then summoned to Al'tshulir's office and was told that unless he accepted the position he would be arrested. (Al'tshulir said, according to Balatskii, that he would uncover the reason for Balatskii's refusal, suggesting that Balatskii had something to hide.) Balatskii emphasised that he had worked under the direction of Al'tshulir and Khvilia, but that neither had told him that he was a member of a counter-revolutionary nationalist organisation, and he knew nothing about the existence of any such body (1:18–22).

Fortunately for Balatskii, the Great Terror was coming to an end. On 21 October 1938 he was convicted of anti-Soviet agitation but was given a remarkably lenient sentence by the standards of the time: five years' exile in Kazakhstan (1:45).

Several months later, on 28 April 1939, Balatskii wrote a letter from Kazakhstan to the Ukrainian Communist Party secretary of the time, Nikita Khrushchev, asking for his case to be re-examined. The letter was written in Ukrainian. This was odd. Balatskii was accused of being a Ukrainian nationalist but he chose to address Khrushchev, a Russian, in Ukrainian. Balatskii knew Russian, and his interrogation records were in Russian, although it is possible that he could not write properly in Russian. Whatever the case, Balatskii wrote that he was an 'honest person and worker'. The methods of investigation 'stunned me', and the indictment was simply 'nonsense'. He had never acted in any way against the Soviet regime. Lutaenko's testimony was all false: he said that he had 'heard anti-Soviet anecdotes in my lectures, but he never attended my lectures'. Balatskii added that he was accused of rejecting a song about Ezhov, but it was rejected by the Union of Composers because its melody, composed by one Sandler, did not correspond to the idea of the text in the vocal as well as piano parts.[21] (Oddly, as discussed earlier, Balatskii was accused by Aronskii of using the song for the Ukrainian nationalist cause.) He went on that there were many other allegations against him, but that he had been in an extremely agitated and nervous state and had been almost forced to sign the interrogation protocol and therefore he did not even know what he had said. Then he concluded: 'I am a young specialist [of music], the son of Haisyn's cartwright, who, thanks to the socialist October Revolution, acquired higher education. I am full of creative power and energy but am deprived of the possibility of being useful to my fatherland' (1:46–47).

Balatskii's letter reached Khrushchev. On 27 July 1939 the prosecutor's office sent a secret and urgent request to the NKVD to send Balatskii's file because the secretary of the party, Khrushchev, was 'interested in the case' (2:7).

In August 1939 the original witnesses were interrogated again. They explained that their earlier testimonies had not been recorded correctly, that they knew of no anti-Soviet remarks by Balatskii, that they knew of no insertion of Ukrainian nationalist songs into the repertory and so on. Thus, interrogated on 23 August 1939, Dziubenko, now released from detention, did not repeat his earlier testimony. He did add, however, that he remembered one incident in late 1937 when Balatskii yelled at the vocal group during a rehearsal, 'Why are you screaming like collective farmers?' Rebuked by one of the members, however, he had stopped and corrected himself (1:50–51)

On 26 August 1939 Aronskii testified that he knew of no anti-Soviet remarks made by Balatskii, but that he had heard anti-Semitic anecdotes from him. For example, 'Two Jews, Moshka and Khaim, went to church to be christened. Khaim went in first. When he came out, Moshka asked him, "So how was it?" In response, Khaim beat him in the face, saying, "Why did you Jews crucify our Christ?"' And also: 'An old Jew is dying and his family has assembled around him. He asks Sur [?], "You're here?", Sur says, "Yes, I'm here." He lists the names of ten to twelve others and then asks, "But who's at the shop?"' Aronskii's testimony made sense because at the time anti-Semitism was still regarded as a grave political offence (although Balatskii was not charged with it). Aronskii added that Balatskii included nationalistic songs, for example, songs by Shevchuk (now repressed) and Haidamak songs. (Haidamaks were peasant and Cossack rebels in eighteenth-century Ukraine.) Balatskii, Aronskii added, also deplored, after the arrest of I. E. Iakir, that 'such a hero' had been taken away, saying that they targeted mainly Ukrainians for terror (1:52–53).

Another witness, Pavel Dmitrievich Lisponenko, a party member and a State Bandura Chorus member, testified on 2 October 1939 that Balatskii did adopt nationalistic songs by Shevchuk, but that he knew of no concrete cases of Balatskii's making anti-Soviet

В. Ш. Микита Сергієвич!

Даруйте мені кілька хвилин на читання цього листа та вибачте за турботи, якими забираю дорогий Ваш час своєю особистою справою. Я зараз в надзвичайно тяжкому морально-...ченому стані, — і пишучи цього листа на Ваше ім'я, може й сплутав адресат. Це лише внаслідок трагедії яка сталась мною і я потрапив з Києва аж до вічного Казахстану адміністративну висилку, якої не заслужив, оскільки все був членом людиною й робітником.

Самий арешт, десятимісячне ув'язнення й методи слідства мене так приголомшили, що й досі важко зібратися думками, щоби вдатись на правдивий шлях для своєї абілітації та позбутись пилли адміністративної висилки.

Коли б хоч на йоту я відчував якусь провину перед своєю країною, я не звертався б ні до кого з проханими по помочу. Але думки, що мене безневинно тяжко покарано, збавлено любимої музичної роботи, — любов до якої я бажав ще з дитячих років пастушка, що мої знання і свід потрібні моїй країні, — не дають мені спокою.

Ні серці не передаваємий їхній і тягар образи від такого куснею моєї праці, бо притаманний мені запал, настрій і любов, з якими я завжди відносився до неї, як є, що нічогісенько антирадянського я ніколи не діяв, бо

22: Balatskii's letter to Khruschchev in Ukrainian.

remarks or telling anti-Soviet anecdotes (1:54–55). On 11 October 1939 Andrei Nikitovich Kononenko, another Bandura Chorus member, gave testimony that Balatskii often told anecdotes, some being anti-Semitic ('Jewish anecdotes'), but that he knew of no cases of anti-Soviet remarks being made by Balatskii (1:56–56zv.)

Based on these testimonies, in 1940 the NKVD concluded that Balatskii's guilt was proved (1:57–59).

Balatskii's subsequent fate is dramatic. On 23 October 1942 he was freed, but in 1943 he was arrested again and sentenced to be shot for his alleged 'anti-Soviet nationalistic activity' (2:21). Then, for some reason, his sentence was commuted to ten years' imprisonment, and in 1944 he was released suddenly (1:72–72zv.). In 1947–48 he worked as the director of the chorus group of the Odesa Philharmonic, in 1949 as the choirmaster of the Song and Dance Ensemble in Kiev, and then as the director of the chorus group of the Poltava Philharmonic.[22] After Stalin died, Balatskii again wrote to the authorities in Kiev, this time in Russian, asking for his rehabilitation (1:72–72zv.).

So testimonies were collected again in 1956. Aronskii and Lutaenko could not be located. Kononenko was interviewed on 14 May. He stated that Balatskii knew nothing about bandura music but was principled. He confirmed his 1939 remark that Balatskii did not like criticism, but he said Balatskii's repertory did not include nationalistic songs, merely old Ukrainian folk songs. He remembered Balatskii saying that he once went hunting with Iakir. This time he did not mention Balatskii's anti-Semitic anecdotes (62–62zv.).

On 16 June 1956 Dziubenko was interviewed again about Balatskii. He testified that Balatskii was a professional man, who knew choral music well but did not know the bandura instrument and was not interested in it. He further noted that at the time, in the 1930s, the repertory changed frequently, and some old Ukrainian folk songs, which were not nationalistic, were banned for a long time. He added that he, too, had been under arrest then (from January 1938 to June 1939) and denied his earlier testimony that in a conversation with him Balatskii had slandered the leaders of the Communist Party and the Soviet government (63–63zv.):

I know nothing about this, because it was such a long time ago and I don't remember. I assume that this was written by the interrogator but without paying attention to it I signed it. As for Balatskii's anti-Soviet or nationalistic activity, I cannot say anything, because I know nothing about it.

In 1956 Baltaskii was rehabilitated (1:74–75). He continued his musical career in Poltava, where he died on 15 March 1981 at the age of seventy-nine.[23]

As it turns out, none of Balatskii's alleged crimes (his slander of party and government leaders, his membership in a nationalist organisation, his inclusion of Ukrainian nationalist songs in the repertory) was proved. He was almost certainly innocent of the crimes of which he was accused. He was lucky not to have been tortured (he probably wasn't). If he had broken down and confessed to his alleged crimes, he would have been executed. He was lucky in another respect too: his case was delayed in 1938, and by the time the police dealt in earnest with it, the political climate had begun to change and the Great Terror was coming to a close. Pleading innocence often did not help, because numerous people were executed even though they denied the charges against them. Still, standing his ground against the formidable prospect of death helped to save him. Otherwise, we might not have been able to retrieve his voice at all.

Many Ukrainian bandurists perished in the Great Terror, although the often-voiced claims by some Ukrainians that the bandurists were completely wiped out by Stalin is not correct. Some well-known bandurists such as Volodymyr A. Kabachok survived.[24] However, the doyen of bandura music, the Kharkiv-based Ukrainian writer and scholar, Hnat Khotkevych, was executed in 1938. Like many Ukrainian intellectuals, he did not initially accept the Bolshevik Revolution. In the 1920s, however, he came to terms with the Soviet government and took an active part in Ukrainian cultural life. Yet suspicion remained that Khotkevych was anti-Soviet and that through his promotion of Ukrainian culture in general and bandura music in particular he was embracing the 'cult' of the Ukrainian Cossacks and Haidamaks (in short, Ukrainian nationalism). Even his musical rendition of 'The Internationale' was banned.[25] Khotkevych was arrested in February 1938, accused of spying for Germany and participation in the Ukrainian nationalist and 'terrorist' organisation UVO, sentenced to be shot on 28 September 1938 and executed on 8 October 1938. In 1956 he was rehabilitated.[26]

Although on the whole Russian musicians escaped the Great Terror lightly,[27] the same cannot be said of their non-Russian peers. Initially the Soviet government accepted that 'national' was not necessarily 'nationalist', hence non-Russian national cultures were allowed to flourish in the 1920s. But in the political atmosphere of the 1930s 'national' became increasingly equated with 'nationalist'. Stalin is said to have liked Ukrainian songs and Ukrainian bandurists.[28] Yet suspicion remained that some of the latter used their music as a method of political subversion. Suspected of Ukrainian nationalism, many were arrested and executed. As artists, the Ukrainian bandurists would not have liked the restrictions placed upon their activity, but they lived by music, not by politics. Their music was their true voice.

Battered and intimidated though they were, many bandurists still survived the terror. Music itself survived in prisons and camps. As one foreign prisoner recalled of his prison time in Ukraine in 1937–38,

> The Ukrainians have a great fund of folk songs, and new ones are constantly springing up in the villages. They are almost always sad and very melodious and beautiful and their text is rarely banal. Our Ukrainian sang them beautifully and we were very grateful. The warders must often have heard him but they never interfered. I even had the impression that sometimes they stood outside the cell door and listened.[29]

As a symbol, the bandura remained important to the Soviet government. In 1939, when Stalin forcibly incorporated Western Ukraine into Soviet Ukraine, he despatched bandurists there as well as the Red Army. They sang Ukrainian songs with texts by Shevchenko, Ivan Franko and other prominent Ukrainian poets, and proved extremely popular.[30]

Whether or not Stalin knew of Socrates' precepts on music, he practised them in his own way: 'rearing in music is most sovereign,' Socrates said, because 'rhythm and harmony most of all insinuate themselves into the inmost part of the soul and most vigorously lay hold of it in bringing grace with them; and they make a man graceful if he is correctly reared, if not, the opposite.'[31] Like Socrates, Stalin discriminated between useful and harmful music, using the Ukrainian bandurists for his political purposes as he saw fit.

CHAPTER 7

Koreans and Chinese in Kiev
Improbable Spies

Sometimes people happen to turn up in improbable places. Ethnic Koreans in Kiev in 1937 are one such case. It is not easy to establish exactly how many ethnic Koreans lived in the Ukrainian capital. According to the 1937 census, 168,259 Koreans lived in the Soviet Union, of whom 167,220 or 99.4 percent lived in the Russian Federation (mainly in the Far East). The same census counted 38,527 ethnic Chinese in the country, of whom 38,489 or 99.9 percent resided in the Russian Federation. According to the census, there was a grand total of one ethnic Japanese in the entire country.[1] These data are not very accurate, however. At the time, owing to the tensions with Japan, many of the Japanese people in the Soviet Union chose to go by Korean names. Already in the early 1930s, in Kharkiv, then the capital of Ukraine, a Civil War veteran and plant director who was married to a Japanese woman had been executed as a Japanese spy.[2] In Ukraine in 1937 alone, thirty-seven ethnic 'Japanese' were arrested for political crimes, although this figure may also include Japanese citizens.[3]

In any case, a few ethnic Koreans and Chinese did live in Kiev in the 1930s. One writer noted of Chinese children in Kiev in the mid-1930s that they spoke Russian without an accent, just the way other children did. (Russian was and still is the dominant language in Kiev.) Yet one summer (apparently in 1937) all of the ethnic Chinese disappeared from Kiev.[4] This was almost certainly connected to the 1937 mass deportations of ethnic Koreans from the Far Eastern border areas on suspicion that they were acting as Japanese spies (just as the ethnic Poles and Germans were suspected of being spies for Poland and Germany). These operations, which followed earlier deportations in 1930–31 and 1935, almost completely uprooted the Soviet Korean population, displacing them to Central Asia, far from the Far Eastern borderlands. The Chinese fared slightly better, perhaps because the Soviet Union supported China in the Sino-Japanese War, which broke out in July 1937. All the same, 11,000 Chinese were arrested and 8,000 deported from the Far East. In addition, more than 1,000 'returnees from Kharbin', 600 ethnic Poles and unspecified numbers of ethnic Germans, Latvians, Lithuanians and others were arrested. (The Soviet Union sold the Chinese Eastern Railway, with its administrative centre in Kharbin, to Manchukuo in 1935.) After the sale most of its employees and their families returned to the Soviet Union where they were called *Kharbinsty*, or 'returnees from Kharbin'.) Birobidzhan, where there were many Jews who had emigrated from abroad, was subjected to special 'cleansing' operations.[5]

According to the head of the NKVD in the Far East, Genrikh Liushkov, who carried out this massive operation, 'Stalin did not trust the Koreans at all. Fearing that as long as they lived near the Soviet borders in the Far East, Japan would use them as spies and infiltrate Soviet territory, Stalin ordered their deportations from the standpoint of counter-intelligence.'[6] Stalin said explicitly, according to Liushkov:

> It is necessary to clean up the army and its rear in the most determined manner from hostile spy and pro-Japanese elements … the Far East is not Soviet, there the Japanese rule … Stalin resumed the conversation by saying that it was necessary in cleansing the rear to terrorise the [Korean] district and the frontier so as to prevent any Japanese [espionage] work.[7]

Judging by Japanese documents, the deportations of Koreans achieved Stalin's goal, at least to an extent: they deprived real Korean spies working for Japan of refuge and assistance in the border areas.[8]

At the time, Korea was under Japanese colonial rule. Japan set up a puppet government in Manchuria in 1932 and expanded deep into China, triggering the Sino-Japanese War in the summer of 1937, all the while setting its sights on the Far Eastern territory of the Soviet Union. Indeed, the Soviet–Manchu (Japanese) border areas had been tense for some time. Spy-hunting was ubiquitous and border incidents frequent. A glance at Soviet reports is revealing. Take late 1934: on 25 December, the Soviet Far Eastern border authorities reported that two Chinese spies sent by the Japanese had been detained on the Soviet side (west of Turii Rog). Three days later, at 4 p.m., a Soviet border sentry near Blagoveshchensk was shot at by four unknown men from the Manchu side. The following day, a Japanese plane invaded Soviet air territory near Grodekovskii. Two days later, on the eve of 1935, a Korean, described as a 'Japanese spy', was detained near Rozanovo-Slavianskii. On the same day, near Slaviansk, two Korean spies, 'despatched by the Japanese', were detained. Similarly, many cases of White (anti-Soviet) Russians being sent across the border into the Soviet Union by the Japanese were reported.[9] The Japanese camp, for its part, counted '152 border disputes with the Soviet Union during the two-and-a-half years between the outbreak of the Manchurian Incident [in 1931] and 1934 but in 1935 the number soared to 136 and in 1936 to 203'.[10] By 1937, according to Stalin, the Soviet Far East was in a 'state of semi-war' with Japan.[11] The hostility only increased in the following years, culminating in the much larger military clashes in 1938 and 1939 (the Lake Khasan and Khalkin Gol incidents).

Many Koreans were terrorised in this explosive international atmosphere. Almost all were suspected of being Japanese spies. The Soviet Union must have been keenly aware of the skilful use by Japan of Koreans, Chinese and others as spies during earlier conflicts, the 1904–5 Russo-Japanese War and the Civil War in Siberia.[12] In addition to deploying its own agents, Japan used ethnic Koreans, Chinese, Mongols/Buriats and émigré Russians to penetrate into, spy on and agitate against the Soviet Union, just as the Soviets infiltrated various organisations in Manchukuo and China. The exact extent to which Japan used them is elusive, nor is it clear whether any of those ethnic Koreans and Chinese who were terrorised by the Soviet regime were actually spies. The effectiveness of spies sent across the borders was by most accounts minimal; they often turned out to be double and triple agents. Most of the émigré Russians sent into Soviet territory failed to return.[13] Still, some cases of ethnic Koreans repressed in the mid-1930s are illustrative. Ben-sun Kim, born in Korea in 1893 and a farmhand in China, was caught crossing the border illegally into the Soviet Union on 21 March 1934. Accused of espionage, he was executed on 29 June 1934. Tiu-er Kim, born in Korea in 1898, was apparently a Soviet citizen. Unemployed, he was arrested on 27 March 1934 for espionage. On 21

May 1934 he was executed.[14] Party membership provided no protection. Khai-ron Kan, born in Daegu, Korea, in 1901, a member of the Soviet Communist Party since 1928 and an instructor in the Japanese language at the Institute of Oriental Studies in Moscow, was arrested on 19 March 1934 and was executed, along with two other ethnic Korean Soviet citizens, on 13 June 1934.[15] Obviously, even those Koreans and Chinese living thousands of miles from the border zones were not safe.

Ben-shu Kim

Kiev, like Moscow, was very far from the Soviet–Manchu border. Yet the few Koreans and Chinese living there appear to have been repressed wholesale. According to Ukrainian police records, in 1937 26 Koreans and 17 Chinese, along with 35 'Japanese', were arrested for political crimes.[16] Ben-shu Kim was among the 26 Koreans. He lived at Aviagorodok, Corpus 6, Flat 18, in Kiev. He was arrested on 22 October 1937, sentenced to death on 18 December 1937 and executed eight days later.[17]

Kim was born in 1905 into a poor peasant family in Pyongan-bukto in Korea, but in 1908 his parents moved to the Ussurii region in Russia's Far East, where he studied from 1915 to 1917. He was forced to leave school and work as a shepherd in the village of Chernigovka, after which he returned to school and finished fourth grade in 1922. In June 1922 he entered the Komsomol (Young Communist League) and worked as an unskilled labourer at a match factory. His entry into the Komsomol helped him. In late 1923 he was despatched to train at a military school in Leningrad. There he entered the Communist Party. Graduating from the military school in 1926, Kim was sent back to the Far East as platoon commander of the Nerchinsk regiment of the Pacific Artillery Division. He continued in that capacity until 1930, when he was sent to the city of Spassk in the Far East to train with 40 Air Squadron for three months. He was then sent to Orenburg (on the Ural River) to train as a pilot. After he completed the training, he worked at the Second Air Division in the city of 'Kirovo' (Kirovohrad in Ukraine?) until 1935. On 15 February of that year he was appointed director of Air Detachment 67 of Dnieper Military Fleet Air Brigade 81 and worked there until his arrest in 1937. At the time Kim was married to Muza, 22, and had a son, German, 4½. Kim stated that he had no relations abroad (namely in Korea under Japanese colonial rule), that his father had died in 1938 (clearly a mistake for an earlier date) and that his mother still lived in the village of Chernigovka in the Far East (1:138, 2:14). (By then, however, his mother had probably been deported to Central Asia.)

When he was interrogated on 21 November 1937, Kim was accused of espionage and membership of a counter-revolutionary nationalist organisation ('Karborovtsy'). He denied all charges: he had never engaged in foreign espionage and did not know those Koreans arrested for counter-revolutionary spying activity with whom he was alleged to have collaborated. When he was asked whether he knew the Japanese language, he said he did not, having never studied it. The only specific crime of which he was accused was that he had caused an aviation accident in which he was injured. The 'accident' was attributed to a deliberate sabotage carried out by order of the Japanese intelligence (1:18–18zv.).

In addition to his Far Eastern connections, Kim was suspected of spying for Germany. One of his colleagues, Georgii Nikolaevich Rogov, a technician at Air Detachment 67, was arrested in August 1937 on suspicion of being a German spy. Rogov often had parties to which both Kim and a certain M. M. Vol'chak were invited. Vol'chak, a Pole, a native of Kirovo in Ukraine, and a German citizen, was a highly educated engineer who worked at the Scientific Research Institute of Electrical Welding in Kiev. He was arrested on 14 August 1937 for alleged 'espionage work for Fascist Germany'. Initially he denied the charges, but later pleaded guilty, confessing that he was an agent of the German consulate in Kiev and had engaged in espionage since 1934. Vol'chak implicated his boss Kuznetsov (who also frequented Rogov's parties) and Rogov. He stated that he had some Chinese and Korean acquaintances, but he did not remember their names or recruit them. In January 1938 Vol'chak was ordered to be deported (1:33, 105–6). Although in 1961, some years after Stalin's death, a special enquiry into his case took place, it was never decided whether he was indeed a foreign spy (160–160zv.).

Rogov, a candidate for Communist Party membership, and his wife, Z. Ia. Rogova, who worked for the city department of justice, were in fact arrested before Vol'chak on charges of embezzlement. Both pleaded guilty. But their problems did not end there. Rogov's wife was said to have been intimately involved with Vol'chak. They were rearrested in August 1937 and accused of espionage for Germany. They categorically denied the charge, but were sentenced to be executed on 11 September 1937. The order was carried out on 16 November 1937 (1:107–8).

In connection with the Rogov-Rogova-Vol'chak affair, F. I. Markov, a witness, accused Kim of giving information about military aviation to Vol'chak and ignoring Rogov's espionage activity: according to Markov, Kim used to say, 'There is no secret from cultured Germans' (1:34, 166). Oddly, K. F. Kuznetsov, who was implicated by Vol'chak, was not arrested. Instead he, a party member since 1932, wrote a statement to the party saying that Kim's relations with Rogov were so close as to be suspicious. He alleged that Rogova found a job for Kim's wife in her office (even though elsewhere Kim's wife was said to be a 'housewife'). Nevertheless, Kuznetsov was not deposed as a witness (1:81). Several witnesses accused Kim of espionage and other political crimes. Kim denied any spying activity as well as the 'criminal nature' of his relations with Rogov and Vol'chak. Probably because Kim did not confess, another kind of charge was hurled at him: wrecking. This accusation was first raised in the summer of 1937, but appears to have led nowhere at the time. Now it was revived. He allegedly had not kept weapons in proper shape, and some of them had become rusty. At one point, a revolver was lost while allegedly under his supervision in the military depot; later a different one in poorer condition mysteriously surfaced in the depot. Kim denied this 'wrecking' charge as well (1:14, 21).

In December 1937 the secretary of the party committee to which Kim belonged wrote a less than favourable character description of him in response to his arrest. According to this report, Kim had dumped his first wife and two small children and refused to help them at all. Nor did he live peacefully with his second wife, frequently causing 'scandals' and coming to blows with her. He was warned by the party over this and in August 1936 was expelled from the party for attempting to rape a woman while intoxicated. After this incident, he corrected his behaviour and his life became generally more stable. All in all, he had several disciplinary actions against him as well as awards for his superior military work (1:131–34).

Without any material evidence and without any confession of crime on Kim's part, he was sentenced to be shot on 18 December 1937. The spectre of execution appears to have changed Kim, who may well have been led to believe that it was not too late and a confession would save his life. At any rate, he must have been desperate. Thus on 25 December, a week after he was sentenced, he broke down and confessed. Told by the interrogator to stop resisting and confess, Kim said:

> Yes, in the course of the entire investigation of this case, I hid my connections with the Japanese intelligence. Now I see the pointlessness of my denial and would like to tell the truth about my traitorous espionage work. I admit that I am an agent of the Japanese intelligence, according to whose assignment I have engaged in espionage on Soviet territory since 1927. In the course of these ten years, I have transmitted to the Japanese intelligence much important confidential military information. I have also recruited several people to espionage work for Japan.

Kim told the interrogator that he was recruited into espionage work by an ethnic Korean named Niokolai An who was the head of the Verkhne-Udinskii regiment. An gave Kim an assignment to get in touch with another Korean called Khan who was a student at the University of the Peoples of the East in Moscow (1:26–26zv.). His confession did not help. Kim was executed the following day.

Any Korean must have been highly visible in a place like Kiev which had so few Asian residents. Kim, like other Koreans and Chinese, had almost certainly been marked out by the police for surveillance. His connection with a German citizen made him even more visible to the secret police. In addition, in the 1930s, in the western borderlands as in the eastern borderlands of the Soviet Union, the Japanese and Poles as well as the Japanese and Estonians were secretly engaged in collaborative subversion against the Soviet Union.[18] (The Soviet Union, in turn, watched the Polish–Japanese alliance closely.)[19] Riga, in Latvia, where Japan had a military attaché, was a major centre for such collaboration, but Berlin, where the Japanese military officer Takanobu Managi had set up a secret organ against the Soviet Union, also promoted clandestine subversive work with the help of the Estonians.[20] Managi and his collaborators used émigré Belarusans to pursue the separation of Belarus from the Soviet Union.[21] They had the same subversive goal for Ukraine and the Caucasian states. According to a Japanese intelligence officer, the 'subversive political activities within the USSR' by Japan (and Germany) were to be used 'later, in time of war ... for fifth column purposes'.[22] Japan targeted ethnic Ukrainians in the Far East for recruitment and maintained contact with Ukrainian nationalists outside the Soviet Union.[23] The Ukrainian nationalists, in turn, pinned their hopes on Japan as a reliable force destined to enter into war against the Soviet Union.[24] Japan's presence was a significant factor even in the western borderlands of the Soviet Union. When the Soviet Army practised military manoeuvres in Ukraine from 30 August to 4 September 1934, the Polish Consul in Kiev opined that it was a 'demonstration against foreign countries, particularly Japan'.[25]

The Japanese army also broadcast Russian-language radio programmes into Soviet territory. It did so in the Far East in order to foment 'uncertainty and anxiety' among the Soviet population, including ethnic Ukrainians in the Far East. On 20 October 1938, for example, it falsely reported an 'uprising of rebels in the capital of Ukraine'.[26] The Soviet Union broadcast Polish-language radio programmes from Kiev, Minsk and other cities to Poland for similar purposes.)[27] Furthermore, Japan maintained a consulate in Odesa, an important port from which the fleet shipped to the Far East, until it was forced to shut down in 1937. Japan placed an intelligence officer at the consulate to observe the Soviet Union (including the movement of the Soviet fleet). Naum Korzhavin, who witnessed the banishment of the ethnic Chinese from Kiev in 1937–38, wondered what danger the Chinese could have posed to the western borderlands.[28] Kiev seemed very far removed from the Japanese threat, but to the secret police it may not have appeared quite so distant.

In other words, as in so many other cases of political repression, the foreign factor was decisive in the case of Kim, even though he lived in Kiev, far from Manchuria, Korea or Japan.

The Perils of Confession

Had Kim stuck to his innocence, would he have escaped execution? It is unlikely, but there are cases in which some Koreans and Chinese arrested in Kiev in 1937 were spared capital punishment. Ivan Nikolaevich Ligai was born in 1906 in Wonsan, Korea, but became a Soviet citizen in 1930 and a member of the Communist Party as well. He was arrested on 13 October 1937 on charges of spying for Japan. At the time he was

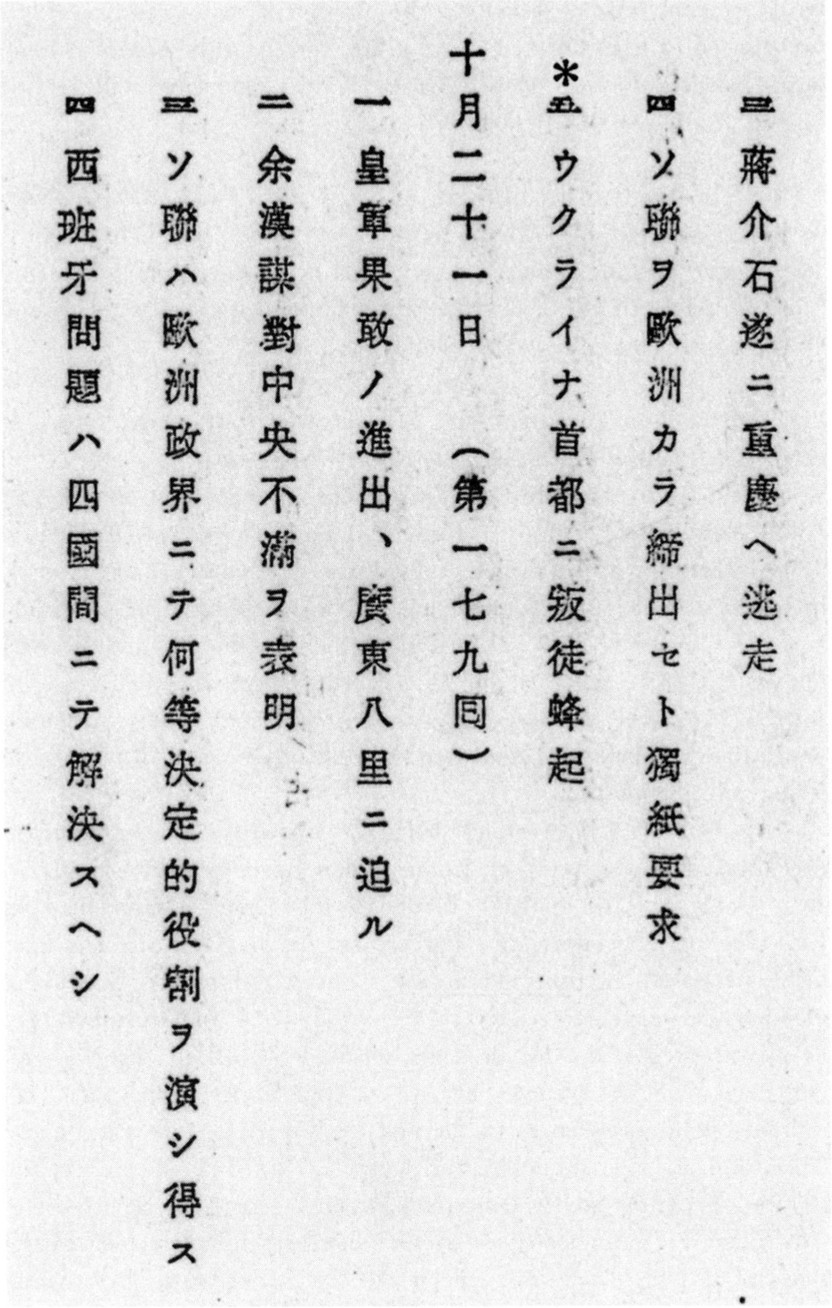

二　蔣介石遂ニ重慶ヘ逃走

四　ソ聯ヲ歐洲カラ締出セト獨紙要求

＊五　ウクライナ首都ニ叛徒蜂起

十月二十一日　（第一七九回）

一　皇軍果敢ノ進出、廣東八里ニ迫ル

二　余漢謀對中央不滿ヲ表明

三　ソ聯ハ歐洲政界ニテ何等決定的役割ヲ演シ得ス

四　西班牙問題ハ四國間ニテ解決スヘシ

23: The Japanese military radio log for 20 October 1938: '5. An uprising of rebels in the capital of Ukraine' (indicated by an asterisk).

working as the head of security at the 'Bolshevik' factory in Kiev. Ligai was alleged to have claimed, 'I want Japan [to beat the Soviet Union]. Japan has already won Manchuria and China, and later will get the Soviet Union.' And:

> In China, particularly in the areas occupied by Japan, they live very well. So I'd like to go there. In the Soviet Union people live poorly, we have nothing here. ... Every year everything gets worse, and evidently Japan will attack the Soviet Union soon and win, because the Soviet Union is weaker than Japan.

Ligai insisted on his innocence and received 'only' eight years of correctional labour (on 4 December 1937) (1:109–11).

Sen-un Kogai (identified as Se-un Ko in some places in the file), an ethnic Korean born in 1905 in Kolsang-dong in Korea, was arrested on 23 December 1937 on charges of espionage. He worked in Zhytomyr, to the west of the Ukrainian capital, but was implicated in an alleged Japanese spy ring. Kogai categorically denied all charges, and received ten years of correctional labour on 2 February 1938. In Kogai's case, in 1939 and 1940 the witnesses against him repudiated their testimonies, which they said had been fabricated by their interrogators. All the same, Kogai was not released (1:111).

Likewise, Ivan Spartsovich Kim, a native of Korea, escaped execution. He was born in Korea under Japanese colonial rule in 1911. Told that things were better in the Soviet Union than in Korea, in 1927 he crossed the border and was arrested. Six days later he was released. In time he became a Soviet citizen and Komsomol member and started to work at a factory in Kiev. In December 1937 he was arrested again. He does not seem to have been charged with espionage, but was instead accused of anti-Soviet propaganda. He insisted on his innocence. In the end he was given ten years in the Gulag and was released in 1947 in Kolyma.[29] (In order to prevent the infiltration of the Soviet Union by foreign agents, the Soviet secret police issued Order 00693 on 23 October 1937 which mandated the arrest of all people who had defected to the Soviet Union by crossing international borders, regardless of the motives and circumstances of their defections. Kim appears to have been rearrested in accordance with this order.)[30]

The only Chinese case that has surfaced in Kiev has a similar narrative arc. Sa-bo Sia was born in China in 1892 but ended up in Kiev. At the time of his arrest on 8 March 1938 he was working as a self-employed handicraftsman and living at 21 Nazarivs'ka Street, Flat 21, in Kiev with his thirty-seven-year-old wife Anna and three children aged from eleven months to fourteen years. He was a party member from 1926 to 1934, when he was expelled owing to his failure to pay membership fees. He appears to have been implicated by Don Sin, an ethnic Chinese who was arrested on 5 March 1938 and executed soon thereafter as a Japanese spy in Kiev. Probably unlike Sin, Sia denied charges of espionage. His file contains his interrogation records only from 23 July 1938. Sia consistently denied any charges of espionage. His case was protracted, which helped him. In the end, the police deposed his wife, Anna, in February 1939, from whom a testimony was extracted that Sia often went away for long periods to the Far East, which ostensibly provided indirect evidence of Sia's clandestine life. Sia rejected his wife's testimony as false, and was exonerated and released in January 1940.[31]

Unlike Ligai and Kogai, Nam-yang Khong-Yi-Pe, a Soviet citizen and party member of Korean descent, was executed. He was arrested on 24 October 1937 in Kiev and, like other ethnic Koreans, was accused of spying for Japan. According to the available records, he was interrogated only once, on the night of 5 January 1938, confessed to his 'crime', was sentenced to be shot on 7 February 1938 and three weeks later was executed (1:112–13).

These cases suggest that Ben-shu Kim might have escaped death had he not confessed to his crime. However, given the numerous cases in which the defendants were executed in spite of their denial of charges, this is speculative at best. Kim, like many others, was almost certainly doomed by his ethnic background.

Post-Stalin Investigations

Ben-shu Kim's case was re-examined in 1954, after Stalin's death, 'in connection with the study of M. M. Krzhimovskii', the husband of Kim's former wife, now Muza Popsueva, at the Ministry of State Security (successor to the NKVD and the predecessor of the KGB). It is not known what the result of the re-examination was (2:1), but it appears that it was favourable towards Kim (2:14–15).

24: One of several memorials in Bykivnia in 2006. The inscription reads: 'These pine trees bear witness to a horrible crime. Buried here are the thousands of innocent killed. Bow down to them. Eternal memory.'

It was only in 1961, after his son, German, turned to the Soviet government for information on the fate of his father in August 1960, that Kim's case was re-examined in detail (1:44). The case against him was so weak that the prosecutor's office did not have much to examine, especially regarding his alleged espionage work for Japan. An enquiry submitted to the KGB in Khabarovsk yielded no evidence of Kim, Kogai, Yi (Yang) or An having belonged to the Japanese intelligence. Markov's 1937 testimony was not supported by any evidence and was refuted by 'subsequent investigations' (1:162, 170). The prosecutor's office concluded that there was insufficient evidence to prove Vol'chak's espionage case, and hence Kim's involvement in German espionage. Nor could the charges of 'wrecking' (improper maintenance of weapons and loss of a revolver) be confirmed. Fortunately, some original witnesses were still alive and were therefore interviewed in 1961. On 26 March 1961 G. N. Sysoev, for example, failed to confirm his 1937 testimony of Kim's 'wrecking' activities (even though he signed it in 1937): he knew nothing about Kim's crime; whatever problems might have existed in the weapons depot, Kim was not responsible (1:47, 167). Another witness,

D. S. Vil'ner, also negated his earlier testimony in his interview with the prosecutor's office on 4 April 1961, stating that he knew nothing about Kim's wrecking, diversionary or espionage activities (1:91–96, 167). Similarly, other witnesses knew of no 'anti-Soviet' activity on the part of Kim.

Kuznetsov, who somewhat mysteriously managed to avoid the fate of Kim, Rogov and others in 1937 and 1938, was also interviewed in 1961. This time he stated that Kim was politically stable and he saw no grounds for speaking of his negative views. Kuznetsov also stated that he did not know the nature of the relations between Kim and Rogov, although Rogov did appear to have lived beyond his means (indeed, he and his wife were indicted for embezzlement). When reminded of his 1937 statement, he responded that when Rogov was declared an enemy of the people, he felt obliged to report that Kim was on friendly terms with him, but that he did not know the nature of their relationship (1:76–80).

In this as in all other cases, the testimonies gathered after Stalin's death in 1953 should not be taken at face value. With the de-Stalinisation campaign under way, the witnesses were under pressure to exonerate the condemned against whom their testimonies had been taken in the 1930s. In fact, few post-Stalin testimonies corroborate earlier versions from the 1930s. At the same time, it is clear that many surviving witnesses wished to set the records straight: their old testimonials were coerced and fabricated. At any rate, in almost all cases, no new proof of the old allegations surfaced after Stalin's death. No proof existed in the 1930s to begin with.

Thus, owing to the lack of *corpus delicti*, on 23 June 1961 Kim was posthumously exonerated of the crimes for which he had been executed in 1937. Immediately thereafter German, who lived in Kiev then, wrote to the government for evidence of his father's death. The KGB recommended that Kim's death be properly registered. Yet, as was typical of the Soviet security organ, it then gave false information: it saw to it that Kim was registered as having died in a labour camp on 17 December 1940 from a stomach ulcer (2: 4–16).

It turns out that Kim had a sister. In 1961, Agaf'ia Kim wrote from Kzyr-Ordinsk in Kazakhstan (where she must have been deported in 1937 from the Far East) to Kiev's military prosecutor's office enquiring about her nephew's (namely German's) whereabouts (2:21–22). It is possible that Ben-shu Kim did not mention his sister to protect her from whatever harm his arrest might cause.

The Mystery of a Vanished Korean 'Spy': The Case of El'-bon Kim

No reliable data of terror against the Koreans and the Chinese in Kiev are found for 1938, but the terror against suspected Japanese spies did not cease. On 19 August 1938 the NKVD issued an arrest warrant for El'-bon Kim, a Soviet citizen and a non-party member born in 1894 in Tsch-hung, Korea. He moved to Kiev from the Far East in 1930 and in 1934 returned to the Far East. When he subsequently moved back to Kiev is not clear. At the time of his arrest, Kim lived at 27 Komintern Street, Flat 8, Kiev, and worked as a guardsman at the Kiev 'Cinema' factory. He was accused of having ties to an executed 'Japanese spy', the ethnic Korean En-ke Kim, and to another ethnic Korean and 'Japanese spy' then under arrest, Don-bin Tsoi, the chairman of a rice collective farm in the Donbas. On 2 September 1938 the NKVD concluded that El'-bon Kim had engaged in espionage for foreign countries.[32]

Oddly, the El'-bon Kim file contains no records of investigation or interrogation. Even more extraordinarily, Kim seems to have disappeared. On 23 December 1938 the NKVD wrote to the Kiev prosecutor's office that it was being sent Kim's case file No. 146602. According to the NKVD's information, the arrested Kim was listed as being held by the prosecutor's office (8). It was a time of much confusion because Stalin had put an end to the Great Terror, the NKVD was being purged and reorganised, and many of the arrested and imprisoned were being released. There is no information on Kim after this communication. Was he being held elsewhere? Was he executed? Or had he been confused with some other Korean, Chinese or Japanese person? Had he disappeared into the depths of the Gulag? Or had he been released or managed to escape?

It was more than a year later that the NKVD began to pursue Kim's case again. On 8 March 1940, it asked the Kiev prosecutor's office where and when Kim's case had been sent for his hearing (9). Five days later the prosecutor's office wrote to the NKVD that Kim's case had been sent to the military prosecutor of the Kiev Special Military District on 27 December 1938 (10). Then, nearly four months later, the

NKVD wrote to the Kiev prosecutor's office again, demanding 'for the third time' that it inform the NKVD where and when case No. 146602 had been sent for hearing (11). Nine days later the prosecutor's office responded that it would like to repeat its missive of 13 March 1940: it had notified the NKVD of the Kim case on 13 March 1940 in writing—missive number 05.11.98 (13). A week later, on 19 July 1940, the NKVD wrote to the military prosecutor of the Kiev Special Military District, asking 'for the second time' that the prosecutor notify it as to where the Kim case stood at the moment (14). The NKVD's reference to 'second time' probably means that between the March and July 1940 correspondence between the NKVD and the Kiev prosecutor's office the NKVD wrote to the military prosecutor and received a reply that the latter knew nothing about the case. But again the NKVD received no clear answer.

After this exchange, the NKVD appears to have been distracted by other matters; soon after, war broke out. Following World War II, the Soviet secret police resumed its investigation of El'-bon Kim's case. It yielded no concrete results. So in May 1958 the Ukrainian KGB decided to close the case: according to a request of the Kiev prosecutor's office, Record No. 4407234, dated 23 December 1938, the case of El'-bon Kim (No. 287660) was sent to the 'above-mentioned organ' (military prosecutor's office), but the Kim file had not been received by the KGB Archive Department. All means to locate his case file had been exhausted. Therefore the case was to be closed (19). In February 1963 the KGB noted that Kim's investigation records were lost: El'-bon Kim was arrested on 19 August 1938 by the NKVD, but there is no other information (2–21zv.).

It is possible that the NKVD somehow mixed up El'-bon Kim's case with someone else's (possibly another ethnic Korean named Kim), because on 23 December 1938 it referred to Kim's case as No. 146602, whereas the May 1958 KGB document refers to the NKVD's action regarding No. 287660. The experience of other regions suggests that mix-ups over prisoners were not uncommon. Sometimes wrong prisoners with the same surnames as those on the death roll were mistakenly executed.[33]

This is an astonishing development. The NKVD, it seems, could lose track of a suspected spy! Is it possible that Kim was mistakenly executed? Is it possible that all ethnic Koreans looked alike to the Kiev NKVD personnel? To compound the problem, many had the same surname (Kim), and the files examined here suggest that NKVD personnel had difficulty with Korean names. Perhaps this case of a 'missing spy' is not so surprising given the fallibility of all organisations. Moreover, after NKVD chief Nikolai Ezhov was removed from his position in the autumn of 1938, the secret police itself was in turmoil owing to the large-scale turnover of its functionaries.

It is not clear whether El'-bon Kim had any relatives. No one appears to have ever made enquiries to the Soviet authorities about his fate. In Kim's case, not only is his voice lost, he has vanished entirely. No trace of him has been found, not even by the secret police.

Like other suspect national groups such as ethnic Germans, Poles, Finns and Kurds, the ethnic Koreans in the Soviet Union were uprooted from their traditional homeland (the Far East). It was terror based solely on ethnicity, because ethnicity itself had become suspect under the gathering clouds of war. Even though ethnic Germans, Poles and others had begun to be deported en masse from the mid-1930s, these deportations were still selective. The 1937 Korean deportation from the Far East, by contrast, came close to 'ethnic cleansing'. It was a precursor of the literally wholesale deportations of the Crimean Tatars and Chechens in the 1940s. (These groups were punished by Stalin for the alleged collaboration of some of their members with the Nazi invaders during the war.)[34] Even Koreans and Chinese living thousands of kilometres away from the Far East were not safe. Some were deported, but others like Ben-shu Kim were arrested and executed as Japanese spies. Those few Koreans and Chinese living in Kiev thus disappeared from the city in 1937 and 1938. Some, like El'-bon Kim, vanished without a trace. Even the seemingly almighty Soviet secret police gave Kim up for lost. No doubt, like many others, El'-bon Kim, Ben-shu Kim and other Korean and Chinese 'spies' for Japan were innocent victims of Stalin's terror, their only crime being their ethnicity.

CHAPTER 8

Foreign Connections
German, Latvian and Romanian Links

By far the most striking aspect of Stalin's terror in the 1930s is the suspicion in which foreign connections were held. Anyone associated with any foreigner or foreign organisation, including philatelists who corresponded with overseas collectors, came under suspicion by the Soviet secret police. Nearly everyone executed in the 1930s for political reasons had something to do with foreigners or foreign countries. Even those who lived far from the borders were not considered free of 'foreign connections' if they appeared to be politically unreliable and thus a threat in the event of war with foreign powers: they were deemed potential fifth columnists and defeatists. Some foreign connections were particularly suspect. The Japanese and Polish connections are discussed elsewhere (in Chapters 7 and 9). Like Japan and Poland, Germany was suspected, with justification, by the Soviet government to be a likely enemy. So were other countries, particularly those that geographically surrounded the Soviet Union: Romania, Finland, Turkey and the Baltic states (Estonia, Latvia and Lithuania).

The Soviet government deemed ethnic Germans a particular threat because of their suspected ties to and sympathies with Nazi Germany. Germans in Ukraine were all the more suspect as throughout the terrible time of the collectivisation campaign and the 1932–33 Great Famine in Ukraine they had corresponded with their relations in Germany and the USA in the hope of receiving material aid and possibly emigrating.[1]

As early as 1934, as a result of the Nazis' ascension to power in Germany, the Central Committee of the Communist Party decided to have full and accurate data collected on all Germans working in industry and in administrative bodies, and to see to it that this survey should not be publicly known.

According to one person who collected this information, already at the end of 1934 the party 'had before it the most precise data on the numbers and occupations of all the Germans living in the USSR. All the secret service work and repressions carried out later were guided by the data we collected and arranged.'[2] Stalin was wont to see a foreign agent in anyone critical of his regime. In 1934, when a mentally unstable soldier (one Nakhaev) was arrested for alleged counter-revolutionary agitation among his peers, Stalin insisted that Nakhaev was 'of course (of course!) ... not alone. He must be a Polish–German (or Japanese) agent.'[3] From 1935, ethnic Germans (along with ethnic Poles) on the western borders began to be deported to remote areas in the east, just as ethnic Finns, Estonians, Latvians and other 'politically suspect' elements began to be deported from the northern borderlands.[4] German 'counter-revolutionary' groups began to be uncovered everywhere.

Ethnic Latvians fared no better: they, like ethnic Germans, composed a 'diaspora nation'. They were targeted for deportation from the northern borderlands in 1935.[5] Their real and imagined connections to Latvia made them potential enemies by default. Indeed, many anti-Soviet elements, foreign as well as émigré, were stationed in Latvia. Before the resumption of diplomatic relations with the Soviet Union in late 1933, the USA maintained a legation in Riga, the capital of Latvia, engaging in intelligence-gathering there. Remarkably, since 1931 Japan had had a full-time military attaché in the three small Baltic states (the attaché in Latvia also served as attaché in Estonia and Lithuania) and collaborated with Baltic intelligence services against the Soviet Union. Romanians may have fared better than Germans and Latvians. Yet Romania and the Soviet Union continued their dispute over Moldova (formerly Bessarabia), incorporated into Romania after World War I. At the time of the Great Terror, Romanians were targeted along with Poles, Germans, Latvians, Estonians, Finns, Greeks, Iranians and others for special treatment.[6]

All foreign connections were suspect in the 1930s, but some were more suspect than others. German, Latvian and Romanian connections were among the most suspect. People with such connections suffered commensurately from Stalin's terror.

Lidiia Eduardovna Kronberg

Lidia Eduardovna Kronberg, as a German and a Latvian, constituted a 'dual suspect'. An ethnic German originally from Latvia, she was arrested on 3 December 1937, convicted of 'espionage and diversion' for Latvia and executed on 19 January 1938. She was one of forty-two people executed in Kiev on that day. Kronberg was fifty-eight years of age according to a christening record dated 20 September 1879 and issued in Russian and German bilingual form by the Evangelical Lutheran parish in Jiukt (Zhuket), Latvia. Her parents were Eduard Kronberg, a farmer, and Annette, both of whom were dead by 1938. Her only surviving close relative was her sister, Mal'vina Eduardovna Shtratsis (Strauss?), who lived in Latvia. At the time of her arrest, Kronberg worked as a cleaner at a barber's in Passenger Railway Station One in Kiev and lived at 73 Korolenko Street, Flat 3. She was a non-party member.[7]

Kronberg had only a secondary education, but like many others of similar background spoke several languages: Latvian, Russian, German and probably some Ukrainian. According to a November 1937 secret police reference to her, Kronberg was 'counter-revolutionarily inclined' and 'systematically communicating libellous fictions in her letters to Latvia'. The police issued an arrest warrant and Kronberg was duly detained. When arrested, she said that her 'nationality' was Latvian, but everywhere else in her case file she is described as an ethnic German. How she ended up in Kiev is not known. When asked about her background by her interrogator on 8 December 1937, five days after her arrest, Kronberg merely said that she had lived with her family in Latvia until 1902 (that is, until she was twenty-three years of age). She then moved to Kiev, where she stayed until she was arrested. It is possible that she married before moving to Kiev (12). She admitted that in 1932 she had re-established contact with her sister in Latvia and that they had maintained communication until her arrest (12).

When she was arrested, letters 'in a foreign language' (Latvian) were impounded along with her passport, trade union membership card, birth certificate and other documents. Moreover, a letter sent to her sister and other 'dear ones' in Latvia dated 13 February 1933 appears to have been intercepted by the police. (This suggests that she had probably been under police surveillance for some time.) The letter was addressed to her sister (here her name is spelt, in Russian and Latvian, Mal'vina

Strauss) and ended up in her case file (36–37). Oddly, the envelope had no stamp on it. Could it be that she paid the postage but the post office forwarded it to the police instead? Or could it be that she never posted it? Whatever the case, this letter made her very vulnerable.

Kronberg's letter was rather damning. An excerpt translated into Russian in her case file shows what her interrogator was interested in. It was the time of the Great Famine, and Kronberg, hoping to return to Latvia, asked her sister for help. She told her that she would go to the German consul in Kiev for advice, because going to Moscow would be very expensive (500 roubles), and she said she could not afford it. She had deposited 200 roubles, apparently in a savings bank, in 1931 towards a trip to Moscow, but now, she lamented, she could not withdraw the money in its entirety, only a certain percentage of it. (This was probably true: banks often refused withdrawals at times of economic crisis. When Kronberg was arrested, a savings bank deposit receipt (No. 12986) for the amount of 165 roubles was impounded. Kronberg said in her letter that she wanted to go back to Latvia whatever happened, because however hard one worked in Ukraine, one starved. In fact, she wrote, come spring, famine would return. When she returned to Latvia, she would tell her sister everything about the 'inhuman life' lived in the Soviet Union. She then recounted a horror story. At a Kiev factory two workers had reportedly been killed by an electric shock. They were buried, but before their wives had had time to stop crying, one of the men turned up at home. His wife went insane from the shock. What had happened was that a doctor, in league with some grave robbers, had falsely certified their deaths and had had them buried. The thieves had excavated the graves and robbed the bodies of clothes, gold teeth and other items of value. One of the factory workers buried alive had regained consciousness and escaped. Kronberg warned her sister that if she told her of all the horror of life in the Soviet Union she would be shocked. She said she was so worn out by life there that she had only one desire—to return to her homeland and die: she had endured hunger and cold and could no longer remember the days when she had drunk coffee with cream (22).

The Latvian original has a little more text. It is dated 30 January (not 13 February, as her interrogation records note) and starts: 'In the Land of Hunger'. (It is possible that Kronberg still used the pre-revolutionary Old Style [Julian] calendar, which was thirteen days behind the New

25: Kronberg's 1936 trade union membership card.

Style [Gregorian] calendar adopted in 1918.) Kronberg wrote with envy that the German consulate in Kiev assisted everyone in need by giving away money and covering their travel expenses, but unfortunately she would have to go to the Latvian consulate in Moscow. For that, she would have to sell some of her silk. The passport alone would cost 250 roubles. Still, she said that she would 'fight and look for any possible way to get to you all as soon as possible'. She then described her dismal life in Kiev: 'One can get only one kilogram of bread and no more. In order to get that one kilogram of bread, one has to queue almost all day.' She continued:

Dear sister, please forgive me for writing so poorly. It is only because I am writing this letter in almost complete darkness. The room has neither light nor water. I have lighted a small lamp, but I still can't see anything. ... I am surprised that Mother didn't want to die. I can't wait to get to the eternal home in Heaven. I am so exhausted and tired of this life. It is my only desire to get to you all and die at Paulits' place. Then I wish to be taken to the graveyard by his horses and wish that Paulits and Alberts would bury me there. That's my longing. ... Oh my God, how I wish I were with you all at this very moment, at your place and peacefully enjoying a cup of coffee with cream. I can't even remember when I had coffee with cream or ate meat last. ... Please write to me as soon as you can. Your letters keep me alive. They are like drops of rain on the thirsty soil.[8]

Kronberg wrote to her sister with some optimism that she should be able to get to Latvia in the spring of that year (1933) (36–37).

Kronberg's attempt to flee the Soviet horror failed. What she did between February and April 1933 is not known. Most likely she was busy just trying to survive. In April 1933, two months after she wrote to her sister, Kronberg visited the German consulate for advice because she 'knew the German language well'. The consulate advised her to go or write to the Latvian consulate in Moscow. In the meantime, her sister intervened to ask the Latvian consul in Moscow to assist Kronberg to return to Latvia, which she considered her homeland. Kronberg then received a letter from the Latvian consul that her exit document had been issued but that she would have to pay 15 roubles. Kronberg, however, did not have the money and so could not receive the document (13–14). (It is possible that '15 roubles' in fact meant 150 roubles. It is also possible that Kronberg did not have even the small sum of 15 roubles at her disposal at the peak of the famine crisis.) Kronberg thus failed to return to Latvia, but by the autumn of 1933 the famine had receded and, possibly, with it her desire to return to Latvia.

At the 8 December 1937 session, Kronberg's interrogator was particularly interested in her visits to foreign consulates. Kronberg told him that she had first gone to the German consulate, before her April visit, in February 1933, to assist her friend Al'bertina Shugial'ter, a Kiev resident and a German citizen. Kronberg visited the German consulate a third time in 1935, this time accompanying Shugial'ter to help her friend 'Sharlot' (Scharlotte) to leave for Danzig, today Gdańsk in Poland, but at the time a free city under the control of the League of Nations and inhabited by a German majority.

As discussed in Chapter 9, anyone who visited foreign consulates in Kiev was put under police surveillance. Combined with her intercepted 1933 letter to Latvia, her three visits to the German consulate must have marked Kronberg out as suspicious. Pressed by the interrogator, Kronberg admitted that when she visited the German consul in April 1933, she had stated that she detested the Soviet government, which had

26: Kronberg's 1933 letter to her sister in Latvia.

led the people to destitution and hunger. However, when further pressed to confess to the crime of espionage, Kronberg drew the line and firmly rejected the allegation: 'I'm not an agent of foreign intelligence services.' Yet she added that she was guilty of visiting the German consulate and giving the consular staff 'fictitious and libellous data' on the Soviet Union—that the Soviet people lived in destitution and famine, that many people were starving to death, that she hated the Soviet regime and that she wanted to flee to her homeland of Latvia (14).

One should note that Kronberg's statements, like those of so many others, may have been distorted by her interrogator. The existence of her unflattering letter about Soviet life clearly put her in a difficult position during the interrogations. Obviously, for example, her statement in the letter that people were starving to death in 1933 in Kiev was neither fiction nor libel. It was fact. The secret police perfected the art of both creating fact out of fiction and creating fiction out of fact. One can assume that Kronberg's admission of guilt and her statements about 'detesting' and 'hating' the Soviet regime were forced from her, or at the very least that there was police intervention in her statements. When she was asked whether she had sent her relations in Latvia 'libellous information on the Soviet Union', Kronberg answered in the affirmative and said she had done so because she was 'embittered' against the Soviet Union. According to her interrogation records, she even itemised the criminal nature of the information she had given to her sister: (1) the Soviet population lived in hunger and many were dying from it; (2) at night the graves were being excavated and the corpses were being eaten 'as if there were no tomorrow'. In addition, she had said that she would tell her about all of the horror of Soviet life when she returned home and that after the 1933 letter she also gave her sister more 'fictitious' stories about 'the high cost of living and the impossibility of living in the Soviet Union' (15). Yet when she was pressed again to confess to the crime of espionage, Kronberg stood her ground: 'I was never recruited by anyone to become a foreign intelligence agent.' Immediately thereafter, however, she added that she had committed the crime of telling 'fictitious stories' about Soviet life (15). She did so probably believing that it was a lesser crime than foreign espionage and that a partial admission of guilt might save her life.

Kronberg's interrogator was not satisfied. In her second interrogation, on 9 December 1937, she was pressed harder. She ended up yielding more ground this time, admitting to 'becoming an informer of the German consulate in the city of Kiev' and conducting 'counter-revolutionary activity' against the Soviet government (in addition to giving 'libellous' information about the Soviet Union to her relations in Latvia). But that was all she said and her interrogation ended there (16).

Her qualified admission of guilt did not help her at all. No witnesses were called. A month later, on 8 January 1938, she was convicted of spying for Latvia (but, oddly, not for Germany, for which she had supposedly become an 'informer') and was sentenced to be shot. Eleven days later, on 19 January 1938 at midnight, her execution was carried out (20). Even though she had nothing to do with Poland, she was executed as part of the Polish Operation.[9] Like so many others executed in Kiev, she was buried in a mass grave in Bykivnia.[10]

In 1989 Kronberg was rehabilitated: only the interrogation records had been used to convict her in 1937–38, and no other evidence was found. At the time it proved impossible to find any information on her relatives (41).

Her rehabilitation was fully justified. Even her 1933 letter to her sister, which the secret police characterised as a 'fiction' and 'libel', was merely an expression of her horror at Soviet life and a reflection of her simple desire to escape Kiev and return to her homeland. It is rare to encounter such honest human voices in case files. It is not an overstatement to say that Kronberg was executed for nostalgia.

Ella Teodorovna Zeibert

Like Kronberg, Ella Teodorovna Zeibert was an ethnic German who was originally from Latvia. In the undated bill of indictment she was alleged to have come to the Soviet Union from Latvia in 1915, but of course there was no Soviet Union in 1915 and Latvia (Courland) was then part of the Russian Empire. She was arrested on 28 November 1937, convicted on 5 January 1938 and executed on 20 January 1938.[11] She was one of fifty-five people executed in Kiev on that day.

Zeibert was born in Riga in 1894. Her father, a lumber factory clerk, died in 1910. During World War I, her mother and her brother Walter moved to Berlin where they lived until 1918. Then they moved to Łódź, Poland. (The bill of indictment against Zeibert mistakenly claimed that her father also lived in Łódź. It is not indicated where another of Ella's brothers, Kurt, lived. It is possible that he did live in Łódź.) Ella Zeibert moved from Riga to Kremenchuk, southeast of Kiev, in 1915 with her first husband, Teodor Ius'fovich (?) Pliashkin-Grinberg. The latter died in 1924. Then she married Dmitrii Ivanovich Gerasimov, with whom she lived until 1926. (At the time of her arrest she was divorced and her former husband was working in Smolensk.) The couple moved to Kiev in 1924. Zeibert taught German throughout her time in Kiev and lived at 8 Tarasiv Street, Flat 22. At the time of her arrest she taught at Middle School No. 143. She also taught at the Kiev Institute of Economic Administrators. She was not a member of the Communist Party. She corresponded with her brother Walter until 1930 (11–12). The bill of indictment, however, insists that she continued to correspond with him in Poland until her arrest in 1937 (23–24).

It is not clear when she was first interrogated. The first such record in her case file is dated 11 December 1937, almost a fortnight after her arrest. There Zeibert was accused of having belonged to a counter-revolutionary organisation and having conducted espionage activity. She categorically denied both charges, but she admitted that she was inclined against the Soviet Union and expressed her dissatisfaction with measures taken by the Soviet government. (The lapse of a fortnight between arrest and first interrogation was not unusual at the time, but it is also possible that the records of an earlier interrogation, where she might have denied all charges against her, were not included in her case file.) She said, 'By conviction I completely shared' the ideas of the Fascist regime in Germany and 'praised it': 'My nationalist, and later Fascist, counter-revolutionary views began to form very early, but most intensely soon after Hitler's ascent to power in Germany' in 1933 (which coincided with the Great Famine in Ukraine). So she said she conducted agitation: 'In Germany, since the Fascists have come to power, workers are living much better than in the Soviet Union' (13–14).

Zeibert implicated one of her German colleagues at school, named as Erika Vil'gel'movna Pliats (in fact her first name was Emma-Irina). According to Zeibert, Pliats praised Fascist Germany and criticised the Soviet Union: 'What is written in Soviet newspapers about Germany is not true. In Germany life is better than in the Soviet Union'; 'It's impossible to go on like this. Some change has to come.' Zeibert added that she had no other 'counter-revolutionary' conversations with anyone else (14zv.–15).

The interrogator asked Zeibert whether she knew Irina Iulianovna Pankevich. Initially she said no, but then admitted that she did: Pankevich

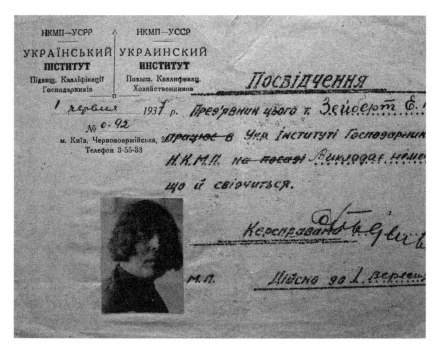

27: Zeibert's 1937 identity card.

had been her student in 1930 or 1931 and they had bumped into one another on a Kiev street in October 1937 and had a conversation. (It is possible that in October 1937 Pankevich was unsuccessfully deployed by the police to entrap Zeibert in a compromising conversation.) Accused of being recruited by Pankevich, Zeibert categorically denied the allegation. According to the November 1937 police records, Pankevich had tried in 1931 to recruit Zeibert to the UVO (which proved to be a police fabrication), but she had refused to join out of fear. Yet the interrogator had added cryptically that the person who refused out of fear turned out to be someone else and not Zeibert and that, subsequently, Zeibert was indeed recruited by Pankevich. According to Pankevich, even though Zeibert was a German, she willingly joined the Ukrainian organisation because she wanted to fight against the Bolsheviks (13, 20, 22). This was in January 1933, at the time of the Great Famine in Ukraine.

Two days later, on 13 December 1937, the interrogator pressed Zeibert: 'In your statement of 11 December you didn't give a truthful

28: An undated photograph of Zeibert and her students.

confession. You hid from the investigator your membership of a counter-revolutionary organisation. Why did you hide this?' Zeibert responded:

> I state once again that I did not belong to a counter-revolutionary organisation. I state once again and confirm my earlier statements that by conviction I indeed shared the ideas of Fascism completely and praised Germany and its Fascist regime and that all of these counter-revolutionary conversations took place in the presence of Irika [can be read 'Irina'] Vil'gemovna [*sic*] Pliats who, like me, praised Hitler and Germany.

When the interrogator insisted that she was not telling the truth, Zeibert stood firm: 'I deny [the allegations of espionage and agitation] categorically, I state again that I was not recruited by anyone into any organisation' (16–16zv.).

Zeibert, like Kronberg, was unable to save her life by making a qualified admission of guilt. It is quite strange that even though her

Latvian connections did not seem to interest her interrogators, she was ultimately accused of espionage and diversion for Latvia and not for Fascist Germany (which did interest her interrogators). She was sentenced to be shot on 5 January 1938 and on 20 January 1938, at midnight, was executed (26–27). Like Kronberg, she was buried in one of Bykivnia's mass graves.[12] Like Kronberg, too, Zeibert was executed as part of the Polish Operation. In 1989, again like Kronberg, Zeibert was rehabilitated: no material evidence was ever found against her. As in Kronberg's case, no relatives were located (41).

Zeibert's fate is illustrative of the almost casual and bureaucratic way in which Soviet citizens were executed. Zeibert was an ethnic German from Latvia. Her alleged 'crime' appears to have been related to her 'connection' with Fascist Germany (and possibly the Ukrainian nationalists), but not to Latvia. In the end, however, she was executed for alleged Latvian espionage connections without a shred of evidence. This suggests that at that particular moment the NKVD in Kiev needed people with Latvian connections to fill a quota. Indeed, quite a few Latvians were executed at that time. Those connected to the Latvian Club in Kiev (founded in 1921 and closed in May 1936) were decimated.[13] Another Latvian in Kiev, Marta Petrovna Kreiman, was also executed in January 1938 for her alleged 'Fascist agitation' ('Life in Latvia is better than in the Soviet Union').[14] To complicate matters, all were executed as part of the Polish Operation discussed here even though they had little or nothing to do directly with Poland.

It is also striking that, as both Kronberg's and Zeibert's cases demonstrate, the Great Famine of 1932–33 continued to cast a long shadow. It was a traumatic experience for the people and a 'defining moment' for the secret police's enemy-hunting.

Zeibert's story does not end there, however. Why did she implicate her colleague Pliats? According to Pliats' statement of 1940, it was due to the fact that she had failed to help Zeibert to secure a job at the Institute of Red Professors in Moscow.[15] (Of course, this may not have been true. At the first interrogation after her arrest, Pliats stated that she had no personal account to settle with Zeibert and that they were good colleagues. At that time Pliats did not know that Zeibert had been arrested.) It is possible that Zeibert was coerced into denouncing Pliats by the police. Pliats was arrested on 16 December 1937. She was born into a German family in 1891 near Łódź. She taught German at the Kiev Pedagogical Institute (8, 27–28). She had no family or relatives at the time of her arrest. Her uncle, her only relative, had died in Łódź in 1923. Under arrest, she was presented with Zeibert's allegations. She was also accused by three students, Ol'shanetskii, Levchuk and Groshchenko, of conducting pro-Fascist and anti-Soviet propaganda. Pliats firmly and categorically denied all the charges. The interrogator repeatedly pressed the charges against her on 23 and 26 December 1937, but she stood firm and denied them again and again. She gave absolutely no ground at all. On 26 December her interrogator demanded 'for the last time' that she confess. Still she categorically denied the charges (13–26). Despite the damaging (and almost certainly false) testimonies against her by four witnesses, Pliats was not executed. Instead she was sentenced to ten years in the Gulag (31–33). She was sent to Karaganda (in Kazakhstan) in April 1938. In 1940 she asked Khrushchev, then the political leader of Ukraine, to reconsider her case. Her request was not met (38–39). Pliats was released in 1948 (33zv., 40). Her subsequent fate is unknown.

Like others who strenuously insisted on their innocence, Pliats could have been executed. The police needed no 'evidence' to sentence her to death. In fact, they had managed to extract damaging testimonies from her students. It is impossible to know why she escaped death when many others like her did not. Perhaps her determination to stand up against (almost certainly) false accusations helped her in the end.

Frida Gershovna Natanzon

Frida Gershovna Natanzon, like Kronberg and Zeibert, was accused of foreign espionage, in her case on behalf of Romania. She was born into a Jewish family in 1888 in Tighina (Bendery) in Moldova, then under Russian rule but from 1918 to 1940 under Romanian control. She had a secondary education and worked in Tighina as a schoolteacher before the 1917 Revolution. Afterwards she married a Kievan mill tenant and came to Kiev, where her daughter, Sara Azar'evna Natanzon, was born in 1918. Her husband died in 1920. In Kiev she worked as a schoolteacher until 1930, after which she worked as a librarian until June 1932. Then, according to the police, she, somewhat oddly, became dependent on her daughter, then fourteen years of age, living at 31 Pushkin Street, Flat 7, Kiev. Nantanzon testified that she worked as a pre-school teacher from 1920 to 1937. She was arrested on 23 April 1938 and executed on 14 October 1938.[16]

Natanzon's case is somewhat different from most others in this book. Her interrogations were recorded longhand and then typed, which suggests that the case was of special import to the Soviet secret police. It appears that it had to be reported to higher bodies and therefore had to be typed. Oddly, however, in her case file there are no records of any interrogation taking place before 3 October 1938; so she may not have been interrogated until five and half months after her arrest. More likely is that she was interrogated, but admitted to no crime and therefore the records of these interrogations were expunged from her file.

Perhaps in order to break Natanzon, her daughter, Sara, was questioned on 29 July 1938, three months after her mother's arrest. Sara stated that her mother's sister lived in Philadelphia, USA, where she had gone before the 1917 Revolution. Natanzon had corresponded with her until 1937. In addition, according to Sara, they had family in Bessarabia, Romania: her mother's sister and father, with whom Natanzon also corresponded until 1937. She and her mother received no monetary help from them. Towards the end of 1937, Natanzon received a postcard that said that if she wanted to know the state of health of her father, she should go to the house of one Rosenblat or Rosenbaum at 6 Engels Street in Kiev. So Natanzon went and there met a Romanian woman called Mul'man who gave her greetings from her father. There were many other people in the house who appeared to be Mul'man's relatives. After a week Mul'man, a sister of the afore-mentioned 'Rosenblat' or Rosenbaum, went back to Romania (8–9).

Natanzon's neighbours were deposed on 29 July 1938. They testified that strangers visited her frequently, that they talked all night and that she received letters from Romania and the USA (31–34). On 1 and 2 October Natanzon was allowed to question her neighbours. The latter simply repeated what they had said in July. Natanzon insisted that no one had visited her from abroad and that she always worked in her flat till late (35–38).

In 1937–38 the arrested were rarely given the opportunity to question witnesses against themselves. In many cases, no testimonies were taken to begin with. In important cases like Natanzon's, such questionings (*ochnye stavki*) were permitted in order to ensure that the prosecution was strong. All the same, these sessions were staged by the police: the witnesses were forced to adhere to their testimonies. There was little substance or even drama to them. They were *pro forma.*

The first extant record of Natanzon's investigation dates from 3 October 1938 (10–15, 16–22), more than two months after her daughter was questioned by the police. She admitted that she knew David Moiseevich Shtern, a resident of Tighina, who was arrested in 1936 in Kiev. She added that her contact with him had been limited, because he lived in Romania and she in the USSR. Yet one day in 1936 he wrote from a Kiev prison to ask for her help. She did not know what to do or why he was in Kiev. On the evening of that day Shtern's relatives, who lived at 26 Mar'iana (?) Street, Kiev, Feiza (?) Leiner and her brother, came to her flat. They persuaded her to send Shtern parcels, which she did on two occasions. Natanzon's interrogator pressed her, asking why she had made no mention of the fact that Shtern had stopped by her flat more than once. Natanzon responded that it was possible that he had stopped by while she was away, but insisted that she did not remember and denied the allegation. As for Mul'man, Natanzon said that she was a wealthy owner of a pharmacy in Romania and that she had somehow used her connections to acquire a legal entry visa to the Soviet Union. Mul'man asked Natanzon what the prices of products were and other questions and praised the 'bourgeois order' in Romania. Asked whether she would admit to her crime of spying for Romania, Natanzon said:

> Yes, I plead guilty. I was indeed in contact with David Shtern and Mul'man (a resident of Romania). They repeatedly asked me to shelter people who carried letters from them in my flat. I did that. This year some people came from Moscow with a note from Mul'man. They told me about my father and asked me about food prices, the mood of the population, about factories and new constructions. I told them all I knew and they left. Who they were I never knew. I know only that they were from Romania. I was pleased to hear that people came from Romania who knew my father, but that they were spies they did not tell me.

The interrogator was not happy with this confession and pressed her to tell the truth. Natanzon responded:

I confirm that the entirety of my espionage activity consisted of the fact that I took in strangers to my flat, accepting the notes from Shtern (before he was arrested) and Mul'man (residing in Bendery, Romania). These ladies and gentlemen, these strangers who were Muscovites, Odesans and Romanians, asked me about everything— what was happening in the Soviet Union, how workers and officials were living, and what their [political] mood was like. What I knew I told them and they took notes and two or three days later they left. I cannot say anything other than this.

She pleaded guilty, but insisted that her only crime was telling visitors from Romania about life in the Soviet Union. She did not herself consider it espionage activity, but conceded that by the Soviet secret police's definition, it was. In other words, Natanzon was not broken completely.

The following day, 4 October 1938, Natanzon was interrogated again. This session was recorded longhand and then typed up (23–25, 26–29). The interrogator insisted that her visitors were Romanian agents. Natanzon responded that some of them asked about everything (life in Kiev, the people's mood, their views of war, arrests in Kiev), but she did not speak about espionage. The interrogator was irritated and asked when and by whom she was recruited into the Romanian intelligence organs. Natanzon gave way. She stated that she was recruited for espionage work at the beginning of 1936 by Shtern, who illegally crossed the Romanian border into the Soviet Union on the Dniester River near the village of Tirnovka just outside Tiraspol. He stayed in her flat in Kiev for three days, and gave her a letter from her father. After her 'daughters' went to bed, Shtern told her that he needed people for espionage and that a lot of money would be given for valuable information. (It is noteworthy that the interrogator wrote 'daughters' even though Natanzon had only one. Natanzon could not have said 'daughters'. This kind of slip can be an eloquent bit of evidence regarding the faking of confessions.) Natanzon agreed and promised to give him whatever information she could obtain and, most importantly, said she agreed to house Romanian agents in her flat. These were the main duties that she fulfilled. When asked how much money she received from Romanian agents for her work, Natanzon responded: 'I received no money. D. Shtern only promised all the time that he'd soon get money and pay. I accepted it. I know nothing more.'

It is not known whether Shtern was actually a Romanian agent. Natanzon probably did receive letters from Romania through him, Mul'man and others. Even so, it is not known for certain whether Shtern or anyone else from Romania stayed in Natanzon's flat. Yet the apparent link between Natanzon and a foreign visitor (possibly an illegal border transgressor) made her case special. No evidence to prove her espionage existed. It appears that she stood up against the accusation for some time, then was coerced into making a qualified admission of her 'crime' and finally was almost broken. Higher-ups were almost certainly involved in her case.

In the end, on 7 October 1938 she was sentenced to be shot. Her execution was carried out a week later (40a, 40b) in accordance with NKVD Secret Order No. 00606 of 17 September 1938. Like Kronberg, Zeibert and others, she was buried in one of Bykivnia's mass graves.[17] When Natanzon was rehabilitated in 1989 owing to the lack of *corpus delicti*, her daughter, Sara, could not be located (46). She would have been seventy-one years of age by then; she may well have been dead.

Plastunova and Litvinov

Sofiia Klement'evna Plastunova was similarly accused of being a Romanian intelligence agent. Like Natanzon, she was born in Moldova (Bessarabia). She was an ethnic Ukrainian who at the time of her arrest in Kiev in September 1937 was fifty years of age. Plastunova lived in Moldova until 1924, then moved to Kiev where two of her brothers lived. (One, Lev Kliment'evich Plastunov, who moved to Kiev in 1919, was said to have served in the anti-Bolshevik Denikin army.) Her move was apparently illegal, and she was arrested but subsequently released after giving a pledge not to leave the city of Kiev and to live at a specified address.[18] In 1937, however, the secret police suspected that Plastunova's move to Kiev had actually been dictated by the Romanian intelligence services. She was not intimidated, however, and fought back in the only interrogation session to which she was subjected, on 24 October 1937. Like the German teacher Pliats discussed earlier, Plastunova categorically denied the charge of espionage. The interrogator repeatedly insisted that he had information about her recruitment by Romanian intelligence, but Plastunova continued to deny the charge (24–26). The interrogation got nowhere.

Plastunova was tried as part of the Polish Operation. What her Romanian connections had to do with Poland is difficult to understand. It is possible that for the sake of bureaucratic convenience the police treated her as a Polish case, just as they treated Zeibert as a Polish case. It is also true that many people suspected of other foreign (Czech, for example) connections were repressed as part of the Polish Operation; likewise, many 'Zionists' were repressed as part of the German and Polish Operations in Ukraine.[19] On 14 November 1937 Plastunova was sentenced to ten years in the Gulag (32). Like Pliats, her firm stand may have helped her to escape a death sentence. In 1940 Plastunova requested a review of her case. She was refused, however (30).

To make matters more complicated, Kievan researchers suggest that Plastunova was ultimately executed.[20] It is not known why, but if it is true, it probably happened in 1941 (she was still alive in 1940), at the beginning of the war, when many prison and camp inmates were put to death. In 1989 no relatives were found. If Plastunova was executed, it is odd that the rehabilitation committee should have noted in 1989 that whether Plastunova was alive or not was not known (37–38). Had she been alive, she would have been 102 years of age.

Abram Mironovich Litvinov, a Jew who, like Plastunova, came to the Soviet Union in 1924, was executed in Kiev in 1937.[21] He was born in Akkerman, Bessarabia (today's Bilhorod-Dnistrovskyi in Ukraine), in 1901. He had little education and was almost illiterate. Conscripted into the Romanian army in 1922, Litvinov deserted after two months. By his own admission, he had engaged in theft and had been arrested about a dozen times, and served several terms in Romanian gaols (12). With no job and hunted by the police, he illegally crossed the border into the Soviet Union and settled in Kiev, leaving his mother and sister in Bessarabia. When he was interrogated after his arrest on 23 September 1937, Litvinov said that he had not maintained contact with them. At the time of his arrest, he was working as a stallholder and lived at 33 Lenin Street, Flat 25, in Kiev with his wife, Maiia Markovna Litvinova, 26, and his daughter, Sara Abramovna Litvinova, 7 (5zv.). Whether he had been convicted of any crime after his arrival in the Soviet Union is not clear, but by and large he appears to have lived an honest life.

Initially Litvinov was accused of being a Romanian spy, working as a courier of intelligence information. In two interrogations, on 7 October and 22 November 1937, he denied the charges. So on 22 November 1937 the police deposed two witnesses, a neighbour and a former colleague. It is not clear whether their depositions took place before or after Litvinov's second interrogation. According to the records, the witnesses maintained that Litvinov complained about life in the Soviet Union being worse than in Romania and said that the Soviet government did not care about the workers. As in so many other cases, these testimonies cannot be taken at face value. In any case, the interrogator did not even question Litvinov about his alleged anti-Soviet remarks (8–14). In the end, he was indicted on charges of anti-Soviet agitation, a charge about which again he was not interrogated. He was sentenced to be shot on 23 December 1937 and six days later, at midnight on 29 December, he was executed (18, 22). Litvinov was buried in a mass grave in Bykivnia.[22] At the time of his rehabilitation in 1989 neither his wife nor his daughter could be found (22–24).

As stated before, foreign connections were the central theme of Stalin's terror in the 1930s. The reason for this is simple: Stalin was certain that international war would come, but he did not know when or with what countries it would be fought. In this context, anyone with foreign connections appeared suspect. If in the Far East Japan posed the greatest threat, then in the west, the greatest threat came from Poland and Germany. But many other countries, such as Latvia, Estonia, Lithuania, Finland and Romania, which together encircled the Soviet Union, also appeared threatening and dangerous.

Many ethnic Germans in the western borderlands (including Kiev) were descendants of settlers whose roots dated back to the eighteenth and nineteenth centuries. Many, like Kronberg and Zeibert, were Baltic Germans. There was therefore a thriving German culture in Ukraine, assisted by the *korenizatsiia* (indigenisation) policy of the 1920s and early 1930s, which was intended to secure the support of non-Russians for the Soviet regime by granting them a degree of cultural autonomy. Valentin M. Berezhkov, who was born in St Petersburg in 1916 but educated at a German school in Kiev, was a master of the German language. (He acquired such a fine Berlin accent that, when he interpreted for Molotov and Hitler in Berlin in 1940, Hitler asked whether Berezhkov was in fact a German. When he told him that he was not, Hitler asked whether he was of German origin. Berezhkov responded, 'No, I'm Russian.' Hitler was surprised, saying, 'It isn't possible'.[23] Deemed politically suspect, many of his school's German-language staff were arrested (the founder and director of the school, Friedrich Fibich, was sent to Siberia as a 'spy' and 'enemy of the people') and the school itself was closed, probably in the mid-1930s. The German church on Lutheran Street in Kiev was also closed.[24] German culture was to disappear almost completely during the war, when almost all ethnic Germans (*Volksdeutsche*) were deported from Ukraine to the east and whoever managed to remain fled west with the retreating German forces towards the end of the fighting.

Kronberg, Zeibert, Natanzon, Litvinov and others were almost certainly innocent of the crimes of which they were accused. No evidence was ever found. It is possible, of course, that they were not happy with their lives in the Soviet Union. Kronberg, for example, wanted to return to her homeland. But they were executed simply because they had connections to countries deemed dangerous.

CHAPTER 9

Consular Affairs
Fatal Visits

As has been discussed in previous chapters, foreign connections were dangerous to Soviet citizens in the 1930s. Visits to foreign consulates and embassies were particularly risky. Already in the 1920s the Soviet authorities monitored visitors to foreign consulates. Then at some point in the 1930s the Soviet secret police intensified and systematised its surveillance. Many visitors to foreign embassies and consulates were subsequently repressed as foreign spies.

In a country as big and as geographically and ethnically diverse as the Soviet Union, a proportion of citizens naturally had connections with people living 'abroad'. After the Russian Empire collapsed in 1917, several independent countries emerged (Poland, Finland, Estonia, Latvia and Lithuania) while other regions (such as Georgia and Ukraine) were reabsorbed back into the 'imperial' hold of the Soviet Union. The demarcation of international borders was complicated by civil and international conflicts such as the 1920 Polish–Bolshevik War, which divided many families. (See Chapters 10 and 11.) The dispersal of entire populations was common, and refugees were to be found everywhere. Moreover, the USSR's thousands of miles of international borders, however tightly controlled, could not be sealed completely and border transgressions happened on a daily basis. Innumerable illegal (as well as legal) immigrants lived in the Soviet Union.

Soviet citizens needed access to foreign authorities to regularise a wide array of personal issues relating to immigration, property, family and other matters. Foreign legations likewise needed Soviet citizens to work as cooks, cleaners, interpreters, repairmen, chauffeurs and so on. They also pursued their own intelligence needs. The Polish consulates in Kharkiv and Kiev were staffed 'right down to (in fact especially) the mechanics and drivers' with their own intelligence agents.[1] In 1932, Polish military intelligence compiled detailed lists of ethnic Poles living in the Soviet Union to be used in case of need.[2]

In 1933, at the time of the Great Famine in Ukraine, the German consulate was inundated by 'thousands upon thousands' of ethnic Germans in need of help. The consulate collaborated with Catholic and Evangelical churches and the charity group 'Brüder in Not' (Brothers in Need) to provide assistance. Some visitors to the consulate made their dissatisfaction with the Soviet government clear to officials. The latter, in turn, feared that such remarks might be deliberate provocation in view of the fact that the Soviet secret police always seemed to be well informed about what took place inside the consulate. Visitors were therefore asked to refrain from having political conversations. All the same, as the German consul of the time, Andor Hencke, stated subsequently, nothing was more dangerous in the Soviet Union than visiting the German consulate—the 'Hitler consulate'. Visitors were suspected of espionage and interrogated by the Soviet secret police. This led to a sharp decline in the number of visitors.[3]

As Hencke observed, contact with consulates proved fatal for many Soviet citizens. Many were caught in a 'diabolical trap', as Timothy Snyder has argued:

> By late 1936, the [Polish] consulate [in Kiev] was dealing with the desperate applications of people caught in a diabolical trap: petitioners who wished to prove, somehow, that they had no contacts at all with Poland. Consular employees knew that these people were innocent of espionage, but how could they certify an absence? From the Soviet point of view, their very attempt to prove their innocence probably proved their guilt. Once they had contacted the Polish consulate, they had contacts (as the Soviet saw matters) with Polish intelligence.[4]

On 10 October 1937 the NKVD, with the sanction of the Politburo of the Central Committee of the Communist Party, issued an operation order which instructed its counter-espionage department to 'arrest all Soviet citizens who are connected to the staff of foreign diplomatic offices and who visit their businesses and private premises' and to 'place under constant surveillance all members of the German, Japanese, Polish and Italian embassies'.[5] Although the full scale of terror against those associated with embassies and consulates in the Soviet Union is not known, it is certain that a very large number of them were arrested and executed in 1937–38.

Diplomats at most major embassies and consulates worked under cover as intelligence specialists. They collected all kinds of information deemed potentially useful. The Japanese consulate in Novosibirsk in Western Siberia, for instance, carefully monitored all sorts of seemingly innocent Soviet activities, including the Siberian railway. In 1937, under cover of going on picnics, some Japanese diplomats spent days on river banks observing freight cars, while others monitored military bases and military factories. Obviously, to carry out such tasks, they needed help from local residents (some of whom may have been double agents). In late 1937 more than a hundred Soviet citizens were arrested as Japanese spies and sixty-three were executed. Among them were the Japanese consular secretary Viacheslav Petrovskii, his sister Ol'ga, the telephone operator at the consulate, Mikhail Mikheev, the chauffeur, and Stepan Bylov, the cleaner. The consulate was shut down in late 1937. Hideo Ōta, the Japanese vice-consul in Novosibirk in 1937 and the head of Japanese intelligence there, was arrested by the Soviet authorities in Manchuria in 1945. He was tried and sentenced in Moscow in 1952 to twenty-five years in the Gulag. After Stalin's death, Ōta was repatriated to Japan.[6]

In the case of the Far East, the arrest of those connected with foreign consulates started much earlier. In Blagoveshchensk, for instance, where there are said to have been as many as 6,000 disenfranchised Soviet exiles, mass arrests began in early 1933, i.e., shortly after the Manchurian incident. In view of the threat of war with Japan these were deemed 'political bombs'. However, it was the Soviet citizens connected with the Japanese consulate in the city, including seamstresses, tailors, tutors and governesses, who were the first to be arrested.[7]

The Soviet secret police sent its own agents to work for foreign embassies and consulates in the country, but foreign missions were careful to weed out Soviet agents. All the same, foreign missions did hire private Soviet citizens when they were convinced that they had nothing to do with the Soviet secret police. This made those private citizens particularly suspect in the eyes of the police. At the same time

Soviet controllers also feared that their own agents might be recruited by foreign missions. In the real world, no one was absolutely certain who was working for whom. Even such low-level employees as cooks and cleaners were suspected by the secret police of working as couriers for foreign missions (indeed, foreign missions did seek to use innocent-looking citizens to perform certain missions to avoid the attentions of the Soviet authorities).

Before the 1934 transfer of the Ukrainian capital from Kharkiv to Kiev, Germany and Poland had already stationed consulates in the latter. This was probably due to the fact that there was a large population of ethnic Poles and Germans in the area. The Polish consulate had a much larger staff than the German consulate. In 1936, however, the German consulate was elevated to the status of a consulate-general.[8]

Those associated in one way or another with the German and Polish consulates in Kiev became targets of special terror in 1937–38. The case of Lidiia Eduardovna Kronberg, who visited the German consulate wishing to return to Latvia, was discussed in Chapter 8. Her case is merely the tip of the iceberg.

A Cook and a Chauffeur

Tat'iana Samsonovna Eshchenko-Monarshukova was a cook at the German consulate-general in Kiev. She was born in 1885 near Kharkiv into a Ukrainian peasant family, and worked in the field before the 1917 Revolution. Afterwards she was variously a homemaker and a cook; she was a non-party member. Her husband, Nikolai Karlovich Eshchenko, born in 1895 in Tula, Russia, was a chauffeur for the German consul-general Georg Wilhelm Grosskopf.[9] Eshchenko-Monarshukova was arrested on 4 February 1938 on suspicion of spying for Germany. She was one of five detained at the time, all of whom had worked for the consul's household.[10] Her husband was also arrested (when is not known) and accused of spying for Germany. They appear to have had their home at 37 Kirov Street, but according to the certificate issued by Grosskopf dated 20 January 1938 (which was confiscated at the time of her arrest along with her passport, 510 roubles in cash and certificates for 395 roubles in government bonds), Eshchenko-Monarshukova lived and worked as a housemaid at the consulate on 3 Voroshylov Street in Kiev.[11]

Interrogated on 21 February 1938, Eshchenko-Monarshukova said that she came to live in Kiev in 1917, married Nikolai in 1919 and became a housewife. In September 1936 she began to work as a cook for Grosskopf at the consulate. She was then asked about someone called Emiliia Khrystanovna Kamerer and her family. She said that she had become acquainted with Kamerer in 1918 at a bazaar where she traded. Her husband, Pavel, was a caretaker, but had died in 1928. Kamerer traded 'by hand' but later opened a stall. From 1918 to July 1936, when Kamerer left for Germany Eshchenko-Monarshukova helped her with running her household. Oddly the interrogator did not press her to confess to her alleged crime of espionage, but rather asked her for the identities of Soviet citizens associated with Kamerer. She named four. She also explained how she came to work for the German consul-general: Kamerer had recommended her and her husband while she was still in the Soviet Union. Asked how Grosskopf and his family treated her, Eshchenko-Monarshukova answered that they were exceptionally good to her: she was paid well and given presents often. It was clear that they trusted her, she said, because in her presence they expressed their suspicions of other people working at the consulate and of their connection with the NKVD. Her story suggests that she was hired independently, without NKVD screening, and that the NKVD was therefore suspicious of her. She was then asked whom she knew among the Soviet citizens who visited Grosskopf. She said she knew no one, but was told that she was lying. Yet she insisted that no Soviet citizen visited Grosskopf (9–15). It is not clear who Kamerer really was—whether she was a German citizen or Soviet citizen. Was she an ethnic German? Or was her late husband a German citizen? Eshchenko-Monarshukova noted that Kamerer and her niece were 'connected' to the officials of the German consulate-general (11).

Interrogated again on 3 April 1938, she was told that according to a 'lackey' of the German consulate, one Beitel'spakher, she had been engaged in provocation in addition to espionage: she had informed Beitel'spakher that her husband had been summoned by the NKVD. Eshchenko-Monarshukova denied the charges firmly and categorically: she had never engaged in espionage or provocation; she had never told Beitel'spakher about her husband's summons by the NKVD. She admitted that she saw Beitel'spakher almost every day because of the nature of her work, she received money from him to buy provisions and she reported to him, but she had never received any espionage assignments from him. Judging by her case files, it was the NKVD interrogators, not Eshchenko-Monarshukova, who engaged in provocation: even though the NKVD confiscated only about 900 roubles in cash and bond certificates, the interrogator inflated the amount and asked why she had such a large sum of money, as much as 3,000 roubles! This was a ruse: the police suggested that Eshchenko-Monarshukova and her husband received cash for their espionage work. She may have responded that they did not have as much as 3,000 roubles, but if she did it was not recorded. What the document says is that she insisted that because she and her husband were fed at the consulate, they were able to save their salaries to buy clothes, presumably to appear respectable as consular employees (17–21—folio 19 is missing, however).

According to the NKVD, both Kamerer and Beitel'spakher were German spies: the former had left for Germany but the latter was 'indicted' (what this means—whether he was actually arrested or, whether, as a diplomat with diplomatic privileges, he was indicted *in absentia*—is not clear). Grosskopf, too, was declared a German spy by the Soviet authorities: he was implicated in a 'German spy ring' in Novosibirsk which he allegedly led before being transferred to Kiev in 1936.[12] Whatever the case, without any material evidence or confession, Eshchenko-Monarshukova was also indicted as a German spy. She was condemned to death on 20 September 1938 (according to NKVD Order No. 00606) and was executed the following day (222–23). Her husband was sentenced to be shot eleven days later, on 2 October 1938. Both were buried in the mass graves of Bykivnia.[13] When they were rehabilitated in 1989, no relatives were found (28). Their only crime was that they had worked at the German consulate-general without first being cleared by the NKVD (not that an NKVD clearance would have given them absolute security anyway).

Eshchenko-Monarshukova was an ordinary Ukrainian living in Kiev: with no special education or skills, she lived by helping a friend with housework, then took up employment with the German consulate-general as a cook. Yet she had the courage to stand up against the accusations of the NKVD. Her fearlessness may mean that she failed to understand the gravity of the charges against her; on the other hand, she may simply have been very courageous. Whatever the case, the police failed to break her.

A Joiner

Efim Vladimirovich Chernomorets was born into a Ukrainian peasant family in the small town of Lysianka near Kiev in 1865. He had little education, but worked independently as a handyman and also for the German and Polish consulates in Kiev. When he began working for the consulates is not known. In 1930, suspected of being a German spy and already working for the German consulate, he was detained for a month and a half. He was not indicted at the time.[14] Then on 29 September 1937 Chernomorets was arrested again on suspicion of espionage. At the time he was living at 55 Gershuni Street, Flat 2, in Kiev, with his wife, Kharetina Vasil'evna Chernomorets, daughter Elena and son Aleksandr.

According to his case file, Chernomorets was interrogated only once, on 27 October 1937, almost a month after his arrest. He told his interrogator that he had lived in Kiev for fifty-four years, working as a joiner, mainly repairing and restoring old furniture. He had also worked briefly in Odesa, Yalta and Katerynoslav (present-day Dnipropetrovs'k), repairing and making furniture. When pressed to admit that he had systematically collected information for the German and Polish consulates in Kiev over the course of many years, Chernomorets said that he had frequented the consulates for 'more than five years', but denied collecting information or working as an informer. Then, asked with whom he had associated at the consulates, he mentioned the following people at the German consulate: the former consul, one Sommer,[15] who had left for Leningrad a few years earlier to become consul there, his successor (whose name Chernomorets could not remember), the vice-consul Gotmar, the secretary Bauman, Vice-Consul Wolwi (?), the consulate caretaker Semen and the doorman Ivan Ivanovich (whose surname he did not remember). He last visited the German consulate in 1936. At the Polish consulate Chernomorets knew the consul Jankowski (who had left for Poland some years earlier) and his successor (whose name he did not remember). He also knew the secretaries there, but not their names. He had visited the Polish consulate repeatedly over the past five to six years for the purpose of repairing and restoring old furniture. Chernomorets visited the consulates many times, and the consuls and other employees visited his home/workshop. That was all there was between them, he insisted (13–14).

The interrogator, however, pressed Chernomorets to confess to crimes of espionage (including informing the consulates about life in the Soviet Union). He again admitted to his frequent visits to the consulates and to the frequent visits of the officials to his workshop, but categorically denied that he had informed them about life in the Soviet Union. (Of course, they must have known about life in Kiev anyway because they lived there and had visited Chernomorets' home/workshop!) He then added that he categorically denied the charges of handing them information of an 'espionage nature' (14–15)

To complicate matters, Polish sources confirm that the Polish consul Henryk Jankowski was indeed involved in intelligence. He founded an intelligence unit (*placówka*) under the name of 'Kh' in Kiev in October 1931. This functioned until November 1936. After he left Kiev in 1933, it was run by his successor.[16] There is no evidence, however, that Chernomorets was an informer.

The interrogator deposed three witnesses. According to the file, their depositions took place on 24 and 25 October 1937. This suggests that Chernomorets was probably first interrogated before 27 October, but that he had denied all the charges and that witnesses were therefore deposed. (No records of any possible earlier interrogations are in his case file.) His neighbour, for instance, testified that Chernomorets praised Tukhachevskii, Iakir and other Red Army leaders who were executed in the summer of 1937: 'They wanted to create a better life for the people.' He was also alleged to have entertained a defeatist position regarding the Soviet Union, saying: 'All the same you [the Soviets] won't win, such weaklings as you' (16–17). As in other cases, these formulaic testimonies were almost certainly fabricated.

Chernomorets was indicted on 2 November 1937 on charges of espionage: in the guise of a furniture repairman he had frequented the German and the Polish consulates and acted as an informer and spy for them. He was sentenced to be shot on 5 November 1937 as part of the Polish Operation. On 16 November 1937 at midnight he was executed (22–23, 25, 33). He was seventy-two years of age. He was buried in a mass grave in Bykivnia.[17] When he was rehabilitated, no relatives were found. Chernomorets, like so many others, was despatched on mere suspicion of having committed a crime. He was in all probability simply a good joiner whose services were appreciated by foreign diplomats, but the police suspected that he was a secret German and Polish agent.

Chernomorets' case file is almost certainly incomplete. The police obviously sought to suppress his voice by editing his records, and his guilt was presumed from the start.

A Pensioner

Mariia Stanislavovna Ditkovskaia worked as a seamstress and lived at 45 Gershuni Street, Flat 23, in Kiev. At the time of her arrest and execution she was a single, uneducated and illiterate pensioner. Born in 1875 in the village of Bezpechna near Kiev, she was an ethnic Pole, a Soviet citizen and a non-party member. On 30 December 1937 she was arrested on suspicion of spying for Poland. On 4 February 1938 she was sentenced to be shot in accordance with the Polish Operation and executed at midnight on 16 February 1938.[18] She was one of forty-four people executed on that day in Kiev.

According to her case records, since 1934 she had frequented and been an informer for the Polish consulate in Kiev. She gave the consul, Henryk Jankowski, information of an 'espionage nature' regarding the political mood of the people in the Soviet Union: the Soviet workers were dissatisfied with the Soviet government and in the event of war would stand up against it. She was also accused of disseminating 'counter-revolutionary Fascist propaganda' in Kiev, praising the Polish nation and saying that it would triumph in a forthcoming war and liberate the Poles from the Communists in Ukraine (16).

Ditkovskaia appears to have been broken relatively easily. Four days after her arrest, on 3 January 1938, she was interrogated. She told the interrogator that on 18 September 1934 someone from the Polish consulate came to her home on Gershuni Street and suggested that she visit the consulate concerning a subject that would interest her. Two days later she met Consul Jankowski there. Jankowski informed her that he had received a letter from someone called Knol' in Warsaw who asked Ditkovskaia to return the belongings she had left with her by way of the Polish consulate. She promised the consul she would do so. Gavriel' Knol' was a widow who had lived on Ditkovskaia's street in 1923, more than ten years earlier, and had left for Warsaw. Two days after her visit to the consulate, the same consular official came to see her again. To him she returned all the belongings of Knol'. Since Ditkovskaia had once worked for her, when Knol' left for Warsaw, she

29: Ditkovskaia's pension book.

had entrusted some of her belongings to Ditkovskaia, and asked that they should be given to her niece, Filitsiia Knol', who was living in the city of Slavuta or Slawuta at the time (9–9zv.). Why Ditkovskaia had not handed them over to Filitsiia is not known. Perhaps she had been tempted to keep them for herself or had been unable to get in touch with Filitsiia for one reason or another. It is possible that Ditkovskaia was embarrassed about this. If so, this was of no interest to the interrogator.

The interrogator pressed her to admit that she was a Polish spy. She denied the charges: 'I was never an agent of foreign intelligence services. I never engaged in espionage activity by order of the Polish intelligence' (9zv.) But when pressed further, she admitted that she had not told the truth. She said that she had told Consul Jankowski about the political mood of the people around her and the residents in her building, especially Communists. She had told him how dissatisfied the workers were with the Soviet government, particularly because of the food shortages at the time. She had said that in the event of war the majority of the population would stand up against the Soviet system. Then Jankowski gave her the task of providing the names of Communists living in her building. She consented, according to the interrogation records. When the consular official appeared at her home, she gave him the names (there were three). After that she never visited the consulate again nor did anyone come to her home from the consulate (10).

Interestingly, the two sheets of paper (folios 9 and 10) in her file used to record this interrogation session are of different quality. Perhaps this can be explained by reference to the general conditions at the time: good materials were in short supply. Yet it is also possible that, after Ditkovskaia was broken following her initial refusal to confess, folio 10 was rewritten completely.

Ditkovskaia was also questioned about a Catholic priest named Sigizmund Karlovich Kvasnevskii (see Chapter 2). She did not know him personally, but she appeared to know of him as a priest (11). Pressed further about her 'counter-revolutionary work', she said,

> [It] consisted only in that as a Polish nationalist I considered it my duty, based on my religious convictions, to conduct agitation among the Poles for the church and to preserve religious sentiments. At the same time I expressed my views that the Polish nation in the future would become a dominant nation, because a war is approaching in which Poland will triumph. Then we Poles will live better than now [11].

Questioned about her foreign connections, Ditkovskaia admitted to a correspondence with her former friend Mariia Glazko, who had emigrated to Poland in 1927. In that year she received a letter from Glazko that was solely about her family. She also wrote to Glazko about her own life. Ditkovskaia drew the line here, however, insisting that she wrote nothing libellous about life in the Soviet Union. She also noted that she had been in contact with the Polish priest Iosif Frantsevich Mruvko, who was arrested on 17 November 1937 and executed a month later on charges of spying for Poland, but that she was not his accomplice (13, 73–74).

Her interrogation records show that she could barely sign her own name. How then was she able to write letters? Did she have someone to write for her? Did the alleged correspondence take place at all? No letters were presented as evidence by the police.

In spite of the absence of any material evidence Ditkovskaia was executed. Apparently a single visit to the Polish consulate in 1934 had proved fatal. She was sixty-three years of age.

In fact, even her 1934 visit may never have taken place. Henryk Jankowski was the Polish consul in Kiev from October 1930 to early 1933. Before that he served as consul in Minsk (Mensk) in Belarus. According to Soviet investigators in 1961, he managed intelligence work at both consulates (42–43). As noted earlier, Polish sources confirm the Soviet conclusions.[19] Yet by 1934, when Ditkovskaia was alleged to have visited the Polish consulate and met him, he was no longer in Kiev. It may be that Ditkovskaia was a faithful Catholic, which would have incurred the suspicion of some (111).

In 1961, twenty-three years after the execution of Ditkovskaia, four people who had been her neighbours in the 1930s were interviewed. They testified that Ditkovskaia, unmarried and without children, was a very modest person who hardly spoke to her neighbours and that they had never heard any anti-Soviet remarks from her (106–13). Ditkovskaia was rehabilitated in 1961 owing to the lack of *corpus delicti* (118).

Clearly this modest woman could not withstand the threats (and possibly torture) of her interrogator. She may have been secretly troubled by something (the personal items of Knol' which should have been handed over to her niece). Otherwise, she lived the quiet life of a pensioner. She may have been religious. In fact, it was her alleged Polish connections that doomed her. Exactly what raised the suspicion of the secret police is unclear. What *is* clear is that she was innocent: she pleaded innocent initially.

A Greek Worker

Polish and German connections were the most dangerous in Kiev. But anyone with foreign connections was suspect in the eyes of the Soviet secret police, and Greeks were no exception. The presence of Greeks in Ukraine went back a long way, to the pre-Christian era, although many were recent immigrants. It is not known how many ethnic Greeks lived in Kiev in 1937, but the census of that year shows that 102,257

Greeks lived in Ukraine, the seventh largest minority after Russians, Jews, Poles, Germans, Moldavians and Belarusans.[20]

Many Greeks were arrested and executed in the terror of 1937–38. What threat they presented to the Soviet Union is not entirely clear, except that some of them were accused of hatching a plan to establish a Greek republic on the shores of the Black Sea and other seemingly fantastic schemes. Some Greek merchants were used by the Japanese in the Far East as informers during the Russo-Japanese War of 1904–5 and in subsequent conflicts between the two countries. But this had happened in the relatively distant past and in a distant land. Others such as Jews, Cherkessians and Turks (not to mention Chinese and Koreans) had also been hired as informers and spies by the Japanese.[21] (This meant that Russia and the Soviet Union also used them, a fact confirmed by Japanese sources.) In the 1930s Japan targeted the ethnic Greeks, as well as other non-Russian ethnic groups, residing in the Black Sea coastal areas in the Soviet Union as potential enemies of the Soviet regime. Stalin was familiar with Japanese strategic thinking on this matter.[22] Even though there is no evidence to show that Japan had managed to achieve even the humblest success in this respect, Moscow treated ethnic Greeks (like Germans and Poles) with much suspicion. The Great Terror struck them as hard as it did Germans and Poles. The execution rate of Greeks (the percentage of those arrested who were then executed) in the case of the Donbas in eastern Ukraine in 1937–38 was very high: 95.6 percent, higher than that for Germans, 84.6 percent.[23] Because the 11 December 1937 secret order against Greeks is still classified,[24] one can only surmise what the Soviet government sought to achieve by this operation.

Ivan Kharlampievich Marangos was a Greek working in Kiev. Born in Athens in 1899, at the age of ten Marangos moved to Warsaw, then a part of the Russian Empire, to work as a shoemaker at a private shop run by his brother-in-law, Nikolai Karpatnos. Karpatnos appears to have died soon after. So Marangos worked until 1912 in Warsaw at the private 'Peros' shoe shop. He then moved to Odesa, and in 1914 to Berdians'k on the northern shore of the Black Sea. In 1922 he moved to Kiev, where he worked as a shoemaker first at a private shop, then, from 1926, at a collective shop (artel'). He was illiterate, according to his statement (although his case file shows that he could sign his own name in Russian) and lived at 8 Borychiv Uzviz, Flat 2, in Kiev with his wife, Klaviia Ivanovna, and daughter, Nitti Ivanovna, who was nine in 1937. Marangos may have kept his Greek citizenship (although this is not entirely clear, as is discussed later). According to his statement, by 1937 he had no relations abroad and was conducting no correspondence with anyone abroad.[25]

Clearly Marangos, a foreigner, was watched by the NKVD, as a memorandum dated 16 December 1937 suggests. According to this, Marangos often went to Moscow, where he allegedly maintained contact with the Greek mission. He knew another Greek, one Berdebes (also arrested), from whom he 'illegally' received 'Greek bourgeois newspapers' which 'libellously discussed life in the Soviet Union'. Alleged to have expressed 'counter-revolutionary sentiments' in conversations, he was arrested on 17 December 1937 on suspicion of foreign espionage (4, 73).

Marangos' case, involving a foreign citizen, was an important and potentially sensitive one. Therefore, unusually, his interrogation records, first made longhand, were typed up for examination by the higher-ups (9–14, 17–22). Four days after his arrest, Marangos was interrogated. He was pressed to confess to the crime of 'counter-revolutionary Fascist espionage activity'. He refused: 'I have never engaged in espionage or counter-revolutionary activity. I have never received any assignment from anyone to do so. I categorically deny the charges.' He was then threatened: 'You are lying. The material in our possession fully exposes your espionage activity. Try not to dispute it because it won't do any good. Confess to your espionage activity.' But Marangos stood his ground: 'I repeat that I never engaged in espionage activity.' Then the interrogator said, 'You are denying the charges in vain, because we have indisputable evidence exposing your counter-revolutionary espionage activity. You visited the Greek mission in Moscow [more than once].' Marangos denied this: 'No, I did not visit it.' Then the interrogator asked him how he had renounced his foreign passport, to which he replied: 'I forwarded it by mail.' The interrogator snapped: 'You're lying again.' It is not clear whether Marangos actually did try to renounce his Greek citizenship and acquire a Soviet passport. The NKVD treated him as a foreign citizen, someone unwilling to become a Soviet citizen after nearly thirty years of working in Russia and the Soviet Union.

How much confrontation (and possibly torture) went on is not known, but Marangos broke down in the end. The change in the handwritten

30a: Marangos' interrogation record, fol. 16zv.

interrogation records between folios 16zv. and 17 is remarkable: the leaves were of a different texture, they differed in the spacing of the writing and in other respects as well (see Illustrations 30a and 30b). The writing on folio 17 (Illustration 30b) is much more animated, perhaps as a result of the interrogator having broken Marangos.

30b: Marangos' interrogation record, fol. 17.

Marangos now confessed: 'I indeed told a lie. Now I have decided to confess to my espionage activity, which I performed as an agent of the Greek mission on an assignment from the Greek consulate and Greek mission in the city of Moscow' (11, 17). Marangos stated: 'Until 1931 I sent my foreign passport by mail to the Greek consulate in Moscow.'

He probably meant 'for renewal'. Yet after 1931, when his good friend
Kuz'ma Konstantinovich Kostis, who knew the Greek language and
worked at the 'Chuziak' collective workshop in Kiev, left for Greece,
Marangos began to go to Moscow in person: Kostis had told him to
go to the Greek consulate there because the consul wanted to discuss
something with him. So he did in September 1931. He was met by
Consul Anisas accompanied by the official Kumbaris. In conversation
Anisas suggested that he conduct espionage for Greece by collecting
information that interested the consulate and giving it personally to
him when he came to Moscow. Marangos agreed. In return Anisas
promised material help.

Anisas gave him three assignments: (1) to collect information
on industry in Kiev, especially on military industry (the quality of
factories; what they produced); (2) to collect information on the
Red Army (the locations, numbers and names of military units);
(3) to collect information on the political mood of the population,
particularly of the Greeks living in Kiev. Marangos was also assigned to
distribute 'bourgeois Greek newspapers' among the Greeks. (Of course,
Marangos was likely to have been illiterate in Greek.) Marangos said
he had visited the Greek consulate 'about four times', once every year
since 1931, the last time being in August–September 1936 (to coincide
with the time of the reregistration of his passport), and handed the
information he had collected to Consul Anisas (and then Consul
Kolumbis who succeeded him in 1933). He gave them information
on: (1) Kiev factories such as 'Bolshevik' and 'Arsenal' working for
the military and their products (Kolumbis was particularly interested
in what 'Arsenal' was making); (2) the presence in the Kiev garrison
of armoured tank, infantry, artillery and anti-aircraft units—including
the approximate numbers of aircraft (1,500) in Solom'ianka; (3) the
presence of the Dnieper military flotilla—about fifteen military ships;
(4) the political mood of Red Army soldiers and of the Greeks and
the population of Kiev (13, 20–20zv.).

Marangos also named five people (two of whom had left the country
and three of whom were Greek citizens in Kiev) to whom he had
distributed 'bourgeois Greek newspapers'. Those in Kiev, Deonisii
Panaiotovich Kolumbis, 59, Marangos' colleague, Dmitrii Denisovich
Berdebes, 48, a baker, and Konstantin Afanasovich Paplomantopulo,
49, a waiter at the 'Panas' Hotel, were arrested and executed on 25

February 1938 (35–36). Yet Marangos was not to blame for their arrests which came *before* he was interrogated. Marangos' implication of them was almost certainly forced upon him.

Marangos told his interrogator that for his espionage activity he received 1,500 roubles from Anisas and Kolumbis (14, 21zv.–22). He repeated his confession in the 24 December 1937 interrogation (23–23zv.).

He was indicted in accordance with the Polish Operation, sentenced to be shot on 5 February 1938 and executed on 25 February 1938, on the same day three other Greeks were executed (24–25, 33). They were all buried in the Bykivnia mass graves.[26] In 1958, Marangos, along with the other Greeks mentioned in his case file, were rehabilitated, owing to the lack of *corpus delicti*. Marangos' death had been falsely registered, however, as acute liver failure on 25 July 1943 (28). His wife, Klavdiia, had been misinformed by the secret police about the cause of her husband's death. It was only in 1990 that his daughter, Nitti Ivanovna Tsutsarina, wrote to the Memorial (a civic organisation to commemorate the victims of terror) in Kiev about her father. Her letter was forwarded to the KGB, which admitted that her father had in fact been executed on 25 February 1938 (42). Personal documents that had been confiscated at the time of Marangos' arrest in 1937 were finally returned to his daughter.

In the end, nothing was proved. It is not even certain whether Marangos ever visited the Greek consulate in Moscow. The record of his interrogation, however detailed and credible it may appear superficially, seems to have been largely the work of the interrogator. Obviously Marangos' foreignness, even after nearly thirty years of work in Russia and the Soviet Union, attracted the attention of the Soviet secret police.

A Former Noble

Few categories of people were more suspect in the eyes of the Soviet secret police than former nobles, the last supporters of the tsarist order. They were, in the view of the Bolsheviks, the embodiment of the counter-revolution. Most of the old nobility voluntarily or involuntarily left the country after the triumph of the Bolsheviks in the Civil War. Those who remained were suspect by default and most were kept on police records. They lived quietly so as not to be noticed.

All this changed with the murder of Sergei Kirov, the party leader of Leningrad, in December 1934. Speculation abounds as to whether Stalin was a party to the crime or not. What is certain is that Stalin took advantage of the assassination to eliminate the politically suspect from the major cities. The old nobles were among the most visible in this group because of their backgrounds. Thus in 1935 almost all noble elements were deported from major Soviet cities.[27] Still some managed to continue living a quiet life until 1937–38.

Nina Nikolaevna Bunge was born into a Russian noble family in 1880 in Vilnius, which was then in the Russian Empire, though it is now the capital of Lithuania. Bunge's case file notes, however, that she was born in Poland.[28] It is true that Vilnius was part of Poland at the time of the Great Terror, but the suggestion that she was born in Poland was one of many subtle tricks used by the secret police to emphasise her foreign connections. Her father was a railway accountant. Bunge herself had only an unfinished secondary education, perhaps somewhat unusually for a noble, although her family was probably a very modest noble family. At the time of her arrest on 16 December 1937, Bunge lived at 9 Mykhailivs'kyi Provulok, Flat 20, in Kiev, with her daughter, Natal'ia Nikolaevna Bunge, 22, a student at Kiev University. Her son, Vsevolod Mikhailovich Grechis (?), 29, was a schoolteacher. The fact that her children had different patronymics suggests that they had different fathers. (Bunge appears to have been her husband's—perhaps second husband's—surname.) Bunge stated that she was married to a professor, but the status of her husband at the time is not known, except that Bunge was his dependant (10, 16). Bunge had extensive connections abroad: her relations lived in Paris, Berlin and Zagreb as well as in Bulgaria and Poland. She maintained a correspondence with her sister and niece in Paris until 1937 (11–11zv.). She had a record of previous arrest: in 1932 she was arrested on suspicion of espionage and held for two months before being released, apparently without being indicted (8zv., 16).

Bunge's noble background and her apparently extensive foreign connections doomed her. According to interrogation records of 24 December 1937, Bunge received 100 francs from a stranger from Poland who brought a letter from Ivan M. Kosakovskii, a pre-revolutionary official in the sugar industry, then living in Warsaw. From other relations and old acquaintances she received money and provisions periodically between 1923 and 1935. In 1928 she also received 20 dollars from the American Society for Scholarly Assistance, based in New York. Between 1924 and 1928 she received money several times from the Paris-based committee De Securi. In 1927 Bunge established contact with the secretary of the committee, S. S. Metal'nikova, who had emigrated from Russia in 1918. Bunge stated that in 1930 she also received food provisions from the committee. Asked about the Polish consulate in Kiev, she acknowledged visiting it once, in 1923, to hand over a letter from her to be forwarded to Kosakovskii. She did not give anything else to the consulate (11–12). Asked why she had used the consulate for that purpose, she said that it was because the stranger who brought the money had suggested she do so. Kosakovskii wanted her to make an inventory of securities he had left in the State Bank in Kiev and send it to him (13).

Could it be that the stranger was a police provocateur sent to entrap her?

Bunge was accused of distributing the money she received from the Paris committee to others who were in need of help in the Soviet Union, and forwarding a list of their names, said to be mainly those of families of former nobles and army officers, to Paris. Yet her actual activity was much more modest, at least in her own account: in 1928 and 1929, when she received money from Paris, she was instructed to give 15 roubles each to two women whose names she could no longer remember in 1937.

The tone of Bunge's statement in her file is direct and straightforward. Even so, it is very difficult to know whether these things actually took place or whether she was forced to admit to things that did not take place. What is certain is that Bunge never admitted to any contact with a foreign consulate other than her 1923 visit to the Polish consulate, or to passing on any information to it. Her interrogation appears perfunctory in comparison with many other cases. This suggests that she was doomed to be executed from the beginning. Her correspondence, which must have been substantial, was not even attached: according to her case file, it was 'held in the Third Department' of the NKVD. The reason was perhaps that it was needed for other investigations into foreign links (the NKVD Third Department was in charge of counter-intelligence), yet oddly her bill of indictment noted that there was 'no material evidence' in her case (17). So even her correspondence provided no evidence of crime.

On 25 January 1938 Bunge was sentenced to death, in accordance with the Polish Operation. On 4 February 1938 she was executed (18). She, too, was buried in the Bykivnia mass graves.[29] In 1989 she was rehabilitated owing to the lack of *corpus delicti*; no relatives were found.

Foreign missions such as embassies and consulates often functioned as a cover for intelligence-gathering. It was precisely at the time of the Great Terror that the Soviet Union forced many foreign countries to close their consulates in return for the closure of its own abroad. The Soviet authorities made the work of foreign diplomats very difficult: they arrested employees of consulates, stopped the delivery of newspapers and periodicals, restricted the travel of consular officers and, in extreme cases, cut their electricity, gas and water.[30] Thus in September 1937 the Japanese consulates in Odesa and Novosibirsk were forced to shut down. A year later, the Japanese consulates in Khabarovsk and Blagoveshchensk met the same fate. By the spring of 1938, Germany, Italy, Britain, Finland, Estonia, Latvia, Sweden, Norway, Denmark and Afghanistan had had all their consulates in the Soviet Union closed. The USA was yet to open any consulates in the USSR. The number of Japanese consulates was reduced from nine to four (Vladivostok, Petropavlovsk, Okha and Aleksandrovsk, although Manchukuo, Japan's puppet state, maintained one in Chita and another in Blagoveshchensk). Poland managed to keep two open, in Kiev and Minsk, while the Soviet Union had one in L'viv and another in Gdańsk (Danzig).[31]

Clearly the closure of foreign missions made intelligence work much more difficult. The impact of such measures is difficult to assess. One thing is certain, however: ordinary Soviet citizens were cut off from almost all contact with foreigners in general and foreign missions in particular. Soviet families divided across the borders lost virtually all means of communication with their relatives abroad.

CHAPTER 10

Across the Borders
Families Divided

Borders divide families. To the extent that the Soviet Union sought to shield itself from the outside world and treated foreign connections as signs of political disloyalty, all divided Soviet families were destined for tragedy. The collapse of the Russian Empire, the emergence of several independent states and numerous wars, civil and international, redefined international borders everywhere when the dust settled in the early 1920s. The coming of independence to Poland and Lithuania, in particular, divided numerous families there and in Ukraine and Belarus, the four territories that, until the partition of Poland in the eighteenth century, had combined to form the Polish–Lithuanian Commonwealth.

The Polish–Ukrainian divide affected the people in Kiev and surrounding areas in particular. Poles in Kiev became politically suspect almost by default, not least because the new Poland, keen to defend its long-coveted independence, regarded the Soviet Union as a great threat, while the Soviet Union considered Poland, along with Germany and Japan, its own most dangerous enemies.[1] (These three countries, particularly Poland and Japan, maintained a close, if informal, cooperation in intelligence matters [see Chapter 7].) The infiltration by Poland of Ukraine and other parts of the Soviet Union greatly concerned the latter,[2] which found the intelligence network of the newly independent Poland to be unwontedly competent. (This perhaps should not have come as a surprise: after all, the Soviet government appointed a Pole as the first head of its own secret police, Feliks Dzerzhinskii, or Dzierżyński.) Poland, in turn, found the presence of Ukrainians a grave threat to its stability. The Ukrainian right, seeking Ukrainian independence, often resorted to political terrorism against the Polish authorities, while the Ukrainian left often appeared as an advance force in the Soviet offensive against Polish independence. As discussed in Chapters 9 and 11, the Polish–Soviet tension destroyed numerous families in Kiev.

It was not just the Polish–Ukrainian border that divided Soviet families. As was the case with Nina Bunge, discussed in the last chapter, the emigration of between 1.5 and 2 million people, both voluntary and involuntary, that followed the Revolution and the Civil War divided untold numbers of Soviet families.

The Dzvinchuks

Iurii Grigor'evich Dzvinchuk was an ethnic Ukrainian who was born into a farmer's family in 1885 in the village of Kosmach, Kolomyia, to the south of Stanislau in Austrian Galicia, which became Stanisławów, part of Poland, in the interwar period and is now Ivano-Frankivs'k in Ukraine. He received seven years of education in Kolomyia in Austria and worked at an insurance company in L'viv (then the Austrian town of Lemberg or Lwów, as it is known in Polish, or L'viv in Ukrainian). He was said to have sympathised with the Polish Socialist Party (PSS), which did not favour Bolshevik power after the Revolution. He fought in the Austrian army in World War I, was taken prisoner and ended up in Kiev. He married Palageia Afanas'eva (who will be discussed later) in 1918. Dzvinchuk knew German and Polish in addition to Ukrainian and Russian, and at some point taught at a technical school in Rzhyshchiv, to the south of Kiev. At the time of his arrest on 4 October 1937, he was working as a guard at a factory in the village of Myrots'ke just outside Kiev. The Dzvinchuks had two sons and a daughter: Platon, 17, Boris, 12, and Valentina, 10.[3]

He had previously been arrested in 1930. He was accused at that time of belonging to a 'counter-revolutionary party' (most likely the SVU, fabricated by the secret police—see Chapter 5) and held in gaol for eleven months. He was then released without being indicted. As it turns out, the records of his 1930 arrest were lost: even the secret police could not find them (40–42).

Before Dzvinchuk's interrogation began on his second arrest, a witness, E. I. Guzerchuk-Manchenko, was deposed on 1 October 1937. The interrogator could not extract any particularly incriminating testimony from him, except for the fact that Dzvinchuk often went to the city of Kiev, his behaviour was strange and the like (16–17).

A fortnight after his arrest, interrogation of Dzvinchuk began. He stated that he had many relatives in Poland, his brothers Petr and Mikhail, sister Evdokiia, cousin Vasilii Ivanovich Dzvinchuk, a distant relative, Ivan Chuntuliak, and others. Questioned about his contacts with them, he stated that they corresponded about family matters and that in 1932 or 1933 (i.e., at the time of the Great Famine) he had received 5 dollars from his brother. His interrogator then quoted a letter from Petr that had been confiscated at the time of Dzvinchuk's arrest: 'You, my brother, live badly among the aliens. Those people don't want to let you come home, in fact can they really be considered human? ... they will drive all of us off the face of the earth.' (The Ukrainian original continues: 'My brother Iuro, it's surprising to me that you've stayed there, that your marriage is so bad, that you took it into your head to take her as your wife'. The interrogator confronted Dzvinchuk with this letter, claiming that his correspondence was not really about family matters but was in fact 'counter-revolutionary'. Dzvinchuk confirmed that it was indeed a letter from his brother in Poland, but insisted that it was not 'counter-revolutionary': it was written in distress at Dzvinchuk's not being allowed out of the country.

The interrogator then presented Dzvinchuk with one of his own letters: 'I have spent all my power and energy on getting released from the hands of alien people. Can I, an honest person, really not be allowed to live there [in Poland]? ... My work is hard, I don't have freedom [*volia*].' Told that this was 'counter-revolutionary', Dzvinchuk defended it as having been written when his spirits were low. He had had no intention of writing a letter of a 'counter-revolutionary' nature, he said (10–10zv.).

To whom Dzvinchuk had written this letter and how the police had obtained it is not known. The letter itself is not in his case file. This may mean that the police intercepted his letter. It is possible that both the letter and Dzvinchuk's admission were fictions. Dzvinchuk's file contains a letter in Ukrainian to his sister Evdokiia, which starts with this phrase: 'From a distant, unfriendly foreign land I send you, Sister, my sincere greetings' (28). This letter, confiscated at the time of his arrest, was never actually posted.

The following day, 20 October 1937, Dzvinchuk was interrogated again. This time, he was grilled about his visit to the Polish consulate in Kiev. He admitted that in the spring of 1932 or 1933 he had gone there once to acquire a visa for Poland. He was then told that the police had information that he had visited the consulate more than once: in August 1933, for instance. Dzvinchuk replied firmly that he had visited the consulate only once. Ordered to detail this visit, Dzvinchuk said that he had been received by an official, whom he had told that he wanted a visa for Poland. When the official realised that Dzvinchuk was not a Polish citizen, he told him that only when he became a Polish citizen could they discuss the matter of his leaving for Poland. What he was told about becoming a Polish citizen is not known, but their conversation lasted for only ten to fifteen minutes, according to Dzvinchuk. Told to give more details, Dzvinchuk said that he was asked by the Polish official whether he had a family, whether they would leave with him and what his financial situation was. To these questions, he answered that there were five people in his family, all of whom would leave with him, that he had no property, that he worked as a security guard at a technical school, that he had been arrested by the secret police and had been released after eleven months in detention, and that he now wanted to go back home (11–12). His statement suggests that, after his arrest, he was no longer able to work as a teacher and so became a guard at the same school instead.

Asked whether he had told the Polish official the reason for his arrest, Dzvinchuk replied that he had not. The interrogator charged that he was lying. Clearly he had wished to return home way back in 1920, shortly after the end of World War I when Poland became independent, and had talked to a Polish official called Raczkowski at the time. Yet he was rejected by Raczkowski, who reasoned: 'Because all Galicians are infected with Bolshevism, we cannot give you any document [for your return home].' True, some, albeit far from all, Galicians were 'infected' with Bolshevism. Clearly, this Raczkowski was not supportive, because Dzvinchuk was a Ukrainian and he saw Ukrainians in general as potential troublemakers in an independent Poland. So Dzvinchuk was abandoned by Poland which housed his home village after the Civil War.

Then the Soviet interrogator began to ask about Dzvinchuk's 'espionage activity', saying that he possessed evidence of his clandestine work. Dzvinchuk denied the charge. Then he was asked why he had stayed in Soviet Ukraine when his own brother, Petr, an Austrian prisoner of war held in Kharkiv, had returned home in 1921. Dzvinchuk's reply was that he had had no particular reason for staying. Not satisfied with Dzvinchuk's reply, the interrogator told him that there was evidence of his espionage work for Poland. Dzvinchuk categorically denied the charge (13–14).

What happened next is not entirely clear. A separate record of his interrogation on the same day (20 October 1937) shows that Dzvinchuk was forced to make a small concession: he now admitted that his correspondence with his brother in Poland was of a 'counter-revolutionary' nature, though he still denied the charges of espionage (15). The NKVD triumphantly noted that Dzvinchuk 'partially confessed to his crime' (18). He was doomed.

Nine days after his last interrogation, Dzvinchuk was sentenced to be shot in accordance with the Polish Operation (33). Shortly thereafter he was executed and was buried in one of Bykivnia's mass graves.[4]

31: A memorial erected among the Bykivnia mass graves. A small icon has been attached to it. The inscription reads: 'Here in the 15[,000] square [meters] of the Bykivnia forest lie the victims of political repression' (photographed in 2006).

In 1967, nearly thirty years after his execution, Dzvinchuk's case was re-examined. Who initiated the process is not clear. Probably an enquiry to the Justice Ministry by one of his sons, Boris, led to the re-examination (35). By then Dzvinchuk's home town had been incorporated into the Soviet Union. His brother Petr died in 1939, at the age of forty-nine. Another brother, Mikhail, died in 1947. Cousin Vasil' had been dead since 1930. His distant relative Ivan Chuntuliak died in 1941 (76). Dzvinchuk's wife, Palageia, died in 1960. Several witnesses were deposed in 1967, among them Boris himself. Boris recounted that after his father's return from gaol in 1931 a dispute had broken out between his parents. His father left (probably for Moscow) and did not live with the family again for several years. In 1934 or 1935, however, he returned and worked first as a construction worker and then as a guard. According to Boris, his mother did not want to go to Poland and his father blamed her for that, but in the end his father stayed in Ukraine even though he wanted to return home very much. His parents did not live together amicably. His father led a secluded life and lost all interest in domestic and international affairs. After his father's arrest, his mother and his elder brother, Platon, were arrested too. He and his little sister were taken to an orphanage. A month or so later Platon was released. A year later his mother was freed, and she collected the children from the orphanage. Platon fought in the war, was wounded and died in 1946 after numerous operations. Boris himself fought at the front throughout the war and was decorated (46–50).

Others who knew Dzvinchuk were interviewed. Their testimonies show that the family was poor but that Dzvinchuk, a quiet man, never expressed any political views (51–56).

Dzvinchuk's own sister, Evdokiia Mokhnachuk, who was seventy-six years of age in 1967, was also interviewed by the secret police. She recalled that in the 1930s her brother had asked her for material help. She sent him 20 dollars in 1935 or 1936. He received the money and thanked her. In 1937 she received a letter from his wife, Palageia, informing her that he had been arrested. Palageia did not know why he had been arrested, but speculated that the authorities did not believe that he was a Ukrainian and had therefore had him detained. In around 1957, after Stalin's death, Evdokiia heard from Palageia that she, too, had been arrested and that her husband had died in gaol (72–73). Almost

certainly the secret police had misinformed Dzvinchuk's wife. Palageia
died without knowing the truth about her husband's death.

In 1967 Dzvinchuk was rehabilitated (62–66).

The case files of Palageia and Platon show that the 1967 accounts
by Boris and Evdokiia are largely accurate. Palageia was arrested in
1937, five weeks after her husband's arrest, on suspicion of 'counter-
revolutionary, Fascist activity'. She was an ethnic Ukrainian who
had been born into a poor peasant family in 1898 in a village near
Rzhyshchiv, to the south of Kiev. According to Palageia's account, her
husband sought to return home in 1922. The Polish consulate agreed
to his repatriation. He tried to persuade her to leave with him, but she
would not consent; consequently the family stayed in Ukraine. Asked
about her husband's previous, eleven-month detention, she said that she
did not know the reason for it. Nor did she know why he had been
arrested recently. Then the interrogator threatened her, claiming that her
husband was a Polish spy and that she had helped him and, moreover,
that she herself had engaged in espionage for Poland. Palageia firmly
stated that she knew nothing about her husband's espionage and that she
had never engaged in espionage herself. Even when pressed further, she
pleaded innocent. The police appear to have taken no further action. In
the summer of 1938 she was released on the grounds that no evidence
of crime had been found.[5]

The couple's eldest son, Platon, was arrested on 11 November 1937,
a day after his mother's arrest. The arrest warrant was issued a day after
the arrest actually took place. The reason was that he had allegedly
assisted his father in his 'counter-revolutionary, Fascist activity'. He
was seventeen years of age and still a student. He stated that he was an
ethnic Ukrainian, but his bill of indictment, issued four days after his
arrest, falsely identified both him and his father as Poles. When Platon
was interrogated, he said that he had been living with his grandmother
in a nearby village since 1934 and that he knew nothing about his
father's activities. Even though he was indicted, he appears to have been
released on 18 November 1937 on condition that he did not leave his
house without the permission of the NKVD. More than a year later, on
9 February 1939, the case against him was finally dropped.[6] As noted
earlier, Platon fought in the war, was wounded and died in 1946.

There is no information available about the fate of Dzvinchuk's other
child, Valentina, who was ten years old in 1937.

The tragedy of the Dzvinchuks is typical of many people from Galicia, a region that changed hands in quick succession from Austria to Poland and then to the Soviet Union. Iurii Dzvinchuk was an Austrian Ukrainian but was regarded by the Soviet authorities as a Pole. He was one of many whose lives were destroyed by the vagaries of international politics. It seems almost certain that Dzvinchuk was innocent. Like many others, he was executed as a Polish spy.

The Shirers

Khaia Shaevna Shirer was born in 1879 in Sierdz, an old town near Kalisz in Poland, then part of the Russian Empire. How Shirer, the daughter of a Jewish medical attendant, came to live in Kiev is not known. At the time of her arrest on 29 November 1937, she lived with her husband, Abram Leibovich Shirer, 62, her adopted daughter, Dora Borisovna (Berovna) Fraiman (Freiman), 26, and Dora's husband, Petr Grigor'evich Gusak, 27, at 11b Pushkin Street, Flat 4, in Kiev. She had a secondary education but stayed at home while her husband worked as a technician at a factory. She was accused of spying for Poland, activities that allegedly began with the 1928 adoption of her niece, Dora Borisovna, from Poland. According to the secret police, Dora was in fact sent to Kiev by the Polish secret police in collaboration with Shirer and Shirer's sister Leokadia Wilner (Lipsker) in Poland, also an agent of the Polish secret police.[7]

Dora was an orphan, having lost her mother, Freide, Shirer's sister, and her father, Beera Fraiman. She had been living with her grandmother, the seventy-four-year-old widow Tsirla Wilner, but the latter could not support her properly. So Shirer and her husband, who were childless, decided to adopt her. Shirer's case file contains a 1927 petition to the Polish consulate written in Russian using a mixture of new and old orthographies (9). She successfully adopted Dora, who moved to Kiev in 1928. She was seventeen years of age at the time.

Dora began to work in 1931. In 1937 she was working at the Kiev city post office. On 17 November of that year she was arrested. According to her statement, her brother Edward, 28, a tailor, lived in the USA; her sister Adelia, 29, a manicurist, in Sieradz, Poland, her uncles Perec Wilner, a medical attendant, in Sieradz, Saul Wilner, a timber industry official, in Kielce, and Szmul Wilner, a grocer, in Zduńska Wola, all in

Poland; and her aunts Leokadia Lipsker in Włocławek, Poland, Tema Bronsztein in Łódź, Poland, Rudka Blibaum in Tomaszów, Poland, and Bronisawa Junt in Chicago in the USA. Dora admitted that she corresponded with her Polish and American relations until 1937 and received packages from Leokadia via Shirer and the Polish consulate in Kiev. At first she rejected the accusation of espionage, but eventually broke down. At her interrogation on 21 November 1937 she said that she had been recruited to the Polish secret police by Leokadia, who had conspired with Shirer, also a Polish agent, to bring her to the Soviet Union. After her arrival in Kiev, Dora had collected information on the political mood of her colleagues and the directives of communications officials (she worked at a post office), and handed what she found to Shirer, who then forwarded it to Poland by way of the Polish consulate in Kiev (15–17).

Now that Dora had implicated her aunt Shirer, a homemaker, in a Polish spy ring, the police arrested her on 29 November 1937. Shirer was interrogated on 1 December 1937 by an NKVD official named Shchitnov, the man who had interrogated Dora. Like Dora, Shirer had also corresponded with her Polish and American relations until 1937. Not much else appears to have been discussed at this session. The interrogation that followed on 2 December 1937 started with the interro-gator's frustrated remark that Shirer had stubbornly refused to admit to espionage (12). Clearly, in the interrogation that had taken place the previous day, she had rejected the charges of espionage firmly. Shchitnov had chosen not to put her rejection on record on that occasion. At the session on 2 December 1937, however, Shirer was broken. No one knows what kind of threat or torture was used against her, but she confessed that when she petitioned the Polish consulate for Dora's adoption in 1925 (sic), she was being used by a consulate official whose name she did not remember but who had recruited her for espionage. He promised a visa for Dora in exchange for information on the mood of people around her. She provided such information to him from that time until Dora's arrival in Kiev in February 1928. After that, she stopped. This admission did not satisfy Shchitnov, who insisted that Shirer continued to spy for Poland afterwards, and not only regarding the political mood of people, but other matters too. (Shchitnov did not specify these matters, but the bill of indictment mentions 'economic data on the city of Kiev'.) Shirer categorically denied the allegations of espionage after 1928. Even before

February 1928 she had provided information only on the political mood of the people and nothing else. The interrogation ended (12–14). That was all.

Shirer was indicted on charges of espionage two days later, on 4 December 1937, without any material evidence. On 19 December 1937 she was sentenced to be shot in accordance with the Polish Operation and a week later was executed (4, 20, 22). She was one of thirty executed on that day in Kiev. Dora was sentenced to be shot on 3 December 1937 and was executed a week later. Both Shirer and Dora were buried in the Bykivnia mass graves.[8] Both were rehabilitated in 1989. No information is available on the fate of their husbands. No relatives were found in any case at the time of their rehabilitation (25). Probably their only crime was to have family living abroad, particularly in Poland.

The Al'bovas

There were as many tragedies as there were divided families. Mariia Vladislavovna Al'bova was an ethnic Pole who was married to Vladimir Iakovlevich Al'bov, a railway clerk in Kiev. Al'bova was born in 1879 in Kiev, completed studies at a gymnasium and before the Revolution worked as an accountant for the Singer company. At the time of Al'bova's arrest on 5 November 1937, she was working as an accountant in the town of Makariv just to the west of Kiev. Her son, Iurii, 24, worked as a disinfection instructor at a district health department, her daughter, Galina, 20, as an accountant in Makariv.[9] The family was well educated by the standards of the time, and everything appeared normal—except that the father was missing.

In 1914, at the beginning of World War I, Vladimir Al'bov was mobilised. He fought at the front as a second lieutenant until 1918, then returned home. As an officer in the military, his experience of the Revolution could not have been a happy one, unless he supported the Bolsheviks. Most likely he was pilloried by his soldiers. Al'bov probably served initially under the command of General Anton Denikin, who was chief of staff in the Kiev military district when the war broke out in 1914. When the White Army led by Denikin occupied Kiev in the autumn of 1919, he appears to have joined it (whether he did so voluntarily is not known). Al'bov then left Kiev with Denikin's army

32: The 'mug shot' of Mariia Vladislavovna Al'bova.

when it was driven out of the city by the Soviets in December 1919. Al'bova never saw her husband again (9).

In 1923, however, she received a letter from someone called Florinskii in Salonika, Greece, enquiring about her husband's whereabouts. She answered that she did not know. Oddly, two or three weeks later she received a letter from her husband, who turned out to be living in Salonika. He worked in the fields there. Then, in 1924, Al'bova received a second letter from her husband in which he said that he was now working as a cook and guard, still in Greece. After that Al'bova never heard from him again and knew nothing of his whereabouts (9zv.).

Nothing is known about the Al'bovs' life together, whether they still loved each other and whether that was the reason why Al'bova never remarried after their separation. Probably Al'bova wanted to remain faithful to her husband even though he had gone abroad. Indeed she never divorced him. From the point of view of the Soviet secret police, however, her failure to remarry meant that she was waiting for the collapse of the Soviet Union and the return of Al'bov to his homeland. However, the fact that the Al'bovs had not been in touch with each other since 1924 frustrated her interrogator, identified as Pavlov. So he chose another sort of incrimination: Al'bova's connections with the Polish church community in Makariv. In the interrogation on 7 November 1937 she was questioned about her role in the community. Al'bova denied that she was a member of it at all: she had merely been the keeper of the church keys from 1925 to 1926, at the request of the church priest, Vonsovich. She was an acquaintance of this Vonsovich and his sister, Khristina. Vonsovich had been arrested in 1928 and exiled, according to Al'bova. (In fact Vonsovich was Bronisław Wąsowicz or Dunin-Wąsowicz, who had been arrested in May 1926, released in December 1926, arrested again in January 1927 and sentenced to three years in the Gulag in the Solovki Islands in the Arctic White Sea.)[10] During her time as the keeper of the keys, the director of the community was one Koliakovskii (Poliakovskii?) who was now dead. Al'bova admitted that in 1926–27 she had signed a letter Koliakovskii had brought to her concerning the repair of the church as mandated by the district authorities (9zv.–11).

The NKVD deposed three witnesses against Al'bova. Their testimonies were formulaic: Al'bova was a member of the church community and an anti-Soviet person who had opposed collectivisation and always complained about life under the Soviet regime; Al'bova praised Poland, saying that people lived better and religion was not persecuted there; Al'bova opposed buying government bonds which were not necessary to her—all the same she had had to live without bread; Al'bova said that the Soviet government would not last long and Ukraine would be taken over by Poland; Al'bova said that she could not stand the Soviet regime; Al'bova corresponded with her husband until 1930, and so on (15–20).

On 13 November 1937 Al'bova was interrogated by a different NKVD officer (whose name cannot be deciphered). She now corrected her earlier statement. The director of the Polish church community was Petrovetskii; he had been arrested and exiled, and had died. The elder of the church was Agelia Frantsovna Milovetskaia, who had also been arrested. Where the latter had lived Al'bova did not know. Al'bova added that she did not know any other members because she did not belong to the community. Pressed harder, she admitted that she knew the Uniate priest Shchepannek (elsewhere spelled 'Stepaniuk') and the church community secretary Galina Vil'gel'movna Vishnevskaia. They and the Vonsoviches visited her home and socialised with her. Then the interrogator demanded that she discuss their 'counter-revolutionary' work. Al'bova responded that she knew nothing about this. She only knew that both Vonsovich and Shchepannek had been arrested, as had Vishnevskaia. Then the interrogator threatened her, claiming that the NKVD had information that she belonged to a 'Polish Fascist organisation'. Al'bova vigorously and repeatedly denied the charges (13–13zv.). Even when presented with the witnesses' testimonies, she stood her ground. She admitted that she knew the priests, but she resolutely denied belonging to the church community. Nor had she opposed the collectivisation of agriculture or conducted any 'counter-revolutionary' activity. She denounced all the testimonies and pleaded innocent, adding that she had nothing more to say (14–14zv.).

Without any material evidence, Al'bova was nevertheless indicted. On 26 November 1937 she was sentenced to be shot in accordance with the Polish Operation. She was executed on 7 December 1937 at midnight (25, 27). Al'bova, one of forty-one people executed in Kiev on that day, was buried in the mass graves of Bykivnia.[11] When she was rehabilitated in 1989, no relatives were found (30).

33: Nikołaj/
Mikołaj Szczepaniuk
(Shchepannek) in the
1930s.

The fact that Al'bova had worked Singer, set up in Russia before
the Revolution by its American parent company, may have made her
suspicious by default.[12] No doubt being an ethnic Pole made her even
more suspicious. Yet it appears that Al'bova's main 'crime' was that her
husband had fled abroad and that she associated with a Catholic and a
Uniate priest. The priest Vansovich (or Wąsowicz) was originally from
Zhytomyr, Ukraine, but he was a Polish citizen. He had illegally crossed
the Polish–Soviet border twice. Ordained in Poland, he was one of the
seven priests whom the Polish archbishop Ignacy Dub-Dubowski sent to
the Zhytomyr area in 1922 'in a conspiratorial fashion'. He was arrested
and released several times. In the end he was executed in January 1938
on charges of espionage.[13] The Uniate priest Shchepannek was in fact
Nikołaj/Mikołaj Wasilewicz Szczepaniuk, originally from Austrian
Poland. He had come to Kiev to study in 1915 and returned home in
1917, only to be sent back to Kiev again by the Uniate Church. He was
first arrested in 1929 and implicated in 1935–36 in the fabricated 'case
of the counter-revolutionary Fascist organisation of Roman-Catholic
and Uniate priests in right-bank Ukraine' (see p. 61). He was sentenced

to five years' correctional labour in the Far East, where he was further punished for refusing to work on Sundays. Like Vonsovich, he was executed, in October 1937, on suspicion of espionage.[14]

Although borders divide families everywhere, the Soviet case is extreme: any foreign connection, even purely familial correspondence, was taken as grounds for capital punishment in the 1930s. In Kiev and Ukraine, Polish connections were the most dangerous: case after case discussed in this book involves a Polish connection of some sort. Although the Al'bova affair initially appeared to be related to her husband's emigration abroad, it soon became a matter of Polish connections.

Other factors also contributed to the destruction of traditional families. As is shown by the famous case of Pavlik Morozov, a boy who was said to have informed on his own father and was killed as a result, children were encouraged to spy on their own parents. Under these conditions, families struggled to be stable and enduring. True, many withstood the terror of the 1930s and survived intact (see Chapter 11). Yet untold numbers of families destroyed in the Great Terror have no survivors. Husbands often disappeared into the nether world of the Soviet prison network, wives were arrested and exiled, children were taken to orphanages and families quickly disintegrated. The Soviet state and the party were meant to function as a substitute family. Deprived of the two traditional pillars of human life, family and religion, many Soviet citizens had nothing to bond with emotionally but the state. The state became a large 'family' for them.[15]

CHAPTER II

Husbands and Wives
From Love to Death

The Soviet government initially treated marriage as a 'bourgeois' concept. Religious ceremonies declined in number and significance, as did civil ceremonies. Many people did not bother to register their unions. As the Soviet government sought to stabilise the country, however, particularly in the wake of the devastating Great Famine of 1932–33, marital union again began to assume a degree of official importance. Yet, as the case of Sa-bo Sia shows (see Chapter 7), the Soviet government never hesitated to exploit marital and family relations in order to terrorise those suspected of political crime. Police interrogators routinely forced spouses to incriminate one another and used the threat of harm against a spouse or other family members to extract confessions of guilt. Not having informed on one's accused spouse became a crime in itself.

When someone was arrested, that person's spouse was often obliged to secure a divorce in order to survive. Stalin took kin relations very seriously. Indeed, at the height of the Great Terror, in the autumn of 1937, a toast made by Stalin at a private banquet included the following statement: 'And we will destroy anyone who, by his deeds or his thoughts—yes, his thoughts—threatens the unity of the socialist state. To the complete destruction of all enemies, themselves and their kin!'[1]

The Soviet practice of terrorising the innocent kin, particularly female kin, of arrested men was so widespread and so absurd that women in camps sang a parody of a well-known Soviet song that praised the country's vastness and freedom:

My country is big,
It has many prisons and camps.
I know no other country
Where they gaol wives and mothers.[2]

Torture was used to break conjugal and familial bonds. The Mishchenkos' case is revealing. Stepan Vasil'evich Mishchenko, an official in the Kiev Cooperative Union, was arrested in the spring of 1938 for having allegedly belonged to a Ukrainian nationalist organisation. Smol'nyi, the NKVD interrogator in charge of the case, 'invited' his wife, Iuliia Kharitonovna Mishchenko, to visit her husband at midnight on 12 April 1938. When she reported to the NKVD office, Smol'nyi told her to wait in the next room. He then went into an adjoining room. She began to hear the crudest profanities, screams and orders. Sensing that something awful was happening, she decided to leave, but Smol'nyi stopped her and commanded her to go and see the man in the next room. There was one condition, however: she could not ask any questions of him. When she went in, she saw her husband sitting with his back towards her. He was not allowed to speak or to turn around. Then Smol'nyi began to ask her a host of questions, none of which had anything to do with her husband's case but which were meant to create a sense of tension and menace: about their daughter's moral and psychological wellbeing (their daughter, Tamara, was thirteen) and other carefully chosen subjects. Unable to restrain himself, Stepan sprang up and began sobbing hysterically; Iuliia passed out. Smol'nyi poured water over her and sent her home. In the end, Stepan was sentenced to be shot, while Iuliia was arrested as a member of the family of a 'traitor of the motherland'. Even under arrest, Iuliia Mishchenko insisted on her and her husband's innocence. She was sentenced to five years in the Gulag. Later in the year, when the Great Terror came to an end, Smol'nyi himself was arrested as an 'enemy of the people'.[3]

Marriages and families were smashed everywhere by the terror. At the same time, as the present chapter will show, many marital bonds proved extraordinarily strong.

Dzevitskii and Dzevitskaia

Sigizmund Mikhailovich Dzevitskii was an ethnic Pole. He was born in 1898 into a worker's family in Lublin, then in the Russian Empire and, after 1918, in Poland. At the time of his arrest on 5 August 1937, he was working as a metalworker at the 'Avtomat' factory in Kiev and was living at 63 Perets' Street, Flat 10, with his wife, Aleksandra, and fifteen-year-old daughter Stanislava. He was a Soviet citizen, a non-party member and had had six years of schooling.[4]

Dzevitskii's case, like others discussed in Chapter 9, involved the Polish consulate in Kiev. He was interrogated four days after his arrest, on 9 August 1937. It appears from the records that Dzevitskii admitted to his 'crime' from the beginning. Questioned about his spying for Poland, he stated that he was indeed an agent of the Polish consulate in Kiev and under its direction had conducted 'espionage work' in Kiev. In 1934 his uncle in Warsaw, Poland, began to petition the Polish consulate in Kiev to allow Dzevitskii to visit Poland. Dzevitskii initially turned down the invitation (perhaps he was afraid of the consequences of dealing with the consulate), but after several requests from his uncle, he finally went to the consulate in 1935. There he was told by an official that to visit Poland he would first have to win the trust of the Polish authorities. This was an odd response on the part of the Polish authorities, but it is possible that the official wanted to test Dzevitskii, a Soviet citizen of Polish background, to see whether he might be of any use for information-gathering purposes or whether he was already a Soviet agent. In any case, when Dzevitskii asked what he needed to do, he was told that the consulate was interested in the political mood of Poles, workers and other people living in Kiev, and in what was being produced in factories and for what purposes. He was asked to spy for Poland and he agreed. Thus did Dzevitskii, according to the 9 August 1937 interrogation records, begin his espionage work (8–10).

Dzevitskii detailed his assignments which were, first, to find out what kind of product was being produced at his factory and for what purposes (he was then working at the 'Rentok' factory); and, second, to give the names and the numbers of people who were 'counter-revolutionarily disposed' and the nature of their 'counter-revolutionary mood'. Although he did keep the Polish consulate informed on these matters, he said that he never provided any figures on factory

34: Dzevitskii's trade union card.

production, or gave any names. After 1935, moreover, he did not visit or meet anyone from the consulate. His interrogator, however, did not accept his last claim (11–12).

It is odd that, although the 9 August 1937 records mention an interrogation conducted on 8 August 1937 (12), all records of the earlier interrogation are missing from the Dzevitskii file. There may simply have been a mix-up over dates, but it is also possible that if an interrogation did take place on 8 August, Dzevitskii had said something quite different from what he confessed the following day. Whatever the case, Dzevitskii was pressed for a frank admission to the further charges on 9 August. Dzevitskii then conceded that he had visited the consulate in early 1936. Regarding his Polish acquaintances, he noted that he had befriended someone called Uzhel, who wanted to return to Poland. He was told by his interrogator that Uzhel was actually a Polish spy, but Dzevitskii stated that he knew nothing about this (13–14).

Without much formality, i.e., without material evidence or witness depositions, Dzevitskii was sentenced to be shot on 14 October 1937. Oddly, he was sentenced in accordance with the German Operation,

NKVD Secret Order No. 00439 dated 25 July 1937, which was concerned with the repression of German citizens suspected of espionage (25). In a reversal of the cases in which ethnic Germans, for instance, were repressed as part of the Polish Operation, Dzevitskii was treated as a 'German case'. It may mean that Dzevitskii had some German connections. (The German Operation initially targeted German citizens, but was subsequently greatly expanded to encompass anyone with connections to Germany or Germans.) In any case, six days later, on 20 October 1937, Dzevitskii was executed (26).

Following Dzevitskii, his wife, Aleksandra Mikhailovna Dzevitskaia, was arrested on 29 September 1937. Dzevitskaia was an ethnic Ukrainian who was born into a worker's family in 1902 in Kiev. (Her father, Mikhail Gavrirovich Shcherbinenko, was a printer who had died in 1922.) She had only an elementary education and was a non-party member; she was now a homemaker. According to her file, her mother, Mariia Danilovna, lived with her. At the time of her arrest, a small golden cross, probably a family heirloom, was confiscated.[5]

According to her bill of indictment, Dzevitskaia knew about her husband's espionage. She even delivered two sealed envelopes to the Polish consulate. (Oddly, this document, dated 13 October 1937, mentions that her husband had already been executed, even though, according to his case file, he was only executed ten days later.) Dzevitskii had persuaded his wife that, as a Pole, he had to help the Polish consulate with its espionage work (23–24).

Dzevitskaia's file reveals further information not contained in her husband's. According to her 9 October 1937 interrogation records, Dzevitskii's uncle Kazimir Dziewicki ran a tobacco business in Warsaw. Until 1936 the Dzevitskiis corresponded with Dziewicki. At the latter's request, the Dzevitskiis began to petition the Polish consulate in Kiev in 1934 for permission for a one-month visit to Poland. Initially they were refused a visa. In early 1935, however, they submitted the appropriate documents a third time and were finally issued with one. Yet they were subsequently refused permission to leave by the Soviet authorities on the grounds that men were not allowed to go abroad. Then Dzevitskaia decided to go by herself, but was again not allowed to go; she stated that she did not know why. Asked how many times she had visited the Polish consulate, Dzevitskaia replied 'three times': once in 1934 with her husband, and twice in 1935 by herself at his request. The interrogator still suspected that the Dzevitskiis had ulterior motives for these activities. When asked why they had wanted to go to Poland, Dzevitskaia plainly stated that they had merely wanted to see her husband's relations. Then the interrogator questioned her about the 'assignments' she had received from the consulate. Dzevitskaia categorically denied that she had ever received any such 'assignments'. Equally categorically she denied carrying out espionage work for Poland. As for her husband, she knew nothing about his work. He had certainly never told her anything about it. She never suspected him of espionage activity, nor did she have any grounds for such suspicions (10–14).

Two days later, on 11 October 1937, Dzevitskaia was interrogated again. Again she was pressed for a confession of her espionage work. Again she categorically rejected the accusation. But she then appears to have given in to some degree. Perhaps she was tortured or threatened with reprisals against her daughter or mother. She now said that she was guilty in that she knew about her husband's espionage work for Poland. He had told her that in 1934 the Polish consulate had promised a visa in exchange for information he had been asked to provide. However, Dzevitskaia added, she did not know the exact nature of the information. According to her, Dzevitskii had visited the consulate 'very often' in 1934–35 and she herself had delivered envelopes there in late 1934 and in 1935. Her partial admission did not satisfy her interrogator, however. Told that she was still lying, Dzevitskaia protested: she had told the truth and she had nothing more to say and knew nothing more (15–17).

How far this last part of Dzevitskaia's statement should be believed is a difficult but interesting question. The statement, though probably forced from her, may not have been truthful. If, as she noted, Dzevitskii visited the Polish consulate 'very often', to what purpose? Is it possible that the NKVD used him, knowing that he wanted to visit Poland? This is legitimate speculation, because the case seems to be somewhat unusual: Dzevitskii, like the ballerina Goroshko (see Chapter 1), was executed without much formality, a sign that the NKVD possessed secret information that could not be disclosed. If so, the secret information concerned would have had to do with Germany. Possibly Dzevitskii was used by the Soviet secret police to spy on the German and Polish consulates. This would explain why he was executed as part of the German Operation. In any case, some vital information appears to be missing from Dzevitskii's case file.

Like her husband, Dzevitskaia was sentenced, without much formality, to be shot. It was eleven days after her second interrogation. Ten days thereafter, on 1 November 1937, she was executed. Unlike her husband, however, she was executed as part of the Polish Operation (24, 26, 42).

In 1989 the Dzevitskiis were both rehabilitated, but no relatives were found to receive the news (43, and 20 in Dzevitskii's file). In the 1990s it became known that both Dzevitskii and Dzevitskaia were buried in the Bykivnia mass graves.[6]

Sosnovskii and Sosnovskaia-Budnitskaia

Had Dzevitskaia not been broken, would she have escaped execution? It is difficult to know, but some wives of executed husbands did survive.

Iosif Frantsevich Sosnovskii was, like Dzevitskii, an ethnic Pole. His father was born in Warsaw but came to Kiev to work. So, unlike Dzevitskii, Sosnovskii was actually born in Ukraine, in the village of Petropavlivs'ka-Borshchahivka near Kiev, in 1891. He was a Soviet citizen, a non-party member and a postal worker. He was accused of associating with Trotskyites and Poles who had been arrested, and of being anti-Soviet and conducting anti-Soviet agitation among postal workers. Even though his wife was Jewish, as is discussed later, he was also accused of anti-Semitism. Sosnovskii was arrested on 24 October 1937, sentenced to be shot on 10 November 1937 as part of the Polish Operation and executed on 19 November 1937.[7]

The records of his first interrogation on 24 October 1937 are purely formal and contain nothing of interest. Of course, it is possible that Sosnovskii refused to admit to the charges against him on that occasion; if so, it is not recorded (8).

Several days later, two of his colleagues were deposed by the NKVD. Izrail' Iakovlevich Krikun testified that Sosnovskii was associated with a host of 'anti-Soviet elements' who had been arrested (Novitskii, Gorokhovskii, Milovshchkii, Zaporovskii and others) and that he often told anti-Semitic anecdotes and had anti-Soviet conversations with other postal workers. For instance, he was said to have commented, 'Today is the Jewish Sukkot [holiday], it means that there is nothing in the bazaar—no Jew, no bazaar' (12–13).

On 2 November 1937 another colleague, Leizer Iankevich Shlepchitskii, was deposed. He said that Sosnovskii was an unmitigated anti-Soviet who systematically circulated anti-Soviet anecdotes against Stalin, Molotov and other Soviet leaders. He did not say what the anecdotes were, because he considered it poor taste to quote them. Shlepchitskii added that Sosnovskii had said the working class lived badly under the Soviet regime but that the Soviet government nevertheless proclaimed that Soviet life was happy and jolly, when in fact hunger and poverty were everywhere. He spoke in this way in queues and everywhere, except when party members were present (14–15).

Interrogated on 3 November 1937, Sosnovskii was asked to admit to his counter-revolutionary activity. He snapped back that he had never engaged in such an activity. He was pressed again, but he denied the charges: 'I repeat that I have never engaged in any counter-revolutionary activity anywhere.' When confronted with the Jewish Sukkot story quoted by Krikun, Sosnovskii said that, yes, he had said that. Apparently he did not consider the remark offensive, for he was married to a Jew and was therefore immune to accusations of anti-Semitism. When further confronted with Krikun's accusation about his close associations with Novitskii and other arrested Poles, Trotskyites and former army officers, Sosnovskii said that, no, he was not associated with them. When presented with Shlepchitskii's testimony, Sosnovskii rejected it as false. He repeated that he was innocent (10–11).

The following day, a third witness and colleague, Andrei Pavlovich Olekh, was deposed. Olekh's testimony was more damaging than the others. According to Olekh, Sosnovskii unequivocally considered Soviet life a disaster. Even though the workers had been exploited before the Revolution, Soviet exploitation of workers had proved even worse: under the bourgeoisie, no one went naked or hungry, but now under the Soviet regime, 'we have lived to see inhuman exploitation, as a result of which we have our own exploitative bourgeoisie and we go naked and hungry'. In a private conversation, Olekh continued, Sosnovskii had said about Trotskii, Zinov'ev and others, 'I'm sorry for those who fought for the ideas of the workers, they should not have been shot, they were the only people who exposed the Soviet system, for which the Soviet regime destroyed them.' The policy of the Soviet system was 'to squeeze the last juice out of the working class' (16–17).

Bearing these details, an indictment was presented to Sosnovskii the following day, 5 November 1937. Five days later, he was sentenced to

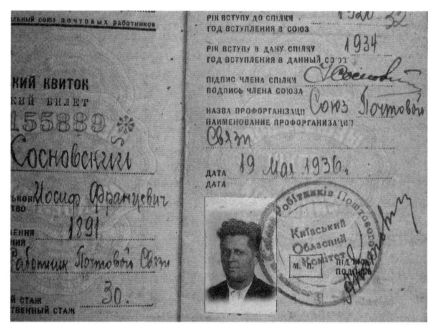

35: Sosnovskii's trade union membership card.

be shot as part of the Polish Operation and on 19 November 1937 at midnight he was executed (20, 37).

In the meantime, Sosnovskii's wife, Fenia Moiseeva Sosnovskaia-Budnitskaia, had been arrested on 16 November 1937. She had been born in Kiev in 1909 into the family of a Jewish handicraftsman. The Sosnovskiis had a daughter, Liubov' Iosifovna, who was nine. At the time of her arrest, Sosnovskaia-Budnitskaia was working at a railway office in Kiev. Before her arrest, two depositions against her, dated 22 and 29 October 1937, had been collected by the secret police. Both were by her bosses. They noted that after her husband's arrest, Sosnovskaia-Budnitskaia, fearing her own arrest, had consulted one of them as to whether she should divorce her husband or wait. The other boss added that she had said, 'Now these parasites have taken my husband, who is not guilty of anything', and had sympathised with others who had been arrested such as Novitskii, remarking that they, too, were guilty of nothing. (This is very odd, because one deposition was taken on 22 October 1937, even before her husband's arrest. This deposition is almost certainly fake. It is also possible that the deposition was simply antedated with no concern for consistency.) Sosnovskaia-Budnitskaia was further quoted as having said that the truth was nowhere to be found in the Soviet Union (10–12).

After her arrest, more evidence was collected against her from three witnesses. This was similar in content to the depositions taken before her arrest except that there was a new allegation: that Sosnovskaia-Budnitskaia was the daughter of a rabbi (17).

After this damning evidence had been collected Sosnovskaia-Budnitskaia was interrogated on 20 November 1937. She was not broken, however. She rejected the testimonies and insisted that she had never engaged in anti-Soviet activity (14–16). Nevertheless, Sosnovskaia-Budnitskaia was indicted on 4 December 1937 on charges of 'counter-revolutionary' activity and sentenced to ten years in the Gulag (31).

Soon after being sent to Karaganda, she began to write to Stalin to demand a re-examination of her case. (According to one witness, she claimed that she was a distant relative of L. M. Kaganovich, Stalin's close aide: Sosnovskii's file, 76.) Her brother, N. M. Gershtein, a Red Army soldier, wrote to Moscow twice in 1939, once to the new secret police chief Lavrentii Beriia, once to the prosecutor Andrei Vyshinskii, asking them to release his sister. According to him, the whole affair was a case of revenge by her first husband, Leonid Budnitskii. Their father, Moisei Iosifovich Gershtein, was not a rabbi but a shoemaker (29–30, 38–39). In 1940 the police revisited the case and in March 1941 interviewed two of the three original witnesses. (The other witness had been executed in 1938.) Both insisted that their testimonies were correct, and one went even further than before to paint Sosnovskaia-Budnitskaia in the worst possible light (44–49). As a result, her appeal was deemed without merit (57–58).

She does not appear to have stopped working on her own behalf. In March 1958, more than twenty years after her arrest, she wrote to the prosecutor's office in Kiev from Karaganda, complaining that her letters had not been answered, that her case had been transferred back and forth between different offices, and that she had now been seeking to prove her innocence for twenty years: her nerves were worn out and it was very difficult to wait any longer (Sosnovskii's file, 36). Shortly after this, the two witnesses who were still alive were again interviewed by the KGB. This time neither confirmed their earlier testimonies (69–70).

One, Isaak Iakovlevich Gutkin, claimed that he did not even remember whether he had been interviewed in 1941. He said that whatever he might have said in 1937 and 1941 had been distorted and exaggerated. She was a 'Soviet person', he added (Sosnovskii's file, 76–77). In 1959 Sosnovskaia-Budnitskaia was rehabilitated (79–80).

Prior to this, Sosnovskaia-Budnitskaia began to investigate her second husband's fate. After she was falsely informed that he had died on 2 May 1943, she wrote back to the KGB asking for details, complaining that she had not been given any. She was told that these were not available but that she could obtain the certificate of his death from the Kiev City Administration (ZAGS) (24–30).[8]

Sosnovskii's case, too, came to be reviewed in 1958, thanks in part to his wife's efforts. Shlepchitskii, whose testimony was used against Sosnovskii in 1937, was still alive and so was interviewed in November 1958 by the KGB. He stated that he did not know why Sosnovskii and his wife had been arrested in 1937. They were both good and honest workers and had never said anything anti-Soviet. Sosnovskii liked telling anecdotes, but they were not anti-Soviet. When asked whether he had testified in Sosnovskii's case, he answered that he had never been called to do so. When shown his 1937 testimony, however, he acknowledged that the signature on it was his and that he had indeed been called by the NKVD to testify. Yet, he stated, the words were not his own. He said that he spoke only positively of Sosnovskii. He did sign the testimony, but had done so without first reading the content at the insistence of the police interrogator (78–80).

Was Shlepchitskii being honest in 1958? Obviously he was worried about the past, as is clear from his statement that he had not been called to testify by the NKVD in 1937. Is it possible that, sensing a change of political wind, he changed his story? Which should one trust, his words of 1958 or 1937? This question is ultimately unimportant, for no proof of Sosnovskii's guilt existed in 1937 or in 1958.

Krikun, another witness and a party member, was killed in the war in September 1941 and so was not available for interview in 1958. Olekh, the third original witness, was said to have been a traitor during the German occupation. Where he went after the war was not known. The KGB could not find him in 1958. Olekh was now characterised by those who had known him as a vengeful person (54–55, 80, 89, 93).

Sosnovskaia-Budnitskaia's brother stated in 1939 that her arrest was the doing of her first husband. In 1958 Budnitskii was interviewed by the KGB. He had nothing but positive things to say about his former wife and her second husband (81–83). Budnitskii may not have been honest in 1959, just as he may not have been truthful in 1937. It is also possible that Sosnovskaia-Budnitskaia's brother, in making the charge against him, had misunderstood the case.

In the end, Sosnovskii was rehabilitated in 1959 because no proof of his guilt existed (101–11). In the 1990s it became known that, like so many others, he was buried in a mass grave in Bykivnia.[9]

Kurovskii and Kurovskaia

Timofei Frantsevich Kurovskii, like Dzevitskii and Sosnovskii, was an ethnic Pole. Also like Sosnovskii, he was born in Ukraine, in the village of Chervone, near Fastiv to the southwest of Kiev, in 1882. He had only a rudimentary education and was a non-party member. At the time of his arrest on 7 October 1937, he was working as a lathe operator at the 'Red October' factory in Fastiv and living at 1a Ovrazhna Street in the same town with his wife, Apoloniia Petrovna Kurovskaia, 53, a son, Vladimir, 19, a worker at the same factory, and a daughter, Kamilia, 13, a schoolgirl. Kurovskii is said to have owned a relatively large farm before the collectivisation of 1929–30, with a house, a barn, a cow, two horses and 4 *desiatinas* (more than 11 acres) of land. When the collectivisation drive began, he gave up his land and began to work at a factory where he had been employed previously. According to the police, he had been arrested twice, in 1930 for misconduct and then again in 1932 for another offence. Yet, at his 1937 arrest, Kurovskii stated that he had no criminal record.[10]

Kurovskii's case is very similar to Sosnovskii's. He was accused of conducting counter-revolutionary agitation among his co-workers. After his arrest, a deposition was taken from his village soviet about his 'counter-revolutionary agitation'. Several witnesses were deposed a fortnight after his arrest. They gave damning testimonies against him, reporting him to have said: 'The Soviet government has begun to shoot its own people, it's got into a muddle'; 'Over there [in Poland] people live very well without any pressure on the workers'; 'Poland is a good country'; 'War will come soon, the Soviet Union will be disbanded and Ukraine will be taken over by Poland'; 'The Soviet government deceives people', and the like (14–21).

Kurovskii may have been interrogated before the depositions were taken, but if so there is no record in his case file. Armed with this damning evidence, the NKVD interrogator questioned Kurovskii on 22 October 1937. The latter admitted that in June 1937, when a medical doctor gave a lecture in the town, in which he said that many workers were suffering from tuberculosis, Kurovskii had added that at his factory, too, many workers had TB. This admission did not satisfy the interrogator, however, who then quoted a witness account of Kurovskii's alleged remark on the Soviet government shooting its own people and its muddled state. Kurovskii responded that it was possible that he had said that, but that he could not say how it had happened because he did not remember it. The interrogator presented further witness accounts against Kurovskii, but the latter categorically denied making any remarks about war and Poland (12–13).

36: Kurovskii's 'mug shot'.

Kurovskii may have said that the Soviet government had begun to shoot its own people. The executions of Tukhachevskii, Iakir and other Red Army commanders in 1937 must have appeared in this light to many people at the time, although few people spoke out, or, if they did, they did so only in a whisper. Yet suspicion that many people entertained such illicit thoughts privately continued unabated (Tukhachevskii and the others were not Soviets but 'enemies of the people', according to the official Soviet view). Whether Kurovskii actually made such a remark or not, the interrogator did not fail to take advantage of the fact that he did not categorically deny the charges made against him on 22 October. The following day, Kurovskii found himself making a further and fatal concession. He now admitted that, in saying, 'The Soviet government has begun to shoot its own people', he was referring to Tukhachevskii, Iakir and the others. Yet he still denied having said that the Soviet government had got into a muddle. He rejected all other witness accounts as false and denied conducting 'counter-revolutionary agitation'. When he was asked of what he was guilty, Kurovskii said that he was guilty of making the remarks about the Red Army commanders and about many workers at his factory suffering from tuberculosis and getting maimed on the job (10–11zv.).

This was all that it took for him to be executed. On 2 November 1937 he was sentenced to be shot as part of the Polish Operation. Eleven days later, on 13 November 1937, Kurovskii was executed (26, 28). Like so many others, Kurovskii, one of forty-eight people executed on that day in Kiev, was buried in a mass grave in Bykivnia.[11] In 1989 he was rehabilitated (33–34).

The day Kurovskii was executed, his wife, Apoloniia, was arrested. Her fate proved different from that of the wives of Dzevitskii and Sosnovskii. She was never broken. In the end Kurovskaia was released without charge. This is a remarkable story, of someone who was so illiterate that she could not sign her own records of interrogation and had to use her right-hand thumb print in place of a signature.

Kurovskaia was born into a Ukrainian peasant family in 1884 in a village not far from Fastiv. She was a non-party member and a homemaker at the time of her arrest. Her arrest warrant, dated 14 November 1937, was issued the day *after* her arrest. This kind of irregularity was not uncommon at the time: no one heeded legal procedures. In any case, the warrant stated the reason for her arrest as her failure to inform on her husband.[12]

Kurovskaia was interrogated the day after her detention. Asked whether she would plead guilty to failure to inform on her husband, Kurovskaia responded, 'My husband, Timofei Frantsevich Kurovskii, did not engage in counter-revolutionary activity, I know nothing about it and I don't plead guilty.' Repeatedly questioned, she stood her ground: 'I categorically deny that my husband engaged in counter-revolutionary work, I don't know what he did and I do not plead guilty in this matter.' The interrogator sought to find other avenues of attack, but she never gave in. When asked whether Kurovskii had had any contact with Poland, she said no. When the interrogator asked whether her husband had any relations in Poland, she said, 'No, my husband was born in the village of Chervone, Fastiv district, and we have no relations in Poland.' The interrogation ended here and Kurovskaia signed the record with her thumb print (13–13zv.).

It appears that she remained in detention without being questioned further for nearly a year after this. It is of course possible that she *was* interrogated, but if so it is not recorded in her case file. Then, in the autumn of 1938, when the Great Terror was coming to an end, two witnesses were deposed against her. On 28 September 1938, Efim Issakovich Aizenberg, a resident of Fastiv who knew the Kurovskiis, was interviewed. He claimed that Kurovskii was a foreign citizen. He also stated that in 1934, when the Polish church in Fastiv was shut down, Kurovskaia had led a campaign against the closure, claiming that the Soviet government pressured 'us Poles' and wouldn't allow 'us' to develop 'our national culture'. (In fact, Kurovskaia was not a Pole, but a Ukrainian.) He also accused her of making anti-Semitic remarks. After her husband's arrest, Aizenberg added, Kurovskaia began to hate the Soviet government and spoke about it to others (19–19 zv.). Aizenberg is identified in the Kurovskaia file as a Ukrainian. Judging by his surname, he was probably Jewish and so may have been brought in principally to support the charges of anti-Semitism against her.

On 2 October 1938 another Fastiv resident, Izrail' Vol'f-Mordtkovych Shapiro, was deposed (21–21zv.). Shapiro was a neighbour of the Kurovskiis. He stated that Kurovskii was a foreign citizen who had come to the Soviet Union during the Civil War and had relations abroad with whom he maintained a correspondence. He had praised Poland and slandered the Soviet Union. After the arrest of her husband, Shapiro stated, Kurovskaia said to him:

> For what does the Soviet government arrest people? My husband is guilty of nothing. They arrested him and are tormenting him in gaol. There are many like him. Maybe the Soviet government doesn't like the Poles. But they'll come to Ukraine soon. Then there'll be no place [for the Soviet government]. The end of the Communists will come. All the arrested will be freed.

Armed with these new allegations, the NKVD resumed its interrogation on 4 October 1938, after what appears to be nearly a year's hiatus. A year of confinement had not broken Kurovskaia. She was neither intimidated nor frightened. She categorically denied the testimonies of Aizenberg and Shapiro. When asked whether she meant to be stubborn, she said no—she merely wanted to state that the testimonies of Aizenberg and Shapiro were false. She added that she had never made anti-Semitic remarks (15–16).

The following day Kurovskaia was interrogated once more. This time she was merely asked when she had married Kurovskii. Kurovskaia stated that she had met him in 1914, married him six months later and lived with him without interruption until the day he was arrested in October 1937. She again signed the records with her thumb print (17).

The firmness of this illiterate woman helped her. Almost certainly, the new, 1938 allegations were either coerced from Aizenberg and Shapiro, or else their testimonies were written by the NKVD and signed by Aizenberg and Shapiro unread under duress. In any case, their statements on Kurovskii (his citizenship, his links to Poland and others) are false. Nevertheless, the NKVD concluded that Kurovskaia's crime was proved and indicted her on 23 October 1938 (24). Remarkably, however, on 14 December 1938, helped by the staff change at the NKVD in the wake of Nikolai Ezhov's dismissal from his post as its chief, Kurovskaia was released on the grounds that the charges were unproven (25).

The subsequent fate of this remarkable woman is not known.

The Bagniuks

The last case in the present chapter involves a divorced couple and, again, consular connections.

Grigorii Zinov'evich Bagniuk (Bahniuk) was an ethnic Belarusan and a Soviet citizen who was born in a village near Brest-Litovsk in Belarus in 1884. He came from a peasant family, had only an elementary education, was a non-party member and worked as a railway switchman at the station in Darnytsia. He lived in Nova Darnytsia, a settlement on the outskirts of Kiev, at 102 Ievheniia Bosh Street, Flat 5. He was arrested on 1 September 1937 on charges of spying for Poland and 'counter-revolutionary activity'. He was sentenced to be shot as part of the Polish Operation on 26 December 1937, and was executed on 5 January 1938. At the time of his arrest, he was living with his forty-five-year-old wife, Dolsenikiia (?), 45. Oddly, a former wife, Domnikiia Fedorovna Mel'nikova, 37, who, as discussed later, testified against him, was recorded as living at the same address as the Bagniuks. At the time, Mel'nikova was married to her second husband Onufrii (?) Vasil'evich Mel'nikov.[13] It is unlikely that the Mel'nikovs really shared a domestic space with the Bagniuks, although it is possible that they may have lived in separate rooms in the same house.

According to the 10 September 1937 interrogation records, Bagniuk came to Ukraine as a war refugee in 1915. In the wake of later events, his home town of Brest-Litovsk ended up in Polish territory. This suddenly made him almost a foreigner, even though Brest-Litovsk had been in the Russian Empire when he was born. He had three brothers who had lived in Poland, but all were now dead, the last one having passed away in 1934. Asked whether he had wanted to go back to Poland, he said yes. Indeed, thirteen years earlier, in 1924, he had decided to go back to his home town, now in Poland. When he found out how much it would cost to secure the necessary documents, however, he had given up.

Asked whether he had ever visited the Polish consulate in Kiev, Bagniuk said no. Pressed further, however, he admitted that he had visited it once in 1924. The interrogator accused him of telling a lie: Bagniuk had visited the consulate not once but several times. Bagniuk defended his statement, maintaining that he had only visited the consulate in 1924, when he had collected two questionnaires, but he had spoilt them and not gone back after that. The interrogator said he was convinced that Bagniuk was not being honest. At the time of his arrest, he insisted, six questionnaires from the Polish consulate had been found at his home. In his case file, four blank copies are attached as evidence (although the list of items confiscated at the time of his arrest indicates only two copies). So whereas Bagniuk may not have been entirely forthcoming with his interrogators in this regard, it is also quite possible that by 1937 he simply did not remember the events of 1924 very precisely. Pressed by his interrogator, Bagniuk now said that he had in fact gone to the consulate twice in 1924. The first time he went to ask to be repatriated because he was a Polish refugee. He was given two questionnaires, which he spoilt. A week later he went to the consulate a second time. He was now given six questionnaires, but was also told that a Polish visa would cost more than 400 roubles. He did not think he could afford such a large amount of money and so did not fill out the questionnaires (9–10).

The interrogator was frustrated by Bagniuk's answers. He insisted that the NKVD had information that Bagniuk had visited the Polish consulate in Kiev more than once in 1934. By way of response, Bagniuk categorically stated that he had never visited the consulate after 1924. The interrogator then threatened him, saying that the NKVD possessed information that he was an agent of the Polish intelligence and had conducted espionage activity for Poland. Bagniuk stated in response, 'I have never been an agent of the Polish intelligence and never engaged in espionage activity' (10).

This seems to have been the only interrogation of Bagniuk. Having failed to break him, the NKVD deposed several witnesses. One was Filipp Moiseevich Kas'ian, apparently his superior at the railway depot, who was interviewed on 19 November 1937. He portrayed Bagniuk as anti-Soviet and anti-Semitic. Bagniuk had allegedly said that everything was better before the Revolution: there were no economic plans and no productivity campaigns. Before they had bowed down before 'pans' (Polish masters), now they bowed down before the 'Yids'. Using the productivity campaigns, the Soviet government was making fools of workers and squeezing the last drop out of them. Regarding the collective farms, Bagniuk had said, 'It's a new form of Polish domination [panshchina]: before peasants worked for their Polish masters and received nothing, now they work day and night and make nothing, they don't even know what leather shoes are' (15–16).

Bagniuk's former wife, Domnikiia, was deposed on 20 November 1937. They had been married for ten years, from 1924 to 1934. There is no information available on why their marriage was dissolved and why they then lived at the same address even though they had both remarried. Was it because they had nowhere else to live? At any rate, Domnikiia testified that her former husband had always wanted to leave for Poland. To this end he had visited the Polish consulate more than once. According to Domnikiia, in 1932–33 Bagniuk told her that he had visited the Polish consul and had had an 'intimate' talk with him. Why did he want to leave for Poland? She said that her husband detested the Soviet government and the Communists, and that he also hated the Jews. In conversations with her, he always said that life in Poland was better and freer than in the Soviet Union—there one could go to church freely, but here it was forbidden. He explained to her why it was necessary to leave the Soviet Union: there would soon be a war and a famine, which would destroy the Communists. He wanted her to go with him to Poland, but she refused. So he beat her. One day in 1933, he came back home particularly angry and yelled at her: 'You scoundrel, you didn't want to leave and now because of you I can't leave. All the same I'll drive you to your grave.' And he threatened to kill her (17–20).

It is likely that there was some domestic strife; they divorced, after all. It is also true that, at the time of Bagniuk's arrest, a Bible was confiscated (6). Still, Domnikiia's testimony concerning Bagniuk's wish to leave for Poland, like so many others taken in similar circumstances, is likely to have been false. Whether Bagniuk was a believer or not (and if so whether he was Catholic, Orthodox or Uniate) is not known. His religion never became an item in the charges against him.

Bagniuk was not allowed to question those who gave incriminating testimonies against him. Without further formality, he was indicted. His bill of indictment states that he confessed to his crimes, although there is no evidence that he ever did (27). Bagniuk was sentenced to be shot on 26 December 1937 and was executed ten days later. Like so many others, he was buried in the Bykivnia mass graves.[14] Bagniuk was rehabilitated in 1989 owing to a lack of *corpus delicti*. No relatives were found at the time (44).

From the point of view of the Soviet government, there was no rationale for marriage being held as sacred. In Stalin's Soviet Union, a husband and wife were not protected from being compelled to testify against each other. In fact, they were obliged to inform the police if they became aware of their spouse's involvement in criminal activity.

Yet the cases examined in this chapter also suggest how strong some marriages and families remained. The case of Iuliia Mishchenko is revealing. Soon after she was despatched to the Gulag in the Urals, her family members (her mother, two brothers and two sisters, one of whom, Evdokiia, adopted her daughter Tamara) began to write petitions on her behalf (her father had died in 1922). Iuliia told her family about the torture the NKVD had inflicted on her husband and herself. They were indignant. They used Stalin's words to fight back: they maintained that her husband, Stepan, was innocent and that, in any case, the arrest of Iuliia directly contradicted Stalin's declaration that 'A son does not answer for his father' (they added, 'let alone a wife for her husband'). (Stalin had said this in 1935, but obviously had not meant it.) The petitions of Mishchenko's family did not bring any immediate results. After Stalin's death, however, both Stepan and Iuliia Mishchenko were rehabilitated (Mishchenko file, note 3, 25–27, 30, 34–36, 45, 46–48).

Marriages and families were destroyed everywhere, but the terror did not always tear apart the bonds between husbands and wives. All kinds of threats and torture were meted out. Even the case files in this chapter fail to convey the full extent of the horror inflicted on spouses. But between the lines of otherwise dry prose littered with spelling and grammatical mistakes, the voice of terror speaks. Dzevitskaia, Sosnovskaia-Budnitskaia and especially Kurovskaia stood firm against intimidation, threats and possibly even physical torture. They defended their husbands and themselves. Dzevitskaia was executed, but Sosnovskaia-Budnitskaia and Kurovskaia survived. These cases are a truly remarkable testament to the power of human relationships.

CHAPTER 12

POW

'The Polish Military Organisation'

Comparing deaths and discussing their relative significance is not the most productive form of scholarly debate. Russians often believe that they suffered the most from Stalin's terror, while Ukrainians believe that they bore the brunt, particularly in the form of the Great Famine of 1932–33. All of the dead deserve to be properly commemorated, of course, and this can make particularistic claims appear moot and hollow.

This does not mean that the question of which groups of people were targeted by Stalin's terror is unimportant. As has been suggested in the preceding chapters, among the 'ordinary' Soviet citizens, the de-kulakised, the priests, the ethnic minorities and those with foreign connections were particularly vulnerable. Regarding the ethnic dimensions of the terror in Ukraine, statistical data can be instructive. Ethnic Ukrainians accounted for the majority of those arrested (and almost certainly executed as well) in 1937–38: 53.2 percent. Russians were the second largest ethnic group among the arrested: 7.7 percent. Yet other national groups do assert that the population shares of ethnic Ukrainians and Russians in Ukraine were greater, 78.2 and 11.3 percent respectively, and so suggest that the suffering of Ukrainians and Russians was proportionately smaller. Ethnic Poles accounted for 1.5 percent of the population of Ukraine, but 18.9 percent of the arrested in 1937–38. This means that the Poles' share among the arrested was more than twelve times higher than their share in the population. The corresponding figures for ethnic Germans were 1.4 and 10.2 percent (more than seven times), and for Greeks 0.4 and 2.3 percent (almost six times). Smaller minorities (Koreans, Chinese, Latvians and others) taken together appear to have suffered to the order of ten times their share in the population (the figures being 0.4 percent and 4.2 percent respectively).[1]

These figures give only rough indications of the ethnic dimensions of the Great Terror, owing to the fact that ethnic data were not always accurate and ethnic identity was not always fixed. Despite differences in language, religion and other aspects of culture, the demarcations between different ethnicities (for instance, Poles and Ukrainians) were far from clear-cut. This problem was all the greater for children of mixed marriages. Nevertheless, Poles occupied a distinct place in the Great Terror in Ukraine and in Kiev. As Marxists, Stalin and his close associates did not regard ethnicity as an absolute determinant of one's political orientation, even though they could not resist making ethnic jokes. Yet certain ethnic groups appeared to them to be politically suspect because they were diaspora groups and maintained special ties to certain foreign countries. Koreans, who did not have a country of their own at the time, were dangerous as potential Japanese spies. Chinese did have their own country, but were suspect for the same reason. The danger posed by ethnic Germans, Poles, Latvians and others was self-evident since their mother countries appeared to be hostile to the Soviet Union.[2]

The ethnic data quoted here suggest that Poles appeared to the Soviet leaders to be the most dangerous. There were several reasons for this. Poland was a relatively large and powerful state. It had been partitioned and had disappeared in the eighteenth century. For this reason, once it achieved independence in 1918 in the wake of the Russian Revolution and World War I, it was fiercely jealous of its autonomy. Many of its statesmen regarded the Soviet Union as its most dangerous enemy and actively engaged in espionage against it, collaborating with the Japanese (see Chapter 7). It is no wonder that Stalin feared a simultaneous Japanese–Polish attack in the 1930s.[3] Unlike another potential enemy, Germany, Poland shared a border with the Soviet Union, raising fears of infiltration by Polish agents into Soviet territory. Poland also shared a long and close, albeit complicated, history with Ukraine. Nearly half a million ethnic Poles lived in Soviet Ukraine before the Great Terror. Their position was precarious. Lack of assimilation gave rise to suspicions of disloyalty, whereas assimilation gave rise to suspicions of trying to pass for Ukrainians or Belarusans. (The linguistic assimilation of ethnic Poles in Ukraine was high, higher than almost all the other major minorities except for Belarusans. In 1926, more than half of the ethnic Poles, 56.9 percent, in Ukraine listed Ukrainian as their mother tongue.)[4]

Preceding chapters have suggested that Poles (and those with Polish connections) were targeted by the Great Terror. Almost all were innocent. The Soviet authorities fabricated numerous anti-Soviet organisations, such as the SVU, the Union for the Liberation of Ukraine. The Polish Military Organisation (Polska Organizacja Wojskowa or POW) was another such invented group. The name was chosen by the Soviet secret police because a real organisation with that name had existed before, from 1914 to 1921. The real POW was founded by the future chief of independent Poland, Marshal Józef Piłsudski. Its main function had been intelligence-gathering and sabotage. After Polish independence in 1918, it was absorbed into the Polish army. The POW remained active in Ukraine, however, because the fate of Ukraine was still being fought out among the Reds, Whites, Ukrainians and Poles. After the Reds' triumph in 1920, the POW virtually ceased to function; its members had been decimated by the Bolsheviks. Yet suspicion died hard and the Soviet secret police suspected that remnants of the POW continued to work underground in Soviet Ukraine. It is true that the Polish intelligence service was active in Ukraine, but the POW was defunct: it existed only in the imagination of the Soviet secret police.[5] Moreover, while it still existed, the Soviet secret police benefited from the POW by recruiting some of its most able agents.[6] All the same, ethnic Poles remained suspect, if only in light of the fact that certain ethnic Poles in Ukraine had worked for and helped the POW during its existence, and many leaders of the POW were natives of Ukraine and thus intimately familiar with Ukraine and Russia. They were now thought to work for the independent Polish intelligence service.[7]

Poland did use former POW members for its intelligence operation. In 1931–32 the Polish intelligence agency (dwójka) collected information on former POW members.[8] Stalin suspected that some of them were active Polish agents. In May 1932 the Japanese military attaché in Moscow, Torashirō Kawabe, enquired of his colleague in Warsaw, Hikosaburō Hata, whether the rumour he had heard in Moscow that two members of the Polish General Staff were executed for espionage for the Soviet Union was true. Two days later, Hata, who worked closely with the Polish intelligence agency, responded: the Polish General Staff recently sent twenty-odd secret agents to Ukraine, all of whom, however, were caught by the GPU. Two 'secretaries' of the General Staff had been bought off by the Soviets and leaked secret information to them. They were court-martialled and sentenced to be shot. The Kawabe–Hata correspondence was intercepted by the Soviet secret police and reported to Stalin.[9] This only heightened Stalin's suspicion of the Poles. After the assassination of Kirov in December 1934, Stalin specifically named a former POW member turned prominent official of the NKVD, Ignacy Dobrzyński (Ignatii Sosnovskii), as politically suspect, and ordered Nikolai Ezhov to remove him ('why do you keep a Pole in such an [important] position?').[10] Suspicions of Poles were such that the Soviet secret police targeted ethnic Poles in the terror. Numerous Poles (and non-Poles with Polish connections) in Ukraine were thus executed as members of the fictitious POW.

Cheslava Nikolaevna Angel'chik

Cheslava Nikolaevna Angel'chik was a native of Warsaw, where she was born into a Jewish worker's family in 1899. The capital of the future independent Poland was then part of the Russian Empire. Angel'chik's family was dispersed between three countries. Two of her brothers, Orlik and Adol'f, worked in the Soviet Union. Her sixty-two-year-old mother, Khaia Ruklia, lived with three of her brothers, Iankel', Aron and Itsak, in Paris. Another brother, Vel'ver, worked in Colombia.[11] At the time of her arrest on 22 August 1937, Cheslava was living at 90 Gershuni Street, Flat 40, in Kiev and was working in the Polish Section of the Ukrainian Pedagogical Institute there as a professor. The Polish Section had been created in the autumn of 1935 when the Polish Pedagogical Institute (PIP) was closed down and absorbed into the Ukrainian Pedagogical Institute.[12] Two years previously, in 1933, at the time of the famine crisis in Ukraine, the PIP was fiercely attacked by the Soviet secret police as the ostensible centre of the POW, and its teaching and administrative staff had been thoroughly purged.[13] This may have helped Angel'chik to obtain the position of professor. In any case, she was appointed to her post by the new director, Ia. Podniak.

Podniak and other new PIP leaders were soon arrested and decimated, however. Subsequently, the leaders of the newly formed Polish Section of the Ukrainian Pedagogical Institute were also arrested as Polish spies and members of the POW. Angel'chik was one of them. It is very likely that, given the suspicion cast upon all Polish institutions at the time, the Polish Section was deeply infiltrated by the secret police. In fact, like Moshinskaia (discussed in Chapter 2), Angel'chik worked for the Soviet secret police, and not just as an informer, but as a secret agent.

After her arrest, Angel'chik wrote a statement to the NKVD chief Nikolai Ezhov dated 27 August 1937, although Ezhov's name has been crossed out by someone (1:9–12). According to this, Angel'chik had completed a classical education in Warsaw. After her father's death in 1920, she went to the provinces to make her living. In 1921, however, one of her brothers, Orlik, who was working in Soviet Ukraine, suggested that she come over to study and start a new life, in order to escape the life of poverty that she had been leading. She received permission to emigrate in 1925 and settled legally in Kiev, where she studied at the Institute of People's Education. She wrote that her father, a worker, took part in the 1905 Revolution against tsarism, as a result of which he was arrested, imprisoned and exiled for three years. All six of her brothers were workers and half-illiterate, but she had managed to study at a gymnasium, where she met one Borovskaia, who later became an influential Communist Party official. (Borovskaia had also emigrated to the Soviet Union and worked at Polish institutions.)[14] Angel'chik added that she had frequented circles sympathetic to Communism at the Warsaw gymnasium.

Upon arrival in Kiev in 1925, Angel'chik had begun to work at Polish School No. 11, which was headed by 'anti-Soviet elements'. She named names. Seeking company (probably she was lonely in her adopted country), she had become involved socially with these 'counter-revolutionary elements', including B. Skarbek, the alleged head of the POW. Yet she had been prevented from securing a position at the PIP by Poles who, she noted, considered her an 'active Soviet person'. It is possible that she was subtly implying that there was anti-Semitism among her Polish colleagues. In the end, after the 1933 crackdown on the POW, she had been able to secure a position at the PIP.

After her appointment, Angel'chik said she was recruited into the POW. To gain her confidence, Podniak had told her that her old friend Borovskaia, a party member, and many others at the institute were also POW members. Her task was to convince the students in the Polish-language faculty that, isolated from Poland where all Polish cultural forces were centred, it would be impossible to build a Polish proletarian culture in the Soviet Union. Therefore, it was imperative that students be taught 'bourgeois' Polish literature and inculcated with Polish patriotic sentiments in order to create a solid beachhead to ensure a Polish victory in a future war between Poland and the Soviet Union.

This logic could only have been devised by the Soviet secret police. The latter were suspicious of the curriculum at the PIP, which appeared 'bourgeois' and 'unproletarian', and so fabricated an anti-Soviet conspiracy there.

Angel'chik stated that in January 1934 she began to work as an NKVD secret agent. The fact that she did not say that she volunteered suggests that she was coerced. It appears that, as a Polish immigrant, Angel'chik attracted the attention of the police, who, exploiting her vulnerability owing to her past, pressed her into service. It is also possible that the secret police targeted Angel'chik, believing that, being Jewish, she might be antipathetic to Polish nationalism. It is also possible, though there is no proof, that the authorities appointed her to the faculty in exchange for her cooperation with the police. Whatever the case, it was then, in 1934, that she met one Prigozhii. Nothing is known about him, but Prigozhii began to suspect her because she went out so many evenings on assignments. He had asked her whether she worked for the NKVD, and she had failed to give a clear answer. As a result, Angel'chik stated, her clandestine work was revealed to him, and he, in turn, informed everyone at the PIP about it. She was unmasked.

In early 1935 (probably a mistake for 1936), by which time the PIP had been closed, her double life ended. She said that she no longer worked for the POW: did she mean by this that she no longer worked as a provocateur? Oddly, she added that even then she did not inform the NKVD about numerous colleagues (she again named names) who were active members of the POW (which did not really exist). By not informing the police, she admitted that she had betrayed their trust. This statement seems to suggest that even though Angel'chik might have been an agent at some point, she was no longer active in police work after 1936. If this is true, it probably means that she came to believe that the intensive terror against the Poles that had begun in 1933 had come to an end by 1936 and it was no longer necessary to inform on her colleagues. By the time of her arrest, however, it had become evident that the terror had not ended, but had returned with a vengeance.

She concluded her statement to Ezhov with a plea (1:12zv.): 'I ask the People's Commissar of Internal Affairs for mercy. If I am permitted to live, I promise to rub off all the counter-revolutionary scum from my face and pay back my adoption into the Soviet family with honest work.' Exactly how she had ended up working for the police and exactly what her role had been is not known, but obviously she knew that she was facing death.

The record of her interrogation does shed some light on her work for the police. Obviously Angel'chik was not the only person at the PIP working for the police. In her interrogation on 31 August 1937 (after her 28 August statement to Ezhov), she stated that she and her colleagues had collected information on the attitudes of Polish peasants in the western border areas concerning the collectivisation of agriculture. (Apparently some of these areas were still not collectivised in 1933.) Their conclusion was that the Polish peasants would cross the borders en masse from the Soviet to the Polish side if they were forced into collective farms. In 1933–34, Angel'chik and her colleagues also visited students' parents, using the need to examine the students' living conditions as a pretext. They then conducted 'anti-Soviet conversations', collecting information on the parents' political mood and their connections to Poland, the Polish consulate and the Polish church. Angel'chik stated that she and others did this work as members of the POW. In fact, they almost certainly did it for the police. It was precisely the kind of information that the Soviet secret police sought. Their findings were unfavourable to the Soviet state. For instance, in the Marchlevs'k Polish Autonomous District near the border with Poland, the residents called the creation of the district a 'puppet comedy': under the guise of protecting Polish culture, it in fact destroyed it.[15] They also reported that the arrest of prominent Soviet Poles (POW leaders) caused much anger among ethnic Poles in Ukraine (1:33, 35, 37, 38–39).

Angel'chik was sentenced to be shot on 13 September 1937 as part of the Polish Operation. Four days later she was executed (1:50, 51). In 1989, she was rehabilitated. Like so many other victims in Kiev, she was buried in the Bykivnia mass graves.[16]

There is a little more to Angel'chik's story. Two days after her execution, the secret police decided to destroy the correspondence confiscated at the time of her arrest (1:44). The reason for this unusual action is not known. It is possible that some of it related to police

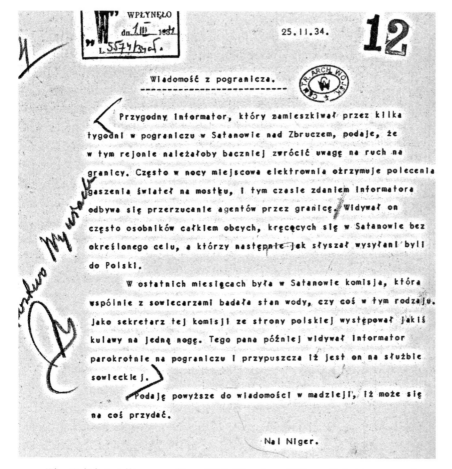

37: The Polish intelligence officer 'Nal Niger', or Wiktor Zaleski, reported to Warsaw on 25 November 1934 that a 'casual informer', who had lived in the border town of Sataniv (in today's Khmel'nyts'kyi Oblast', Ukraine) for a few weeks, suggested that closer attention might be paid to the border traffic in the region. At night, the local power plant frequently received an order to turn off the light on a bridge over the Zbruch River which constituted the Soviet–Polish border. When the light went off, in the opinion of the informer, Soviet agents crossed (see also Illustrations 6, 17 and 19 above).

operations. Another odd detail is that Angel'chik's marital status is not known. When she was arrested, however, two men were present to witness the search of her flat: Vladimir A … (indecipherable) Kondratenko, who lived at 7a Zakharivs'ka Street, Flat 1, and Nikolai Pavlovich Davidiuk (address not known) (2:1). The presence of

Kondratenko is unusual, since he was unlikely to have been the manager of her building. (Davidiuk was probably the manager.) Three months after Angel'chik's execution, Kondratenko wrote a petition to the NKVD, asking that some of Angel'chik's personal belongings, which were still in her sealed apartment, be given to him: an EKL–4 radio receiver valued at 450 roubles, twenty volumes of the *Great Soviet Encyclopedia* and a mattress valued at 100 roubles. In addition, he said that, of the government bonds worth 3,190 roubles that were confiscated from her, 1,350 roubles' worth belonged to him (2:5, 13). Why were Kondratenko's bonds with Angel'chik's? Perhaps she was married to him at one point. Maybe Kondratenko was in some way associated with the secret police, and that was why he was present at the search of her flat. It is possible that he had denounced her to obtain her personal possessions. The truth is elusive. It is not known whether he got what he wanted: at least some of Angel'chik's belongings were transferred to the state in the spring of 1938 (2:6).

Emiliia Kazimirovna Iatskevich

Like Angel'chik, Emiliia Kazimirovna Iatskevich was a Polish-language teacher in Kiev. She was an ethnic Pole, born in 1899 into a worker's family in Rzhyshchiv, to the south of Kiev. She had partially completed higher education (she studied at the PIP until it was abolished in 1935). Afterwards she worked as a teacher at Polish School No. 114 in Kiev until she was arrested on 23 November 1937. She was divorced and, at the time of her arrest, was living with her son Anatolii Vladimirovich Andreev at 4 Victims of Revolution Street, Corpus 1, Flat 55, in Kiev. She stated that she had no criminal record, but the secret police listed her as having been arrested in 1920 for 'speculation' (which probably meant small-time peddling).[17]

In her 25 November 1937 interrogation, Iatskevich was first questioned as to whether she had relations abroad and, if so, whether she corresponded with them. Her answer was negative: no relatives and no correspondence, although she added that the husband of her sister had emigrated to the Soviet Union from Poland in 1920—but, in any case, they were divorced now and where he lived she did not know. Then the interrogator told her that she was under arrest for being a Polish spy and that she should tell him the truth. She categorically denied the charge. The interrogator told her that the police had evidence of her conducting 'counter-revolutionary Fascist agitation' and demanded that she confess. She rejected this charge as well. The interrogation ended at that point (13–14).

The following day, Iatskevich was interrogated again. This time she was told to admit that she had been recruited into the POW while studying at the PIP. Iatskevich stood her ground, maintaining that no one had recruited her. Unable to break Iatskevich, the interrogator again demanded that she admit to 'counter-revolutionary Fascist agitation' (i.e., praising Poland and criticising the Soviet Union). She responded that she had not engaged in such agitation, nor had she praised Poland (15–16). Another session of interrogation took place on the same day. Again and again Iatskevich denied all the charges against her (17).

She might have been sentenced to be shot at this point, without evidence or confession, as happened with others. Yet the police deposed several witnesses in an apparent effort to bolster the case against her. On 28 November 1937, the school superintendent, Nikolai Ignat'evich Sakhovskii, was interviewed. He stated that, in her third-year class, there were incidents in which pupils had blotted out the eyes in the portraits of the Communist Party leaders and that Iatskevich had not reported them. It was only after a considerable lapse of time that he found out about them. And only then did Iatskevich come and explain to him that the father of one particular student had been arrested and that was why he had done it: she had had nothing to do with it. Sakhovskii then stated that Iatskevich was verbally abusive towards her own pupils, calling some of them Trotskyites. Sakhovskii also alleged that one Bogdanovich, a colleague of Iatskevich at the Institute, had been arrested. Sakhovskii added that Iatskevich was an anti-Soviet element (18–19).

The incidents with the portraits of Soviet leaders are significant. At the time, there were reports from all over the country of children tearing down Soviet leaders' portraits or blackening their eyes or attaching swastikas to them. Many 'counter-revolutionary songs' were reportedly sung by youngsters, particularly after the murder of the Leningrad party leader Sergei Kirov in December 1934: 'Kirov was killed, it's not enough, Stalin should have been killed'; 'Kirov was killed—food rationing was abolished; if Stalin is killed—people will begin to live', and the like.[18] Reading different meanings into acronyms was also a common pastime: for instance, taking SSSR (the Russian acronym for the USSR) to stand for '*Smert' Stalina Spaset Rossiiu*' ('The Death of Stalin Will Save Russia').[19] Like so many other reports, these may have been fabricated. Yet it is also true that Soviet children, like children everywhere, enjoyed making mischief, in this case at the expense of the Soviet leaders.[20] Naum Korzhavin, who was a pupil in Kiev in the 1930s, recalled what he did, probably a day or two after Kirov was assassinated: bored and tired, he grabbed a scrap of newspaper with a portrait of the assassinated man and raced down the hall screaming 'Kirov! Kirov!' for no particular reason until he was stopped by a frightened teacher. He sensed that his conduct might somehow be interpreted by someone somewhere as that of an enemy of the people. He also noted that at the time all of the children drew swastikas out of curiosity in play.[21]

After the Kirov murder, party and Komsomol leaders, concerned about the implications of children's games, sent investigative teams to the provinces in Ukraine. The teams came back with reports of a multitude of plays, songs and games that appeared to be politically sensitive.[22] Taken literally, they appeared to include calls for terrorism against the Soviet leaders. The blackening of the eyes of leaders in portraits appeared to observers to carry a hidden message that the Soviet leaders were unable to see how hard the lives of the Soviet people were. It is possible that some of the acts were intentionally political. Some children, observing their surroundings, must have understood the political situation. Others simply took their cues from political life and created games, perhaps brutal and savage in some respects, but nonetheless otherwise characteristic of the games of innocent children. Yet in the political atmosphere of the time any remark, song or game could assume a sinister meaning. Those who missed such hidden meanings were blamed for their lack of political vigilance. If Sakhovskii's account is right, Iatskevich had protected the children but at the same time had sought to protect herself by labelling them Trotskyites just in case.

On 29 November 1937, Iatskevich's colleague Liudmila Stanislavna Serikova was deposed by the secret police. She repeated more or less what Sakhovskii had stated, with some variations and additions: Iatskevich was an anti-Soviet element; she did not inform the superintendent or other colleagues about her pupils defacing the portraits of Soviet leaders and drawing swastikas on them (because Iatskevich did not attach much meaning to these incidents); she was an anti-Semite who insulted a colleague simply because she was Jewish; she praised

Poland and denounced the Soviet Union ('People are now dying from hunger here') (20–21).

On the same day, two more witnesses described the same incidents in almost identical phrases but with new details: a Jewish teacher left the school because Iatskevich had allegedly harassed her; Iatskevich praised 'Fascist Poland', saying that whereas the Soviet people died from hunger, the Polish people lived much better and much more freely; a relative of Iatskevich's with whom she was in close contact was arrested by the NKVD as an 'enemy of the people' (22–25).

Without being given an opportunity to refute the witness testimonies, Iatskevich was sentenced, in accordance with the Polish Operation, to be shot on 15 December 1937 and was executed six days later (29–30). She too was buried in the Bykivnia mass graves.[23] Iatskevich was rehabilitated in 1989. At that time no relatives were found (32).

The POW 'Insurgent Group'

Not everyone in the imagined POW was a professor. In fact, many peasants and workers were arrested as soldiers and insurgents of the POW. For example, a band of 'POW insurgents' consisting of fifteen farmers in several villages of the Ivankiv district to the northwest of Kiev were executed in the autumn of 1938. It was the second such incident involving the alleged POW groups in the villages.

This affair involved both collective and independent farmers, all of whom were arrested in the villages of Makariv, Ordzhonikidze and other rural settlements of the Ivankiv-Rozvazhiv area between 17 and 19 May 1938. According to the police files, they were: (1) Anton Denisovich Navrotskii, 45, said to have participated in a kulak uprising against the Soviet government in 1919. At the time of his arrest, he was an ordinary collective farmer with a wife and three children. He had served a three-year sentence in 1932–35 for 'lack of discipline' at work. His brother Ivan was arrested as a member of the POW in 1937; (2) Tsezar' Ivanovich Il'nitskii, 34, de-kulakised in 1931, who subsequently joined a collective farm. He, like Navrotskii, was sentenced to three years of correctional labour in 1934 for 'lax discipline' at work. At the time of his arrest, he lived with his wife and three children. Two of his brothers had been arrested; (3) Vladimir Denisovich Navrotskii, 57, said, like his brother Anton Denisovich, to have taken part in a kulak uprising in

1919. At the time of his arrest, he was a rank-and-file collective farmer and lived with his wife and three kids. He was completely illiterate and used his fingerprint to sign all documents (including the records of interrogation); (4) Stanislav Aleksandrovich Adamenko, 36, also alleged to have been a kulak. Before he was de-kulakised, however, he sold his property and left his village. In 1934 he returned. At the time of his arrest, he was a collective farmer and lived with his wife and daughter; (5) Denis Frantsevich Adamenko, 33, the 'son of a kulak', still an independent farmer at the time of his arrest, having refused to join a collective farm. He lived with his wife; (6) Bronislav Dominkovich Adamenko, 45, formerly a kulak, now an independent farmer. He lived with his wife and two children; (7) Bronislav Frantsevich Adamenko, 26, the 'son of a kulak', a brother of Denis Frantsevich and a rank-and-file collective farmer who lived with his wife and two children.

The list continues: (8) Martyn Boleslavovich Glenbotskii, 58, formerly a kulak, a rank-and-file collective farmer who lived with his wife and four children; (9) Vladimir Romanovich Veres, 36, a collective farmer who lived with his wife and three children; (10) Nikolai Ivanovich Singaevskii, 41, formerly a kulak, who had served a five-year gaol sentence. At the time of his arrest, he was an independent farmer who lived with his wife and four children; (11) Petr Vekent'evich Gurnevich, 42, formerly a 'middle peasant' (i.e., neither a kulak nor a poor peasant), an 'active Catholic Church member' and a collective farmer. At the time of his arrest, he was living with his wife and five children; (12) Lavrentii Ivanovich Repik, 32, the 'son of a kulak', an independent farmer who lived with his wife and two children; (13) Ivan Il'ich Repik, 34, formerly a 'poor peasant' and then a collective farm accountant, with a record of two arrests and three years of detention for embezzlement. He lived with his wife and daughter; (14) Stanislav Ivanovich Andrienko, 42, formerly a 'middle peasant', now a rank-and-file collective farmer who lived with his wife and three daughters; (15) Petr Ivanovich Andrienko, 46, probably Stanislav Ivanovich's elder brother, formerly a 'middle peasant', now a rank-and-file collective farmer who lived with his wife and three children.[24]

Many of these defendants had additional extended family members living with them. All but two, Singaevskii and I. I. Repik (both of whom were Ukrainians), were ethnic Poles. They were all born in the Ivankiv district and were Soviet citizens. None was a party member.

Although their bill of indictment stated that all had confessed and pleaded guilty to the charges (1:254–63), this does not seem to have been the case.

The crimes of which they were accused, as was often the case, were formulaically described. The fifteen villagers were allegedly recruited into the POW cells founded in the Ivankiv-Rozvazhiv area by the Catholic priest Zygmunt Żych, a native of Kiev, who was arrested in 1930 and sentenced to five years. (In 1932 Żych and seventeen other Polish Catholic priests were released in a prisoner exchange between Poland and the Soviet Union. His subsequent fate in Poland is not known.)[25] In 1930 Żych does not seem to have been accused of POW activity, but, rather, of anti-Soviet agitation. Later the NKVD claimed that he was an agent of the Polish intelligence. According to one witness, he preached love for the motherland Poland, urged Poles to educate their children in a patriotic Polish spirit and warned that the Soviet government, the 'government of the Antichrist', should not be trusted and that Poland would beat the Soviet Union and take over Ukraine in a future war, in which the duty of Poles in Ukraine would be to help the Polish troops. Żych rejected the charges. The police described him as having fled to Poland. There is no mention of the prisoner exchange (1:171, 2:486–95).

The main purpose of the Ivanivka-Rozvazhiv POW group, according to the NKVD, had been to remove Soviet power by way of an armed uprising, detach Ukraine from the Soviet Union and restore the Polish borders to their pre-1772 state (i.e., the reinstatement of the Polish territory of the pre-partition era). The armed uprising was to coincide with a military assault by Poland on the Soviet Union. For this purpose, the POW group engaged in systematic diversionary and wrecking activities and 'counter-revolutionary' agitation, spread defeatist sentiments among collective farmers and formed military detachments from Polish 'bandits' and 'counter-revolutionary kulak elements'. (This was meant to explain the presence of the two Ukrainians. Singaevskii was formerly a kulak but I. I. Repik was a poor Ukrainian peasant. Both, however, had criminal records.) Numerous 'counter-revolutionary' remarks were attributed to them: 'War will start soon between Poland and the Soviet Union and the Poles will beat the Soviet Union, take power and punish collective farmers severely' and the like (1:257).

Ostensibly before the arrests, the secret police had collected 'references' (*dovidky*) condemning the targeted villagers. (Often they were actually collected after arrests.) The testimonies were mainly obtained from the village soviet chairmen, who alleged, sometimes in a mixture of Ukrainian and Russian, that so-and-so was an 'anti-Soviet' element who had said this or that. They also listed anyone linked to the arrested. Arrest warrants were then issued against the fifteen villagers in the Ukrainian language (1:16–30, 76–89). Almost all interrogations were conducted in Russian, however.

Some of the fifteen arrested rejected the charges initially. When accused of being a POW member, A. D. Navrotskii categorically denied it. Later he was broken and confessed to having been a POW member since 1928 (1:105–10). Il'nitskii appears to have been broken from the beginning. He admitted that being de-kulakised had made him anti-Soviet and that he had agitated among the collective farmers by asserting: 'The Soviet peasants are living like an enslaved people'; 'The collective farms are a yoke for the peasants' (1:111–14). V. D. Navrotskii, like Kurovskaia (see Chapter 11), was illiterate and had to use his fingerprint instead of a signature. But unlike Kurovskaia, who stood up to the false accusations, he was broken from the beginning, according to the records of his 21 July 1938 interrogation (1:115–19). B. D. Adamenko was also broken and confessed to political crimes. He had agitated among the collective farmers by saying,

> Look how we Poles are being mocked by the Soviet government. I've been without bread for several days and my children are doomed to starvation, but it's all right—an end will come soon to this barbarian government. Poland will capture Ukraine soon, and we'll begin to live well as we did before the Revolution (1:125zv.).

Glenbotskii, like A. D. Navrotskii, initially denied all the charges against him and then gave in. He confessed to having engaged in 'counter-revolutionary agitation': 'Poland with Japan will beat the Soviet Union' (1:135–37).

Witnesses were also deposed. One quoted many 'criminal' remarks allegedly made by Gurnevich, an 'active Catholic Church member':

> The Soviet government is a dragon. They don't recognise God, but God exists and He'll fight against them in war. Sooner or later the Soviet government will be beaten and captured by our faithful Poles.

... In capitalist countries like America life is much better than here in the Soviet Union. ... My brother lives in America, he drives a [indecipherable] car. He got it [for himself] and it is his own property, but here, owning one's own car is out of the question. We'll be without a shirt (1:203–203zv.).

When, however, the accused were allowed to question the witnesses against them, Gurnevich, for example, disputed the account of one Rafael'skii who had implicated him in the POW. Rafael'skii had not recruited him to the POW, he said. Asked who did then, Gurnevich said, 'No one recruited me. I was not a participant in the counter-revolutionary Polish organisation' (1:231).

The arrested did not understand what their interrogators meant when they spoke of the POW (or POV in Russia and Ukrainian) as if it were some kind of foreign word: the alleged members of the POW did not know that the letters stood for 'Polish Military Organisation'.

The interrogators could not cope with the complexity of the case, which involved more than a dozen people. A close reading of the documents reveals numerous unresolved issues. The question of 'who recruited whom' was never answered. In fact, many contradictions exist in the case file. A confessed that he was recruited by B in 1934, whereas B confessed that he was recruited by A in 1928, and so on. The group was allegedly going to stage an armed uprising, but no one had a weapon or knew where to acquire one. There was no evidence beyond obviously forced confessions of guilt. Nevertheless, on 28 September 1938 all fifteen were sentenced to be shot in accordance with NKVD Order No. 00606 dated 17 September 1938. They were executed on 2 October 1938 (1:265–67, 268, 282) and buried in the mass graves of Bykivnia.[26]

Mass arrests and executions of this sort must have devastated the villages. After Stalin's death, there was a serious investigation into this POW affair by the prosecutor's office and the KGB in Ukraine. They found numerous contradictions in the case file, particularly in terms of who recruited whom. Surviving villagers were interviewed. Their accounts showed the case to be a complete fabrication. According to the 21 April 1956 testimony of their former colleague on the collective farm, I. I. Kostiatchuk, the Navrotskiis were not kulaks, as had been alleged, but poor peasants. They joined the collective farm in 1930

38: The death certificate of a Polish victim of Stalin's terror, along with a small flag of Poland, bound to a pine tree at the Bykivnia mass grave site (2006).

and worked conscientiously, grateful to the Soviet regime for the fact that the collective farm had brought them a good life (2:10). Another witness, Viktor Ippolitovich Tsudzinovich, testified that he, too, had been arrested on 18 May 1938. He was beaten by his interrogators, but he had withstood the torture and not confessed to any crime. In the end, he was released after a year, on 11 May 1939 (2:41).

Bronislav Adamovich Glembotskii, who had been the soviet secretary in the village of Ordzhonikidze in 1938, testified in 1956 that he had written 'references' against some of the fifteen executed. (He could no longer read them for himself, because he was almost blind, so they were now read to him.) He added that they had been dictated by NKVD officials: he had been young (twenty-two), inexperienced and 'feared the

NKVD', so he had written down what he was told. Nina Antonovna Kotusenko confirmed that the 'references' were written by Glembotskii and that it was she who had signed them. A policeman named Khutornoi had come to the village on 21 July 1938 (two months after the arrests) for 'references'. When she said that she did not know the arrested men, the policeman began to yell at her. Depositions were then taken, some from her deputy, Ivan Gerasimovich Khoroshun (who was killed in World War II) (2:61–62). According to another witness, Mikhail Vasil'evich Antoshchenko, who was illiterate and had not signed his testimony, Khoroshun was not well disposed towards S. A. Adamenko. Adamenko, who was said to have been a kulak, had taken part in the de-kulakisation of Khorshun's father-in-law, probably in 1930. Khoroshun had told people that he would never forgive Adamenko for that and, when Adamenko was arrested, Khoroshun was pleased. Rumour had it in the village that Khoroshun had helped to have Adamenko put in gaol (2:65). The writers of other 'references', those found alive in 1956, also confirmed that they had been dictated by the NKVD (2:84, 109).

Some testimonies reveal details about village life in the 1930s. D. F. Adamenko had never joined the collective farm because he followed the faith of his wife, who was a devout Catholic. In fact, she somehow survived the Stalin years and was still not a member of the collective farm in 1956 (2:72). Another witness, Viktoriia Grigor'evna Zaichenko, a Catholic, said that Catholic priests in Ivankiv (she did not name Żych) preached that 'each government is given by God, therefore one has to submit oneself to the government' (2:99). The church appears to have been closed in 1931.

Some witnesses deposed by the police in 1938 were still alive in 1956 and were interviewed. They repudiated their old testimonies. Ivan Vasil'evich Loban, for example, stated in 1956 that when he was summoned to the NKVD in 1938, his testimony had already been written and he was told to sign it. 'Frightened by the events of the time', he signed as told (2:119). Another witness said that D. F. Adamenko was not a kulak but a poor illiterate peasant who was also deaf (2:72, 77). Adamenko's signature in the file was clearly written by someone who was literate (1:65zv., 124 and following lists). This suggests that it was not Adamenko who signed the documents in 1938.

The Ivankiv district prosecutor at the time of the 1938 affair was also found alive in 1956. Evtikhii Onufr'evich Litvin, a Ukrainian and party member since 1927, was thirty-five years of age in 1938. In 1938, he had been presented by the NKVD district chief, Aleksandr Ivanovich Dunaev, with documents listing the alleged crimes of the arrested and the testimonies against them. Litvin stated in 1956 that at that time he had believed Dunaev: he had been young and had no experience as a prosecutor (he had only assumed his position in January 1938) and thought that the prosecutor should not interfere with the work of the NKVD. At the time, in 1938, he had received no instruction from above to supervise the investigative work of the district NKVD. Asked whether he had been aware that the NKVD officials had beaten the arrested and extracted confessions using impermissible methods, Litvin answered that he had received no official reports on this matter but that when some of the arrested were released in late 1938 and early 1939, and their cases were returned to him for further investigation, he had overheard them discuss being beaten (2:123–29).

The KGB reached the conclusion that there was no evidence that the alleged organiser of the POW, the priest Żych, was a Polish spy and determined that the 'references' used to convict the fifteen arrested were fictitious. Owing to the lack of *corpus delicti*, the fifteen executed were rehabilitated in 1956 (2:486–95, 513). This action was accompanied by the characteristic deceptions of the KGB. In response to enquiries from the relatives of the executed, the KGB gave false reports of their deaths: 'Your father' died on 14 November 1942 from liver cancer in the Gulag; 'Your husband' died in a labour camp on 28 July 1948 from a stomach ulcer, and the like (3:33, 42, 59 and the following lists).

The Ivankiv POW story did not end here. The file includes a rare set of documents from 1956 examining the responsibility of the former NKVD officials in the case. The former district NKVD chief, Dunaev, was living in Ivanovo, Russia, in 1956. He was fifty-six years of age then. Two years earlier, he had been dismissed from the secret police owing to illness. The Kiev military tribunal determined in 1956 that Dunaev should account for the 1938 affair: he had ordered the arrests of the fifteen men, had interrogated most of them himself and had indicted them. Other NKVD officials, A. A. Cherniak, V. A. Dubovoi, M. A. Khrapinskii, L. M. Pavlichev, I. D. Riaboi, I. B. Muspenko, Ia. A. Kudrik, Dolgushev and Novgorodskii, had played only secondary roles: therefore the KGB decided not to pursue them. (Some had died in the war or could not be located in 1956, in any case.) The

Kiev military tribunal sent Dunaev's material to Ivanovo for further action (2:560–63). What action, if any, was taken against him is not known.

Like ethnic Koreans in the Far East, ethnic Poles were politically suspect simply because of who they were. In a sense, the Poles were worse from the Soviet point of view, because they had a motherland to look to, whereas the Koreans did not at the time. It would not have been surprising if the ethnic Poles had been uprooted from Ukraine (and Belarus) and deported to the hinterland en masse in 1937–38, just as the Koreans were in 1937 from the Far East, the ethnic Germans in 1941 from Ukraine and Russia, and the Chechens in 1944 from Chechnya. In fact, in 1935 Poles on the western border, like Finns on the northern border, did begin to be deported. By the autumn of 1936, 15,000 families (69,283 ethnic Poles and Germans) had been deported.[27] These deportations did not extend to the Poles in the heartland, however. Why were the Poles not deported wholesale as the Koreans were?

In some respects, the terror campaign of 1937–38 was an extension of the borderland operations to the heartlands of Ukraine, Belarus and Russia. The Polish Operation targeted anyone with Polish connections. Yet it did not uproot the Poles. Perhaps there were too many (about half a million in Ukraine alone). It is also a fact that the ethnic Poles in Ukraine were far more integrated than the Koreans in the Far East. In other words, Poles were part and parcel of Ukrainian society at the time. (Indeed, the head of the Ukrainian Communist Party from 1928 to 1938, Stanislav Vikent'evich Kosior, was an ethnic Pole born in Wegrów, which had been part of Imperial Russia but is now in Poland. He was arrested in 1938 and executed in 1939 as a Polish spy and a POW leader.) Likewise, for all the ethnic, religious and linguistic differences between Poles and Ukrainians (and Belarusans), distinctions were often not evident even to those directly concerned. Determining who the Poles were was no easy matter. In all likelihood, a wholesale deportation appeared unrealisable.

The terror of 1937–38 in general and the Polish Operation in particular were reflections of the tense international situation in which the Soviet Union found itself in the 1930s. The Soviet people knew that they could not speak their minds freely. None of the alleged 'counter-revolutionary remarks' quoted in the present chapter ('Poland will capture Ukraine soon, and we'll begin to live well as we did before the Revolution' and the like) can be confirmed as actually having been spoken. But the ideas no doubt circulated widely in Soviet society, and the NKVD officials would have been familiar with them.

The circulation of these 'counter-revolutionary' ideas meant that war was the central theme of Soviet political life in the 1930s. For many, war was something to be feared, for it would bring death and destruction. However, for others war was to be welcomed, for it might bring down the Soviet government just as World War I had brought down the tsarist government. Stalin suspected that there were many people who entertained such hopes. In his view Poles stood out among them. In the midst of the Polish Operation, he received word from Ezhov on its progress. A 14 September 1937 report stated that as of 10 September 23,216 people had been arrested in the country as a whole, 7,651 in Ukraine. Stalin cheerfully added his note: 'To Ezhov. Very good! Dig up and clean out, henceforth too, this Polish espionage filth. Eliminate it *in the interests of the Soviet Union.*'[28] In 1940, not long after Stalin had invaded Poland in collusion with Hitler, he had most of the captured Poles (mainly officers) executed in the infamous Katyn Massacre).[29] The victims numbered almost 22,000. Alongside them, numerous residents of former Polish territory were executed as well. They were all deemed spies and subversives.

As he said of the Far East in 1937 (see p. 126), Stalin feared that Ukraine's western borderlands were 'not Soviet': there the Poles ruled. So it was necessary to terrorise the areas in the most determined manner. It is telling that of the 225,039 people arrested in 1937–38 on charges of espionage, as many as 101,965 or 45 percent were arrested as 'Polish spies'. The latter constituted by far the largest 'espionage contingent', followed by 'Japanese spies' (52,906, or 23.5 percent), 'German spies' (39,300, or 17.5 percent) and 'Latvian spies' (18,861, or 8.4 percent).[30] The terror was a pre-emptive strike in preparation for war.

CHAPTER 13

The Case of a Trotskii

What's in a Name?

Lev Davidovich Bronshtein (Trotskii) was a famous Russian revolutionary, often credited alongside Vladimir Il'ich Ul'ianov (Lenin) for the success of the October 1917 Revolution which laid the foundations for the first socialist state in history. Trotskii is the name that Bronshtein adopted before the Revolution. Like most revolutionaries, he did so for both pragmatic (he had to work underground) and symbolic reasons. Trotskii is said to have adopted his new name because it implied 'resistance' and 'defiance' (from the German word *Trotz* meaning defiance). Ul'ianov adopted 'Lenin' (which may have come from the Siberian Lena River or from the Russian word *lenivyi*, meaning 'lazy' and 'idle') and Iosif Vissarionovich Dzhugashvili adopted 'Stalin' (derived from the Russian word *stal'*, meaning 'steel'). After Lenin's death in 1924 Trotskii was defeated in a power struggle with Stalin and expelled in 1929. From that time the name of the October hero Trotskii was considered an official curse word in the Soviet Union. Trotskii was branded a Fascist spy and conspirator against the Soviet Union. Untold numbers of Soviet citizens were subsequently arrested and executed as Trotskyites. In 1940, on the order of Stalin, Trotskii was assassinated in exile in Mexico. The name and face of Trotskii disappeared so completely from the Soviet Union that most people did not even know what he looked like until his photographs and portraits began to be published again at the time of *glasnost'* in the late 1980s.

Almost all of Trotskii's kin who stayed in the Soviet Union fell victim to Stalin's terror. In spite of Stalin's 1935 dictum, 'A son does not answer for his father', by 1937, the year of the Great Terror, he had declared that he meant to destroy the kin of all of his enemies: 'we will destroy each and every enemy even if he is an old Bolshevik; we will destroy all his kin, his family.'[1]

What if one were indeed a Trotskii? Although the name was not widespread, there were people whose real surname was Trotskii. For a number of real Trotskiis, their name became their nemesis, drawing the attention of the authorities to them and resulting in their repression for alleged anti-Soviet activities in the 1930s. When their cases were revisited in the 1980s and 1990s, each without exception was declared innocent and rehabilitated. Other than the fact that none was a party member, all that they appear to have had in common is the Trotskii surname.

Frantsishek Trotskii (Franciszek Trocki), born in 1889 in Berdychiv, Ukraine, was a Catholic parish administrator for small towns near Proskuriv (present-day Khmel'nyts'kyi). He was arrested in 1928 and sentenced to ten years in a labour camp for anti-Soviet, anti-Semitic and pro-Polish propaganda. In 1932 he was sentenced to death for allegedly being part of an anti-Soviet group of Catholic priests in the Gulag. As part of an exchange of political prisoners, however, Trotskii was released and returned to Poland shortly thereafter. His subsequent fate is unknown.[2] Veniamin Vasil'evich Trotskii was born into a priest's family in Tver', Russia, in 1906. On 21 March 1930 he was arrested, charged with anti-Soviet propaganda and on 3 December 1930 was sentenced to ten years in the Gulag. His subsequent fate is unknown.[3] Isaak Moiseevich Trotskii was born in Odesa in 1906. Like his revolutionary namesake, he was a Jew, but he did not belong to the Communist Party. He had received a higher education and had become a historian in Leningrad. On 23 December 1936 he was sentenced to ten years' imprisonment on charges of terrorism. Like many others who escaped death in 1936, Isaak Trotskii was sentenced to be shot in October 1937 during the Great Terror campaign in the famous prison camp on the Solovki Islands, which had formerly been an equally famous old monastery.[4] Like Isaak Trotskii, Mikhail Nikolaevich Trotskii, a Ukrainian born in 1882 in Novhorod-Sivers'kyi in Ukraine, was not a party member. He worked as an accountant in Leningrad. Mikhail Trotskii was arrested on 8 October 1937, accused of terrorism and other crimes, and sentenced to death. He was executed on 20 December 1937.[5] According to data obtained in Kiev, another Trotskii, a religious man, D. V. Trotskii, born in 1904, was executed on 29 September 1937.[6]

Leonid Pavlovich Trotskii

Fortunately for historians, there is one Trotskii who survived the Stalin years in labour camps and whose file provides substantial information about his alleged political crimes. His case supports the conjecture that, like many others, he was repressed largely because of his name: he was declared guilty by association.

Leonid Pavlovich Trotskii lived in Kiev in the 1930s.[7] He was born in Białystok, Poland, in 1911. (The city was part of the Russian Empire then.) According to his own account, he moved to Russia proper in 1914 as a war refugee, but in 1915 his mother died, leaving him and his siblings (a brother and a sister) in the custody of their father, an accountant. The latter was too busy to supervise his children, and Leonid Trotskii ran away from home in 1917 at the age of six, living the life of a waif until 1921, when he was found by his father. He then lived with him until 1928, completing five years at a village school. From 1929 he worked to support himself. In his confession, he stated that he had been a waif and a 'degenerate' and had hated the Soviet government. He was 'parasitically minded' but, forced by necessity (apparently a reference to his marriage to Galina Petrovna), had begun to work (15–15z.v).

In his file Trotskii is described as an ethnic Russian even though his parents, like himself, were born and raised in Poland (21). (At one point, however, he is said to be a Pole, perhaps because he was born in Poland.) At one time he was a member of the Komsomol, but his membership lapsed, most likely because he failed to pay his membership dues. Relatively well educated for the time, he worked as a clerk for the Paramilitary Defence of Water Transport in Kiev until 20 July 1938, when he was arrested. At the time of his arrest, his daughter was one and a half years old. Accused of having entertained hostility towards the Soviet government and engaged in anti-Soviet activity, he was sentenced on 4 December 1939, nearly a year and a half later, to five years of correctional labour, which he served in Tavda in the Urals (76). It is not clear when he was released, but three times, in 1939, 1948 and 1949, he appealed in vain for rehabilitation. After Stalin's death, in 1960–61 the KGB and the prosecutor's office re-examined his case but found no grounds for rehabilitation. On 8 September 1988 Trotskii died at the age of seventy-seven without rehabilitation. In 1989, when

39: The 'mug shot' of Leonid Pavlovich Trotskii.

the Soviet government finally began the process of his rehabilitation, it could not find his wife and daughter. In March 1990, however, his wife, now signing herself Galina Petrovna Kiprova, wrote to the KGB regarding Trotskii. (It is not known whether their marriage ended in divorce and, if so, when.) As part of her communication, Kiprova included a letter (and drafts) Trotskii had written (but never sent) to the Soviet leader Mikhail Sergeevich Gorbachev before his death. Kiprova added that Trotskii had worked all his life even though he was not in good health and that one day in 1988 he had gone to work, collapsed and two days later died (183). What kind of job he held at the age of seventy-seven she did not specify.

The letter to Gorbachev was dated 10 October 1987 and bore his home address, 21 Amal'chyk Street, Flat 75, Kiev. In it, Trotskii expressed his desire to have the brand of 'enemy of the people' removed from his name. Aware that he did not have much longer to live, he wrote, 'I have absolutely no time left' and 'the time for life has gone'. He was desperate. He said that he needed to continue to work, but that

Москва - Кремль Ц.К. КПСС тов. Горбачёву
Михаилу Сергеевичу.

от гр. Троцкого Леонида Павловича
рожд. 1911 г. VIII м. прожив. Киев-206, А.Малышк, 21-75
Просьба.

По необходимости хотел еще поработать, по годам
и самочувствию, работа сторожем для меня приемлема.
В отделе кадров сторожей мне сказали прийти через
неделю - пришёл мне ответили Вас проверяли и вот из-за
прошлого зачислить на работу не можем, я бы уже не
писал о далёком прошлом, прошло 50 лет тому назад.
В 1938 году я был арестован как враг народа, пол года
четыре "следователя"-садиста, уничтожая морально
и физически требуя какие-то дикие и непостижимые
уму признания - добили меня до создания полного безразли-
чия к жизни, я плакал как ребёнок не от физической боли
а от морального уничтожения и о невозможности дока-
зать невиновность перед Родиной. Описать ужасы след-
ствия не возможно, это фашистские пытки я под-
писывал чистые листы бумаги, а садисты писали что
хотели, мне было безразлично лишь бы скорей закончились муки
Без суда пробыл в заключении пять лет.
Я прожил в труде много лет и как каждый человек
заканчиваю своё земное существование, инициативы
чувствую осталось немного, очень прошу снять с меня
прикреплённый пол века тому назад ярлык "враг народа".

40: The letter Trotskii addressed to Gorbachev in 1987.

when he applied for a security guard job, he was denied on the grounds of his 'past'. He recalled how four 'sadistic' interrogators (Kornberg, Kamenev, Kniazev and 'S-something') had destroyed him morally and physically, demanding 'wild and incomprehensible confessions'. The torture he suffered had reduced him to a state of total indifference to life, leaving him to 'cry like a baby not from physical or moral pain but from moral devastation and from the impossibility of showing his innocence'. It is impossible, Trotskii emphasised, to describe the horror of 'Fascist' torture. In the end, he had put his signature on clean sheets of paper on which the 'Fascists' then wrote whatever they wanted, but he was indifferent, only wishing to get the torture over with as soon as possible. This letter, according to Trotskii, was 'the last cry of my soul' (184–86). Sadly, the last cry of his soul was not heard at the time. In April 1990, Kiprova received a letter from the KGB declaring Trotskii's rehabilitation (the accusations against him were 'without foundation') (177).

Trotskii's 'Crime'

Trotskii's 'crime' was that he allegedly composed and propagated an anti-Soviet poem, a rephrasing of Aleksandr Pushkin's famous 'Ruslan and Liudmila' (1820) (which inspired Mikhail Glinka's opera *Ruslan and Liudmila* [1842]). The original poem starts with:

> By the sea stands a green oak tree;
> A golden chain strung round it:
> And on the chain a learned cat
> Day and night circles round it;
> Walking right, he sings a song,
> Walking left, he tells a tale.
> Such marvels! There, a woodsprite wonders,
> A mermaid sits in the tree.[8]

The verses were so well known that any Soviet citizen could recite them by heart. But, as was often the case, the famous lines were rephrased to other ends too. Trotskii was accused of paraphrasing the classic Russian poem in the following way (74zv.):

> By the sea stands a green oak tree;
> The golden chain was taken to Torgsin;
> The water-nymph was not given a passport
> And the wood-sprite was exiled to the Solovki
> Now no sea is there
> There now shines a star
> And Stalin tells fairy tales
> About the achievements of the Five-Year Plan.

This was sharply critical of the state of affairs in the 1930s. At the time of the Great Famine, people sold their valuables to Torgsin to survive, making it a symbol of the way the state exploited its citizens' hidden resources for the sake of industrialisation. (For Torgsin, see p. 274, note 6.) During the famine years of 1932–33, people traded their valuables for food provisions at the Torgsin stores simply to survive. The Soviet government made a profit of 6 million roubles through trading in Torgsin in 1931; the figure then increased dramatically to 49.2 million in 1932 and 106.3 million in 1933, almost eighteen times the 1931 level.[9] Therefore people are said to have read Torgsin as an acronym: *Tovarishchi Rossiia Gibnet Stalin Istrebliaet Narod* ('Comrades, Russia Is Perishing, Stalin Exterminates the People'). In a similar vein, the passport in the poem refers to an internal passport system introduced at the time of the Great Famine, whereby those without a passport were prohibited from living in the cities. Peasants were not issued with passports. By fiat, therefore, all peasants were relegated to second-class citizenship. Many peasants, suspected of opposition to collectivisation and de-kulakisation as well as to the government's harsh grain procurements, were arrested and exiled to the Gulag on the Solovki Islands. Stalin boasted of having fulfilled the first Five-Year Plan (1928–32) of economic development in just four years, but insofar as it was accomplished it was done at the cost of famine, destitution and death. Stalin's tales of success are described in this poem as fairy tales.

Given that numerous people were arrested and executed for similar satirical poems and anecdotes, Trotskii was actually very lucky to have survived, having been arrested towards the end of the Great Terror. Had he been arrested in, say, the autumn of 1937, he would certainly have been executed. Because Trotskii suffered from tuberculosis and his condition worsened in detention, he was spared interrogations for a month (143–55). This also helped. By the time they resumed, the mass terror operations were coming to an end, with Stalin's chief executioner, Nikolai Ezhov, removed from his position as the head of the NKVD. As a result, in the relatively lenient post-Great Terror climate, Trotskii's case was examined by the Special Board of the NKVD in Moscow, which sentenced him to 'merely' five years of correctional labour.

In the end Trotskii was exonerated of his alleged 'anti-Soviet' activities. The poem itself was critical of Stalin and the Soviet regime and could be characterised as 'anti-Soviet', according to the definition in use at the time. The question remains, however, who actually wrote and recited the poem in question.

Poems, songs and anecdotes critical of Stalin and the Soviet regime were legion. Traditionally, Ukraine, the 'land of free Cossacks', was a fertile ground for such popular artistic creations directed against the central government. After the collectivisation and de-kulakisation of the countryside, and particularly at the time of the Great Famine in which millions of people died, such 'anti-Soviet' utterances were reported widely. For example, one such ditty goes:

> They've signed men up for the kolkhoz
> Now they lay their plans
> Potatoes the men will eat
> Without butter, without cream.[10]

Another one runs:

> Lenin plays the accordion,
> Stalin dances the hopak,
> Whilst Ukraine lives
> On but one hundred grams [a day].[11]

Yet another:

> I joined the kolkhoz
> In a new skirt
> I leave the kolkhoz
> Naked up to the bellybutton.[12]

People knew that one could be arrested for expressing such sentiments:

> I was summoned to the NKVD
> And yelled at for songs
> I complained that I was starving
> But they did not give me bread.[13]

Clearly, songs such as that allegedly written by Trotskii were not uncommon.

Who composed the poem in question? Almost certainly not Trotskii. According to the case file, it first surfaced when a witness, Nadezhda Nishchenko (Mal'tseva), an assistant bookkeeper in Trotskii's workplace, wrote it down while being interrogated by the NKVD.

The secret police worked hard to find subversive political meanings in songs sung by people. Yet they also knew that silence could be just as expressive. When people cautiously kept silence, the police found it suspicious. Whether Trotskii was vocal or silent, it seems likely that he attracted the attention of the police because of his name.

Interrogations and Testimonies

An examination of Trotskii's file reveals the way in which the case was constructed out of bits of fabricated evidence from two main witnesses. Initially, Nishchenko, interrogated on 13 February 1939, maintained that she personally had not heard any anti-Soviet songs, remarks or anecdotes from Trotskii. Then she noted that she did remember an occasion, a meeting with him, during which she had recited a paraphrased poem of Pushkin to him. It was of an anti-Soviet nature. She insisted that she had slandered the Soviet government and the Communist Party without realising it. In Kharkiv in 1933, someone whose name she did not remember had recited the poem to her by chance. She admitted that she had later recited it to Trotskii but to no one else. When asked why she had recited it to him, Nishchenko responded that as they strolled in a park together Trotskii had cited Pushkin's 'Ruslan and Liudmila', which reminded her of the reworked version she had heard in Kharkiv. Asked how Trotskii reacted to the poem when she recited it, Nishchenko answered, 'I don't remember, but in any case, he made no remarks to me.' Further interrogated about Trotskii's 'anti-Soviet manifestations', Nishchenko responded that there were no such incidents (48–51).

Before Nishchenko was interrogated, however, another witness, Tamara V. Murashko, an office worker in Trotskii's workplace, had told an incriminating story against him. Interrogated on 5 September 1938, Murashko noted (35zv.):

> For the purpose of inciting hostility towards the organs of the NKVD [Trotskii] said that arrests were being made wrongly, that innocent people were being arrested—this embitters people and creates an army of the discontented with the Soviet government. He made various remarks about the organs of the NKVD shooting numerous arrested people on Lysa Hill [in Kiev] and said that he himself was an eyewitness.

Murashko provided further incriminating evidence against Trotskii, saying that he had called the 1937 Supreme Soviet elections 'puppet comedies' which were of no benefit to the Soviet people. Murashko accused Trotskii of not wanting to change his surname: even though his superiors had provided him with the money to do so legally, he had failed to change it. She alleged that it was useful for him to live and conduct 'counter-revolutionary' agitation under the name of Trotskii (16, 35zv.).

Trotskii's initial interrogation records are missing from his case file. In fact, his case file is in poor shape generally, the pagination having been mixed up by an archivist. Trotskii was first interrogated by someone called Kornberg. In his 25 April 1961 rehabilitation testimony Trotskii noted that he did not know why he had been arrested in 1938. Kornberg tortured him over several months to extract confessions from him that he was a Polish military officer and had collected intelligence information. He was forced to sign such confessions (143–46). However, the records of his interrogation by Kornberg are missing from Trotskii's case file. When questioning resumed after Trotskii's tuberculosis break, he had a new interrogator, Kniazev. On 4 September 1938 Trotskii confessed further (16):

> In order to arouse hostility towards the organs of the NKVD among colleagues, I tried to show that arrests were made wrongly and that in most cases innocent people were being arrested, defending the enemy of the people Kossior [Stanislav Vinkent'evich, a former leader

of Ukraine, then under arrest and in 1939 executed] and others. I also
tried to show that the members of the government lived as did the
ministers in the old days, not caring about the good of the people. I
hinted at a quick death for the Soviet government and lauded Fascist
Germany, slandering the situation of workers in the Soviet Union.

Some phrases in Murashko's testimony and Trotskii's confession are
almost identical. Surely both were written by their interrogators.

In 1961, Trotskii maintained that his second and third interrogators
did not torture him since, after being broken by Kornberg, he simply
signed all of the confessions the interrogators submitted to him. It was
from the second and third interrogators that he first learned about the
paraphrased Pushkin poem. There was another variation as well: 'At
an oak tree Comrade Stalin tells fables about the Five-Year Plan ...'.
Trotskii insisted that he had never heard such poems and never recited
them to anyone. He knew Nishchenko, but she had never recited the
Pushkin paraphrase to him (147–48, 150)

In 1961 the witnesses were interrogated again. The first police
interrogator, Kornberg, could not be located: suffering from tuberculosis,
he had been fired from the NKVD before the war (167). (It is not known
whether Kornberg caught tuberculosis from Trotskii.) Nishchenko was
interrogated in February 1961. She testified that she and Trotskii had
never discussed political subjects and that she had never heard any anti-
Soviet anecdotes or remarks from him. She acknowledged that Trotskii
liked poems. When he recited Pushkin's famous poem to her, she in
turn recited, 'without any malicious intent', the paraphrased anti-Soviet
poem she had heard in Kharkiv. After that, according to Nishchenko,
Trotskii recited it to other people (106–12). In other words, Nishchenko
confirmed her 1939 testimony.

Like Nishchenko, Murashko was interrogated in February 1961. This
time she testified that her husband had been arrested in December 1937.
(Most likely he had been executed.) Murashko said that Trotskii must
have believed that she was ill-disposed towards the Soviet government
because of her husband's arrest and he therefore recited the 'anti-Soviet'
poem in question. She added, however, that she did not remember
where this took place or who the poem's author was. There is no
indication in the records that she was familiar with the actual content
of the poem (96–103).

Other witnesses were also interrogated in 1961. They all testified that they had never heard anti-Soviet anecdotes or remarks from Trotskii. Some added that Trotskii was 'not serious' and was fond of inconsequential chattering (120).

The most trustworthy testimony would appear to be Nishchenko's. She was more or less consistent in 1939 and 1961. So Trotskii might have heard the 'anti-Soviet' poem from her. Yet it is also possible that Nishchenko was wrong in both 1939 and 1961: in the first case (1939), she might have been frightened and therefore implicated Trotskii; in the second (1961), she might have feared contradicting her earlier testimony. In 1961 Trotskii himself rejected Nishchenko's account. As noted earlier, in 1961 the KGB found no grounds for rehabilitation because Murashko and Nishchenko confirmed their earlier testimonies.

A perusal of the Trotskii file suggests that he was originally arrested as a Polish spy or agent because he was born in Poland. He was then tortured into confessing his 'crime'. Trotskii was not originally accused of reciting the paraphrased anti-Soviet Pushkin poem. As for Murashko's original testimony, it had nothing to do with the alleged anti-Soviet poem. In any case, it lacks specificity and is full of the set phrases that constituted the standard Soviet police language of the time. By late 1938, the political climate had changed significantly, with the removal of NKVD chief Ezhov and the beginning of an attack on his 'excessive' terror. Trotskii might have been released then, but he was not. Most likely, the reason lay with his surname. Meanwhile, his colleague Nishchenko was interrogated. It is likely that Nishchenko had been intimidated (or threatened) into providing compromising evidence against Trotskii. The fact that she is referred to in the records by both her maiden name (Mal'tseva) and her husband's name (Nishchenko) probably means that her husband had been arrested and that she had been forced to revert to her maiden name (almost certainly she had divorced her husband). It is also likely that she had been recruited by the secret police and that she wanted to protect herself, fearing that her knowledge of the 'anti-Soviet' poem might be exposed by someone else. Equally probably she was a reluctant witness: this may explain why in her 1939 testimony Nishchenko did not initially accuse Trotskii outright. Whatever the case, the charges against Trotskii changed abruptly. Mention of his Polish connections was dropped and a charge of 'anti-Soviet' propaganda was introduced instead. Trotskii pleaded guilty and, owing to the new political circumstances, received 'merely' five years. Immediately thereafter, Trotskii began to appeal for rehabilitation, but failed to obtain it before his death in 1988.

Interestingly, it is noted in Trotskii's 8 August 1939 bill of indictment that 'in view of the fact that the main witnesses cannot be summoned to the court for operational reasons ([for fear of] disclosing the work methods of the NKVD), the case is to be subject to the Special Board of the NKVD of the USSR' in Moscow (75–76). This almost certainly means that Murashko and Nishchenko were NKVD agents or informers. They were obliged to work for the secret police because Murashko's husband (and possibly Nishchenko's as well) had been arrested. All in all, it is certain that Trotskii was innocent of the crime of which he was accused in 1939. Indeed, he was exonerated of all charges in 1990, more than half a century after his conviction.

This leaves us with the question: where did the alleged anti-Soviet poem originate? If Nishchenko's testimony is credible, then it originated in Kharkiv in 1933. This may well be true, because, as discussed earlier, similar poems, songs and anecdotes circulated quietly and often clandestinely throughout the country. Yet it is more likely that it was an invention of Nishchenko or of some other NKVD functionary and that Nishchenko acted as a provocateur to entrap Trotskii, who was fond of poems, with a politically paraphrased poem of Pushkin. In 1961 Trotskii testified that he first heard it from his interrogators. It is possible, however, that he actually did first hear it from Nishchenko and understood that it was a provocation and therefore made no comment on it.

In this case, as in numerous others, the truth is elusive. However, the voice of a man whose life was ruined by Stalin's terror machine still comes through. He demanded rehabilitation from the Gulag and continued to do so until his death half a century later. He was rehabilitated posthumously.

The Realm of the Unknowable

It is tempting to believe that 'Stalin tells fairy tales/ About the achievements of the Five-Year Plan' was the creation of a powerless, 'ordinary' Soviet citizen such as Trotskii. If that were the case, Soviet citizens, far from being politically integrated into the Stalinist regime or silenced by the terror machine, retained a critical sense and continued to give voice to it, if only indirectly.

Here, however, one enters the realm of the unknowable. If, on the one hand, the poem *was* a popular creation, it reflected the suffering of at least one nameless person. If, on the other hand, it was an NKVD fabrication or embellishment, the functionary or functionaries responsible might have imagined that it reflected the sentiments of those whose political loyalty they suspected. In that case, clearly they believed that it was the true voice of 'enemies of the people'. Most likely Trotskii was no such 'enemy of the people'. Yet it is certain that there were people who were critical of the policies of the Soviet government and the Communist Party. To assume otherwise would mean vastly underestimating the humanity of those now dead. Of course, being critical did not mean being an 'enemy' or even being rebellious, although the NKVD considered otherwise.[14] The vast majority of people had by the 1930s learnt to endure in apparent silence. The NKVD, in turn, made every effort to uncover the true feelings of the people, even if that meant inventing them. It is quite likely that the NKVD inventions were then in turn appropriated by the people.

Oddly, Soviet leaders themselves knew about and enjoyed singing 'counter-revolutionary' songs of the following sort:

> Tell us, Kalinin, my boy,
> How the Five-Year Plan f[ucked] us up.[15]

While the leaders were laughing, the Soviet people sat in gaol or, if they were lucky, simply lived in fear. In the summer of 1937, a dark joke circulated in Moscow: '"How are you?"—"It's like being on a bus: half [of us] are standing and shaking, and the other half are sitting [in gaol]."'[16] One knows virtually nothing about Leonid Pavlovich Trotskii's actual thoughts concerning the paraphrased Pushkin poem. In private he may well have thought that it had merit. In all likelihood, he did not voice such a thought, because to do so would have meant losing his voice for ever. Trotskii, like many others who survived the worst phase of Stalin's terror, might have been released in 1939. He was not. His name predetermined his fate.

Epilogue

The cases examined here represent the tip of a massive iceberg. For each person discussed in these pages, at least ten thousand more died in the Great Terror of 1937–38 alone; millions more Soviet citizens died in the Great Famine, in exile and in the Gulag. However many people Stalin had killed by the secret police, many more were treated as suspects. Thus, in March 1941 the Soviet secret police had as many as 1,263,000 Soviet citizens on their register as possible 'anti-Soviet elements'.[1] Although Stalin never stopped politically motivated terror and killings, he did not repeat the Great Terror. Why this is so is as complex a question as why he started the Great Terror in the first place. For one thing, even though Stalin trusted no one, he could not kill everyone: the mass killings had to stop at some point. For another, Stalin probably concluded by late 1938 that the Great Terror had sufficiently terrorised those harbouring disloyal feelings towards his regime. In 1929 he had defended the famous play by Mikhail Bulgakov *Days of the Turbins* (an adaptation of his novel *The White Guard*), which described in sympathetic terms the anti-Red Turbins in Kiev during the Civil War of 1918–20, saying that it demonstrated to the audience the 'all-conquering power of Bolshevism' (*vsesokrushaiushchaia sila bolshevizma*).[2] In 1935 he said capital punishment instilled a sense of terror in the Soviet population.[3] In 1937, Stalin had reportedly said that 'it was necessary in cleansing the rear to terrorise the [Korean] district and the frontier so as to prevent any Japanese [espionage] work' (see p. 126). Judging by the cases discussed in this book, people were indeed scared and rendered helpless by the terror, however courageous and strong they may otherwise have been.

A perusal of police files shows that even the seemingly clearest cases involving foreign spies and anti-Soviet elements discussed in this book are not clear at all. The 'swan song' of the alleged monarchist Antonina Ivanovna Zhelikhovskaia, if at all genuine, was no more than a decade-old private musing. Nina Nikolaevna Bunge, of noble origin, was simply involved in private charity if her case file is to be believed. Lidiia Eduardovna Kronberg, horrified by the famine of 1932–33, was guilty of nothing more than wanting to escape and return to her homeland to die. The priest Andrei Grigor'evich Nademskii may have been unfavourably disposed to the atheist Soviet regime in the privacy of his mind, but available evidence suggests that he had nonetheless accepted, and worked within, the boundaries set by it. Leonid Pavlovich Trotskii enjoyed jokes, true, but there is no evidence to suggest that he harboured anti-Soviet designs. A substantial number of people discussed in the present book worked willingly or, more likely, unwillingly for the secret police. Yet they and all the other people discussed here were exonerated in the end, for there was no proof of the allegations against them. Certainly the rote phrases attributed to them were forced and the testimonies against them were fake (although some people may well have willingly given false testimonies to obtain material gains or settle personal scores).

The importance of the question of evidence cannot be overemphasised, for it is much too easy to read anti-Stalin resistance into police files and contend that the Great Terror was Stalin's response to 'a perceived immediate political threat' that was 'reaching dangerous levels'.[4] Stalin manipulated and fabricated evidence to prove the existence of 'enemies of the people' who 'posed such a serious threat that they had to be destroyed physically'. This was Stalin's elaborate trap for the world, including future historians. Stalin was a lover of history. He was conscious of his own historical legacy. He even kept in archives numerous execution orders he had signed. No historian should fall into Stalin's trap.[5]

The only 'crime' of the people discussed in the present book is that they came under suspicion of political disloyalty for various reasons during the 1930s. Critical or even subversive thoughts no doubt existed in Soviet society; so did dreams and fantasies of alternative political orders. Some even fantasised about killing Stalin.[6] In almost all cases, dreams and fantasies remained just that, though, and critical thoughts remained private. Sometimes people did whisper and confide privately.[7] Yet the very act of whispering aroused instant suspicion. True, loose tongues existed. The singing of songs like 'Kirov was killed, it's not enough, Stalin should have been killed' (see p. 227) was reported in many places; the perpetrators were mainly schoolchildren who did not yet know fear and simply enjoyed the irreverence of the words. Those with secret dreams and desires tended to keep silent in the 1930s. Instead, provocateurs used such illicit remarks and dreams for their own sinister ends. Indeed, the case files examined in the present book point to a widespread deployment of provocateurs by the police.

It seems mistaken to argue that in the 1930s the private sphere was unknown to the Soviet subject.[8] Stalin obviously did not think so. It was precisely the existence of this impenetrable private sphere that made him so suspicious of so many people. However, officially, the private as distinct from the public did not exist in Stalinist society. Therefore any suggestion of the private was taken as a sign of political deviance and, by implication, disloyalty. The public could not really subsume the private completely, but the private became deeply secretive. The 'secret' private sphere became part and parcel of the Soviet system, and individual citizens past masters of 'dissimulation'.[9] One of the key political words of the 1930s was 'double-dealing' (*dvurushnichestvo*)—public compliance and private doubt. Stalin equated critical thought with disloyalty and treason. Ever vigilant, he exhorted his entourage to follow his lead: 'You cannot daydream and sleep when you are in power.'[10] Taking no chances, Stalin had the politically suspect physically destroyed.

Ironically, forbidden thoughts and ideas were widely propagated by the official Soviet press through their reports on terrorist schemes, a fact often overlooked by historians of the Stalin era. Even school textbooks spread illicit ideas through their discussion of, for instance, the 1881 assassination of the 'Tsar Liberator' (Alexander II was so called because he emancipated the Russian serfs in 1861). This 'subversion' did not escape the attention of the powers-that-were. In 1937, Kaganovich denounced a newspaper article on the assassination of Alexander II as a signal to terrorists.[11]

Almost everyone terrorised was innocent of the crimes of which they were accused. Stalin, like his closest associates such as Molotov and Kaganovich, may have come to understand later that many innocent people had been killed in the terror. Yet he never hesitated to kill a hundred people to catch the one among them who really was a spy. In 1937, Stalin contended that if only 5 percent of the alleged enemies were genuinely enemies, it was still a big deal ('*esli budet pravda khotia by na 5%, to i eto khleb*').[12] According to Nikita Khrushchev, Stalin said at the time: 'Ten percent of the truth is still the truth. It requires decisive action on our part, and we will pay for it if we don't act accordingly.'[13] The cases discussed in this book suggest that even a ratio of 1:100 would be a vast exaggeration. In fact, there is not a single genuine case here.

It is not that spies and anti-Soviet elements did not exist. Poland, Japan, Germany and other countries worked hard to penetrate the Soviet Union. The master Japanese spy, Major General Shun Akikusa, who was head of the intelligence department of the Kwantung army in Manchuria in 1945, was taken prisoner by the invading Soviet army. Interrogated in Moscow, Akikusa confessed that when most Soviet citizens in Manchukuo returned to the Soviet Union in the wake of the 1935 sale of the East China Railway to Manchukuo, he managed to hire approximately twenty of them for espionage work. (It is estimated that approximately 25,000 *Kharbintsy* returned to the Soviet Union in 1935–36. The twenty 'spies', then, constitute fewer than one in every thousand.) And only three of those actually reported back, the first one from Irkutsk, the second from Vladivostok and the third from somewhere Akikusa could no longer remember. He had no further contact with these three, however, and received no information from them. Between 1933 and 1936 he sent twelve spies (mostly émigré Russians) into Soviet territory. Although they were supposed to return after collecting military information, 'almost no one' did.[14] Akikusa's confessions cannot be taken unquestioningly at face value, but parts of them (concerning the despatching of émigré Russians into Soviet territory and its very limited utility, for example) can be confirmed by reference to the statements made by others involved in anti-Soviet espionage in Manchukuo.[15] Perhaps the spies Akikusa mentioned were caught and executed by the Soviet secret police. Yet it is also quite possible that some, if not most, were in fact Soviet agents. It is now known that in the 1930s in Eastern Siberia and the Far East the Soviet Union successfully operated counter-intelligence groups, fake anti-Soviet organisations working with the Japanese intelligence, eastern versions of the famous 'Trest' operation (see p. 284, note 6) called 'Dreamers', 'Maki-Mirage' and the like.[16] In any case, the Japanese feared that their spies were double or triple agents. The Soviets had the same fear regarding the spies they themselves sent to Manchukuo, Japan, Poland and elsewhere. Like Akikusa, Hans Pickenbrock, the head of espionage in the German military intelligence, testified that the German use of spies (mainly Poles, Latvians and Lithuanians despatched to Soviet territory) failed to yield satisfactory results.[17]

How many actual spies and convinced anti-Soviet elements were among those executed in 1937–38 is now impossible to determine, for at the time mere suspicion was taken as evidence of crime. According to Artem Sergeev, Stalin's adopted son, Stalin was capable of seeing sinister intentions behind simple accidents, including the aeroplane crash in which Sergeev's father was killed in 1921, if they had political consequences.[18] Exactly the same logic operated in an April 1937 decision taken by the Politburo regarding a fire that had broken out at the residence of one of its members, Kaganovich: the Politburo announced that it 'consider[ed] this fire not an accidental event but one organised by enemies'.[19] Almost certainly Stalin dictated this resolution. According to Molotov, speaking in defence of Stalin, evidence was not important since 'there is no smoke without fire'. Stalin 'played it safe' by letting 'an extra head fall' so that there would be 'no vacillation at the time of war and after the war'.[20] It is very telling that while Molotov denied the very existence of, let alone having signed, the infamous 'imperialist' secret protocol to the 1939 Non-Aggression Pact with Nazi Germany (which dismembered Poland and divided much of Eastern Europe between the Soviet Union and Germany), he readily acknowledged having signed death warrants against untold numbers of Soviet citizens in 1937–38.[21]

Some people who were repressed under Stalin have never been rehabilitated. Some were former secret police officials who were actively involved in Stalin's terror. According to an estimate by the Ukrainian journal *V mire spetssluzhb*, those who have not been rehabilitated were mainly 'Polish and German spies' and those who collaborated with the German occupiers during World War II. In Russia, it is said that 90,000 such people were denied rehabilitation in the 1990s. In Ukraine, some had their rehabilitations subsequently annulled.[22] A 1946 report from Luhan'sk, a city in eastern Ukraine, suggests that most collaborators were not those assumed to have been disaffected with the Soviet system such as former kulaks and repressed people. 'The majority, according to the NKVD, were those who at first glance had no reason to be disaffected.'[23] Yet at least some, like the individuals discussed in this book, may have been innocent. A perusal of their interrogation records shows that the same mechanism of torture, manipulation and fabrication of evidence was at work.[24] Access to the case files of those who have not been rehabilitated is still restricted. Until all evidence is subject to open scrutiny, one cannot take any allegation at face value.[25]

Foreign factors were the leitmotiv of the Great Terror. In terrorising the country, Stalin was fighting both for his own power and for the regime he had created. Using the spectre of war, he sought to disarm and destroy suspected enemies of the Soviet regime and thereby maximise internal security. The lives of untold numbers of people were ruined and terminated in the name of national security. Certain categories were hit particularly hard: people from formerly privileged classes such as nobles (Bunge and Zhelikhovskaia), immigrants from foreign countries (Ben-shu Kim, Angel'chik, Litvinov), fugitives and de-kulakised peasants (Gorodovenko, Stashchenko, Bigotskii), marginal people such as the poor and unemployed (Kravchenko), priests and their families (Moshinskaia, Nademskii, Zakharevich, Polishchuk), ethnic minorities (Poles, Germans, Latvians, Greeks, Koreans and others), people associated with foreigners (Goroshko, Vasil'eva, Al'bova, Shirer, Natanzon and many others, including foreign-born citizens and former prisoners of war). The secret police descended on these politically vulnerable people like vultures and sought to recruit them as informers, provocateurs and secret agents. The clergy were the ideal target. Some priests volunteered in order to protect themselves and their families, others were coerced. In either case, the police made full use of them to identify and incriminate others belonging to the same politically suspect categories. The latter constituted the majority of the alleged 'spies', 'traitors', 'anti-Soviet elements' and, more generally, 'enemies of the people' destroyed in 1937–38. The Great Terror was focused in design if not in its implementation.

The wide deployment of the politically suspect as informers and provocateurs was dangerous and self-defeating, for the police often did not trust the information supplied by those whose political loyalty they questioned in the first place. As a result, the police ended up destroying their own agents en masse.

The Great Terror came to a halt in late 1938, but political terror in the USSR in general did not: people continued to be arrested and executed, albeit on a more reduced scale. Nor did the outbreak of war in September 1939 (the Polish Campaign), the Winter War with Finland in November 1939 or war with Germany in June 1941 (Operation Barbarossa) stop the terror. The case of a woman who was executed in Kiev in July 1941 illustrates well the extraordinary callousness, brutality and inhumanity with which Stalin and his regime treated individual lives. On this occasion, it was not the spectre of war but a real war with rapidly advancing enemy forces that was used to justify her destruction. Like the other case files discussed in the present book, hers reveals a life, now utterly forgotten, that contained its own dramas but that meant nothing to the authorities. Like other files, upon close examination, this one also reveals the awful mechanism of terror.

Zoia Grigor'evna Vikhoreva

Zoia Grigor'evna Vikhoreva was born in Vologda, Russia, in 1899. Arrested on 28 June 1941, a few days after Hitler launched his Blitzkrieg against the Soviet Union, she was executed on 17 July 1941. Her alleged crime was 'anti-Soviet agitation'.[26] At the time of her arrest, she was working as a cleaner and errand woman (*kur'er*) at the Central Grocery Depot in Kiev, and was living in a dormitory at 94 Korolenko Street in Kiev. She was a non-party member and had only an elementary education. She came from a family of poor peasants and eked out a living as a cook before the October Revolution. According to her own account, her parents died when she was four. She was then taken to Kiev by a Mr Ershov. When Ershov died in 1913, his sisters did not wish to support her. Therefore she began to work as a maid at the Kaufmans. From 1917 to 1925 she performed day-labour work. Until 1930 she sometimes worked as a day labourer and at other times as a maid. In 1930–31 she then worked as a nurse and cleaner in 'Stalinka' (Stalino in eastern Ukraine?). From 1931 to 1938 she again worked as a day labourer. After this she was employed as a cleaner and errand woman at the 'Graviurchas' clock workshops at 2 Sofiia Street, Kiev. From 1941 until her arrest Vikhoreva worked at the Central Grocery Depot in the same capacity. She had no relatives in the Soviet Union or abroad, although from 1924 to 1927 she was married to Mikhail Iakovlevich Shukovak, a veterinary doctor. He abandoned her and their baby in 1927. The baby died in the same year (11–11zv.).

On 30 June 1941 Vikhoreva was interrogated. She was told to confess to having 'anti-Soviet conversations' in her workplace. Vikhoreva firmly denied the charges against her. Her interrogator, Sergeant Gofman, responded that he had evidence that on 22 June, the day of the German invasion, Vikhoreva had engaged in 'anti-Soviet conversations' in the office of the director of the depot. Told to confess, Vikhoreva still refused: she did not have any 'anti-Soviet conversations' there on 22 June 1941. She had talked to Aron Iu. Perepechai, a colleague. The conversation had concerned Perepechai's leaving to serve in the Red Army (11zv.).

It turned out that before Vikhoreva was arrested, Perepechai had been deposed by Gofman. Perepechai testified on 26 June 1941 that Vikhoreva had come to the director's office (where the depot commandant, Gersh Ovseevich Savorovskii, was also present) 'in an elevated mood'. This was shortly after Molotov's speech on 22 June 1941.[27] Without greeting anyone, Vikhoreva said, 'Thank God, Hitler'll come here soon.' To this Savorovskii said, 'You think that things'll get easier if Hitler comes to power. How about people, for example, with large families like Perepechai?' Vikhoreva, according to Perepechai, said, 'Well, but he's not a Communist, he won't be killed.' Perepechai reported this incident to the director Finkelshtein, who was apparently not in his office at the time (12–12zv.).

On the same day Savorovskii was deposed. He gave essentially the same testimony as Perepechai, though he added that in November or December 1940 Vikhoreva had uttered an 'anti-Soviet' remark in the presence of himself and his colleagues: 'What kind of life is there in the Soviet Union now when the working class cannot get anything? But in the old days one could get everything. In the old days I got 15 kg of meat [for] beefsteak and cooked it with sour cream, now we workers don't know life.' Savorovskii, like Perepechai, claimed that he had no personal score to settle with Vikhoreva (13–14).

Apparently these testimonies were not enough. On the day Vikhoreva was interrogated, another witness, Leiba Iankelevich Konoplianik, a cabinetmaker at the depot, was deposed. According to Konoplianik, Vikhoreva had complained in late 1940 at the office of the construction workers' union that she lived badly, saying, 'If the Germans came here, things would be better and there would be order' (15–15zv.).

On the same day, 30 June 1941, Vikhoreva was allowed to confront the three witnesses. The same secret police official, Gofman, was in charge of all three sessions. Perepechai confirmed his earlier testimony, which Vikhoreva denied (16–17). Savorovskii confirmed his testimony as well. This time Vikhoreva admitted that she had said in his presence, 'What kind of life is this when the working class cannot get anything? But in the old days one could get everything.' She denied his accusations regarding her alleged remarks about Germans, however (18–20). Konoplianik slightly modified Vikhoreva's alleged pro-German remarks: 'If the Germans came here, things would be better, there would be order and I'd live better.' Vikhoreva denied Konoplianik's testimony (21). In each session, Vikhoreva was asked whether she had any questions for her three accusers, to which she said no. She could have challenged the three accusers more aggressively.

Did Vikhoreva actually complain that her life in 1940 was worse than her life before the Revolution? No doubt her material existence in 1940 was impoverished. It would be surprising if she had nothing to complain about. Given her life as an orphan and a day labourer before the Revolution, however, it is hard to imagine that her pre-revolutionary life was better than her life in 1940. It is possible that, working as a maid at the Kaufmans, she could have bought 15 kg of meat and cooked beefsteak with sour cream. She may have told such a story to her colleagues at one point or another. The story could well have been misinterpreted, or interpreted with malice, by others. It is also possible that Vikhoreva's testimony was distorted or falsified by Gofman, that Vikhoreva gave up resisting during a moment of weakness, or that she felt threatened by Gofman. There is no compelling reason to believe her accusers' testimonies. They may have had personal scores to settle with her, even though they denied it. It is possible that they, like other 'witnesses', were forced by the police to give false accounts or that they were police agents or provocateurs. Most likely, Vikhoreva had been on the police list for some time as disgruntled and politically unreliable, and therefore potentially anti-Soviet.

The case file contains a subtle clue to understanding Vikhoreva's mind. She stood her ground on all points but one. The only concession she made concerned the testimony of her superior, Commandant Savorovskii. This may suggest that she was worried about losing her job, and so admitted to her alleged remark about the difference between pre-revolutionary and Soviet life. Given the events of 1937–38 Vikhoreva probably sensed instinctively that she faced execution for such an admission. Hoping against hope, though, she ignored the prospect of death and concentrated on retaining her job. However threatened she may have felt, she drew the line at admitting to false charges concerning Hitler and the Germans. Like many others in Kiev and elsewhere, she may have looked to the expected war with trepidation as well as with an unarticulated hope for release from a stifling life. Since 1933, people in Ukraine were often reported to have asked with expectation, 'When will Hitler come?' The question was often a provocation, just as the allegation against Vikhoreva may well have been a provocation.[28] Whatever private expectations she may have had, they would have remained private. There was suspicion, nonetheless, that her private sentiments were anti-Soviet. Her every utterance was therefore interpreted with suspicion.

Whatever the case, Vikhoreva was indicted in an extraordinarily speedy fashion; that is, on the day she was interrogated, 30 June 1941, two days after she was arrested. The process appears to have been accelerated by the circumstances of the war. The bill of indictment noted that, although there was no material evidence, her guilt had been 'sufficiently fully' established by three witnesses (25–26). Fortunately for Vikhoreva, this was not a time of extra-judiciary justice such as that which characterised 1937–38. The Soviet regime sought to establish a degree of legality in the wake of the Great Terror. So Vikhoreva was to be tried at the military tribunal of the NKVD in Kiev.

On 7 July 1941, when the German forces were making rapid advances on all western fronts, the military tribunal jurist Lupalo gave an order to the director of the Kiev prison where Vikhoreva was held that she be handed over to Convoy 227 of the NKVD troops and delivered for trial by 1 p.m. (33). It would seem that all traces of Vikhoreva ended there. Her case file has no records to show whether she was tried and, if so, what the result was.

Almost four years later, towards the end of the war when Kiev, liberated from the German occupiers, was struggling to return to normal, the military tribunal found time to revisit Vikhoreva's case. On 23 April 1945 it met for forty minutes, but could not proceed because the defendant, Zoia Grigor'evna Vikhoreva, could not be located (34). Vikhoreva appears not to have been tried as ordered in 1941 but evacuated in the face of advancing German troops. So, on that day four years later, the military tribunal made enquiries of the relevant offices

41: A monument stands on the former premises of the NKVD in the centre of Kiev (see above, Illustration 1). The inscription reads: 'To the Victims of Terror: the 1930s to the beginning of the 1950s' (photographed in 2006).

of the security forces and internal affairs (35). The government offices in Kiev could not locate Vikhoreva (39–40). The tribunal's efforts to find her continued into 1947. (Vikhoreva was not the only person it wanted to find. Its July 1947 enquiry to the First Special Department of the Ministry of Internal Affairs concerned another woman too, Ekaterina Nikonovna Ponomareva.)

Two months later (and more than two years after the initial enquiry), on 30 September 1947, an astonishing note was finally issued by the First Special Department in Moscow: according to the information it had, Vikhoreva was executed on 17 July 1941 following 'the resolution of a committee of the NKVD and the prosecutor's office of Ukraine' (44). Vikhoreva was thus executed nineteen days after she was arrested.

Why is it that Kiev had no record of Vikhoreva's fate but Moscow did, if it was Kiev that sealed it? Moscow did not clarify which committee made the decision to execute Vikhoreva. Did both Moscow and Kiev seek to pass the buck? There is no answer to these questions.

42: A grave pit in Bykivnia in the 1980s.

Vikhoreva was one of numerous prisoners in Kiev and elsewhere whom the Soviet government chose not to evacuate to the east but to shoot because it did not deem them worthy of life: it presumed her and others to be guilty without trial. Instead of expending resources on evacuating them, it had them shot. Under Stalin, a trial was a legal luxury in any case, particularly at a time of emergency.

Vikhoreva was officially rehabilitated in 1989 (50). It turns out that, like so many others discussed in this book, she, too, was buried in one of the Bykivnia mass graves.[29] So in the end she became part of the statistics of those executed under Stalin. She had no relatives and no one appeared interested in her fate.

Killings continued even when the country faced the mortal danger of defeat in the war against Germany. Following the logic of Stalinist politics, the killings continued precisely because of people like Vikhoreva who, the police alleged, aided the external enemy from within through 'subversive' remarks and actions, thereby putting the country in greater danger.

Stalin retained power, won the war and kept the Soviet regime intact. He insisted that the Great Terror saved the country. His critics reject

43: A large cross that stands on the main site of the Bykivnia mass grave (photographed in 2006). The inscription reads 'Eternal Memory'.

the claim as preposterous, contending that the Soviet Union won the war *in spite of* Stalin and his terror.

The dead cannot speak. Consequently some people find it convenient to blame them. Some say with Molotov that 'there is no smoke without fire': someone like Vikhoreva must have been disposed against the Soviet regime, however cleverly she may have hidden her true sentiments. Others, like some former secret police interrogators, portray themselves as the true victims, maintaining that they were misled by the false confessions of those whom they had interrogated.[30] Of course, they do not speak of the intimidation, threats and torture to which they subjected people like Vikhoreva.

Historians may not be much better at deciphering the complex web of truth and untruth. Some see 'anti-Stalinist elements' everywhere and take 'fiction in the archives' for fact. (Thus they may present people like Vikhoreva as outspoken opponents of the Soviet regime.) Others, failing to comprehend the meaning of the forced silence of the dead, posit the 'Stalinist subject' as devoid of a private sphere. (They may depict people like Vikhoreva as incapable of entertaining their own private thoughts independent of the Stalinist universe.) The voices of the dead get lost in either case.

In Vikhoreva's case, as in nearly all others, the only records of the lives of the executed that are left are in their case files. Instead of 'spies', 'traitors' and 'anti-Soviet elements' who are so standardised and demonised as to appear faceless, one finds in these records concrete, individual lives with human faces. A scrutiny of the files, particularly the handwritten records that few have cared to read before, turns up subtle signs of forced confessions and false testimonies. It also yields the silenced voices of the dead which are buried in the detail. Although Vikhoreva, for instance, made a calculated concession to her accusers, she protested her innocence against charges of being a Hitler sympathiser. Many others voiced their innocence in their own way. Even when the arrested were completely broken, their forced confessions reveal their fear, despair and resignation.

The voices of the dead recovered in this book are those of men and women who faced unwarranted death in their own desperate ways. Stalin was certain that no one would remember them. The 'all-conquering power of Bolshevism' condemned them to oblivion, but it could not suppress their voices completely. Ironically, Stalin's efforts to extinguish their voices helped preserve them, in the depths of their case files.

Notes

Introduction

1. The classic work is Alexander Solzhenitsyn, *The Gulag Archipelago, 1918–1956*, 3 vols (New York, 1974–78). For more recent works, see Anne Applebaum, *Gulag: A History* (New York, 2003) and O. V. Khlevniuk, *The History of the Gulag: From Collectivization to the Great Terror* (New Haven, Conn., 2004).

2. See Michael Ellman, 'Soviet Repression Statistics: Some Comments', *Europe-Asia Studies*, 54:7 (2002).

3. V. P. Popov, 'Gosudarstvennyi terror v sovetskoi Rossii. 1923–1953 gg. (istochniki i ikh interpretatsiia)', *Otechestvennyi arkhiv*, 1992, no. 2, 28.

4. For the Soviet source, see RGASPI (Rossiiskii gosudarstvennyi arkhiv sotsial'no-politicheskoi istorii), f. 17, op. 162, d. 21, l. 149 and d. 22, l. 7. For a Mongolian account, see Mandafu Ariunsaihan (Mandah Ariunsaihan), 'Mongoru ni okeru daishukusei no shinsō to sono haikei', *Hitotsubashi ronsō*, 126:2 (2001). See also Shagdariin Sandag and Harry H. Kendall, *Poisoned Arrows: The Stalin–Choibalsan Mongolian Massacres, 1921–1941* (Boulder, Colo., 2000).

5. Rolf Binner and Marc Junge, 'Wie der Terror "Gross" Wurde: Massenmord und Lagerhaft nach Befehl 00447', *Cahiers du monde russe*, 2001, nos 2–4, 587–89.

6. See my 'Accounting for the Great Terror', *Jahrbücher für Geschichte Osteuropas*, 53:1 (2005).

7. See J. Arch Getty, '"Excesses Are Not Permitted": Mass Terror and Stalinist Governance in the Late 1930s', *Russian Review*, 61:1 (2002).

8. See, for instance, Vitaly Shentalinskii, *Arrested Voices: Resurrecting the Disappeared Writers of the Soviet Regime* (New York, 1993), A. L. Litvin (ed.), *Dva sledstvennykh dela Evgenii Ginzburg* (Kazan, 1994) and Pavel Chinsky, *Micro-histoire de la Grande Terreur: la fabrique de culpabilité à l'ère stalinienne* (Paris, 2005).

9. Catherine Merridale, *Night of Stone: Death and Memory in Russia* (London, 2000).

10. V. A. Nevezhin, *Zastol'nye rechi Stalina* (Moscow, 2003), 262.

11. Quoted in Dmitri Volkogonov, *Stalin: Triumph and Tragedy* (New York, 1991), 210.

12. See my *Stalin* (Harlow, 2005).

13. On 21 July 1937 Stalin sent a coded telegram to provincial party leaders and secret police officials, scolding some of them for treating torture as 'something criminal':

torture had been permitted by the Central Committee of the Communist Party (i.e., Stalin), 'as an exception', against suspected 'enemies of the people' who, even under detention, 'continued to fight against the Soviet government' (i.e., those who refused to confess). Stalin asked rhetorically why the socialist secret service should be more humane in torturing the 'inveterate agents of the bourgeoisie and the enemies of workers and peasants' than the bourgeois secret services were in torturing the 'representatives of the socialist proletariat'. (Reproduced in Oleg Mikhailov, 'Limit na rasstrel', Sovershenno sekretno, 1993, no. 7, 5.) Soon after torture began to be applied systematically. Stalin explicitly demanded torture in the case of certain individuals. On 13 September 1937, for example, he ordered: 'Beat up Unshlikht for not giving up the Polish agents.' On 13 March 1938 he directed: 'Beat Riabinin very hard—why did he not give up Vareikis?' (Lubianka. Stalin i glavnoe upravlenie gosbezopasnosti NKVD. 1937–1938 (Moscow, 2004), 352, 499. On 10 January 1939, i.e., after the end of the Great Terror, Stalin sent a coded telegram to the provinces, which praised the use of torture for accelerating the discovery of 'enemies of the people', but accused the NKVD of abusing the 1937 authorisation of torture in 'exceptional circumstances' and of 'converting an exception into a rule'. (Lubianka. Stalin i NKVD-NKGB-GUKR 'Smersh'. 1939–mart 1946 [Moscow, 2006], 14–15.) For Stalin's sanctioning of executions, see Dmitri Volkogonov, Stalin: Triumph and Tragedy (New York, 1991), 308, 323, 338–39, 422.

14. Carlo Ginzburg, The Cheese and the Worms: The Cosmos of a Sixteenth-Century Miller (Harmondsworth, 1982), ix.

15. In Soviet parlance, acts of political coercion (arrest, imprisonment, exile, forced labour and execution) were called 'repressions' and those who suffered them the 'repressed'. Where better English terms are wanting, these Russian terms are used in the present book.

16. For this point of view, see Stephen Kotkin, Magnetic Mountain: Stalinism as a Civilization (Berkeley, Calif., 1997), 336.

17. Oleg Kharkhordin, The Collective and the Individual in Russia (Berkeley, Calif., 1999), 270–78.

18. Quoted from my 'Communism and Terror', Journal of Contemporary History, 36:1 (2001), 199–200.

19. One survivor noted that a 'prisoner who capitulated could erect a fantastic guilt edifice which was much more convincing than anything the G.P.U. could have produced because he used real experiences and respected the laws of logic and chronology' (see Alex Weissberg, Conspiracy of Silence [London, 1952], 107). This may well be true of those tried at the show trials, but it is hardly the case with the 'ordinary people' discussed in the present book.

20. Natalie Zemon Davis, Fiction in the Archives: Pardon Tales and their Tellers in Sixteenth-Century France (Stanford, Calif., 1987).

21. See my 'How Do We Know What the People Thought under Stalin?' in Timo Vihavainen (ed.), Sovetskaia vlast'—narodnaia vlast'? (St Petersburg, 2003).

22. For an eloquent critique of such a false sense, see V. A. Tvardovskaia, 'Poet i vozhd'. Po povodu stat'i E. G. Primaka "Poet Aleksandr Tvardovskii i Verkhovnyi v gody Velikoi Otechestvennoi i posle nee"', Otechestvennaia istoriia, 2006, no. 4, 170–73.

23. See, for example, Jochen Hellbeck, Tagebuch aus Maskau 1931–1939 (Munich, 1996).

24. This was true of many earlier cases of Soviet terror, including the 1929–30 'Spilka Vyzvolennia Ukrainy' (Union for the Liberation of Ukraine) affair in which Ukrainian academics, teachers and others were implicated. See the vast volumes covering the case: Derzhavnyi arkhiv Sluzhby bezpeky Ukrainy (in Kiev), f. 67098fp.

25. *Vsesoiuznaia perepis' naseleniia 1937 g. Kratkie itogi* (Moscow, 1991), 59, 66. There is a concise history of pre-revolutionary Kiev in English: Michael F. Hamm, *Kiev: A Portrait, 1800–1917* (Princeton, New Jersey, 1993).

26. V. M. Nikol's'kyi, *Represyvna diial'nist' orhaniv derzhavnoi bezpeky SRSR v Ukraini (kinets' 1920-kh–1950-ti rr.): istoryko-statystychne doslidzhennia* (Donets'k, 2003), 402–4.

27. Computed from *Vsesoiuznaia perepis'*, 45, 47.

28. Mykola Rozhenko, *Sosny Bykivni svidchat': zlochyn proty liudstva*, vol. 2 (Kiev, 2001), 13–14.

29. For deportations from Kiev, see RGASPI, f. 17, op. 162, d. 21, l. 45.

30. *Memoirs of Nikita Khrushchev*, vol. 1 (University Park, Penn., 2004), 29. 'Mensheviks' and 'Socialists Revolutionaries' were socialist groups opposed to the Bolshevik regime. They had been banned. 'Trotskyist' (or 'Trotskyite') refers to supporters of L. D. Trotskii, a principal opponent of Stalin. Trotskii lost the power struggle to Stalin in 1927, was expelled from the country in 1929 and was assassinated in 1940 in Mexico on Stalin's order.

31. *Khrushchev Remembers* (Boston, Mass., 1970), 172.

32. Quoted in *Z arkhiviv VUChK-HPU-NKVD-KHB*, 1998, nos 1–2, 215.

33. Naum Korzhavin, *V soblaznakh krovavoi epokhi*, vol. 1 (Moscow, 2006), 92.

34. George O. Liber, *Soviet Nationality Policy, Urban Growth, and Identity Change in the Ukrainian SSR 1923–1934* (Cambridge, 1992), 189.

35. Quoted in *Z arkhiviv VUChK-HPU-NKVD-KHB*, 1998, nos 1–2, 215.

36. *Vsesoiuznaia perepis' naseleniia 1939 goda. Osnovnye itogi* (Moscow, 1992), 69.

37. For torture in a Kiev prison in 1937, see the account by a survivor, Mojshe Salzman, *Als Mosche Kommunist war: die Lebensgeschichte eines jüdischen Arbeiters in Polen und in der Sowjetunion unter Stalin* (Darmstadt, 1982), 213–43. Women, too, were tortured. See Iryna Boshko, 'Rik 1938-i, Kyiv, Luk'ianivs'ka v'iaznytsia', *Ukraina* (Kyiv), 1989, no. 20, 2–3.

38. Weissberg, *Conspiracy of Silence*, 421. This book has an arresting account of the torture he suffered in 1937 and 1938 in the NKVD prison in Kharkiv, Ukraine.

39. RGASPI, f. 17, op. 162, d. 21, l. 14.

40. *Pravo na repressii. Vnesudebnye polnomochiia organov gosudarstvennoi bezopasnosti (1918–1953)* (Moscow, 2006), 173–74.

41. Iurii Shapoval, Volodymyr Prystaiko and Vadym Zolotar'ev, *ChK-HPU-NKVD v Ukraini: osoby, fakty, dokumenty* (Kiev, 1997), 176.

42. Marc Jansen and Nikita Petrov, *Stalin's Loyal Executioner: People's Commissar Nikolai Ezhov, 1895–1940* (Stanford, Calif., 2002), 134, and *Tragediia sovetskoi derevni: kollektivizatsiia i raskulachivanie*, 5:2 (Moscow, 2006), 50–56, 550–51.

43. Quoted in Valerii Vasiliev, 'The Great Terror in the Ukraine, 1936–38', in Melanie Ilič (ed.), *Stalin's Terror Revisited* (Basingstoke, 2006), 153.

44. Nikol'skyi, *Represyvna*, 402–4.

45. Shapoval, Prystaiko and Zolotar'ev, *ChK-HPU-NKVD*, 437, 478, 502, 562.

46. No comprehensive statistics on the sexual ratio are available. An examination of

the executed in Leningrad in 1937–38 notes that less than 4 percent were women. Melanie Ilič, 'The Great Terror in Leningrad: A Quantitative Analysis', *Europe-Asia Studies*, 52:8 (2000), 1518. Ses also *idem*, 'The Forgotten Five Per Cent: Women, Political Repression and the Purges', in Ilič (ed.), *Stalin's Terror Revisited*, 131. The figure for Kiev is probably similar. When the bodies in mass graves in Vinnytsia to the southwest of Kiev were unearthed and counted by the German authorities during World War II, there were only 169 female ones out of a total of 9,432, or slightly less than 2 percent. See Ihor Kamenetsky (ed.), *The Tragedy of Vinnytsia: Materials on Stalin's Policy of Extermination in Ukraine during the Great Purge 1936–1938* (Toronto/New York, 1989), 104.

47. Mykola Rozhenko and Edit Bohats'ka, *Sosny Bykivni svidchat': zlochyn proty liudstva*, vol. 1 (Kiev, 1999), 12, Rozhenko, *Sosny Bykivni svidchat'*, vol. 2, 12, and A. I. Amons, *Bykivnians'ka trahediia* (Kiev, 2006), 133, 158–59, 163, 166.

48. Amons, *Bykivnians'ka trahediia*, 133. Note Musorks'kyi still used the term 'enemies of the people' in 1989.

49. Rozhenko, *Sosny Bykivni svidchat'*, vol. 4 (Kiev, 2003), 8.

50. For Moscow, see, for example, *Rasstrel'nye spiski. Moskva 1935–1953. Donskoe kladbishche* (Moscow, 2005).

51. *Pam'iat' Bykivnia. Dokumenty ta materialy* (Kiev, 2000), 17.

52. Rozhenko, *Sosny Bykivni svidchat'*, vol. 3 (Kiev, 2002), 3, and Rozhenko and Bohats'ka, *Sosny Bykivni svidchat'*, 11–12.

53. See Kamenetsky, *The Tragedy of Vinnytsia*.

54. For an earlier, 1990 visit to this site, see Marco Carynnyk, 'The Killing Fields of Kiev', *Commentary*, 1990, no. 4.

55. J. A. E. Curtis, *Manuscripts Don't Burn: Mikhail Bulgakov: A Life in Letters and Diaries* (London, 1991).

56. A good description of a similar case file is in Chinsky, *Micro-histoire de la Grande Terreur*, 23–42.

Chapter 1: Love with Foreign Diplomats

1. I have discussed this in my *Stalin* (London, 2005).

2. *Zimniaia voina 1939–1940*, vol. 2 (Moscow, 1999), 207.

3. Erik van Ree, *The Political Thought of Joseph Stalin* (London, 2002), 300.

4. *Zimniaia voina*, 206.

5. See Chapter 9.

6. Czechoslovakia opened its consulate in Kiev in 1936, only to be forced to close it down in early 1938.

7. TsDAHO, f. 263, op. 1, spr. 58438fp, 1:15, 19. Hereafter references to this archival source are made in the main text with the volume and folio number.

8. CAW, I:303.4.1929. According to *Rocznik służby zagranicznej Rzeczypospolitej Polskiej według stanu na 1 kwietnia 1935* (Warsaw, 1935), Zaleski was born in 1899 and recalled to Warsaw on 1 April 1935.

9. Andor Hencke, *Erinnerungen als Deutscher Konsul in Kiew in den Jahren 1933–1936* (Munich, 1979), 11.

10. Andrzej Pepłoński, *Wywiad polski na ZSRR 1921–1939* (Warsaw, 1996), 110, 126–27, 149, 171, and CAW, I:303.4.1913 (Tbilisi file), I:303.4.1964, 1965 (Istanbul files). Karszo-Siedlewski worked as a *chargé d'affaires* of the Polish embassy in

Moscow (see RGVA, f. 308k, op. 3, d. 299, ll. 1–9) and as consul-general in Kharkiv before he moved to Kiev as consul.

11. Timothy Snyder, *Sketches from a Secret War: A Polish Artist's Mission to Liberate Soviet Ukraine* (New Haven, Conn., 2005), 40.

12. CAW, I:303.4.1929.

13. *Ibid.*, I:303.4.1965 (report of 1 Nov. 1937).

14. This is probably a mistake by Goroshko or the interrogator for Aleksander Stpiczyński.

15. Whether Zaleski was married when he was posted to Kiev is not known. However, his Istanbul file shows that in 1938, when he was posted to Istanbul, he was married to 'Lucyna'. See CAW, I:303.4.1965 (18 Aug. 1938 correspondence).

16. See my *Freedom and Terror in the Donbas: A Ukrainian–Russian Borderland, 1870s–1990s* (Cambridge, 1998), ch. 6.

17. *Repressii protiv poliakov i pol'skikh grazhdan* (Moscow, 1997), 33.

18. Mykola Rozhenko, *Sosny Bykivni svidchat': zlochyn proty liudstva*, vol. 2 (Kiev, 2001), 126.

19. I was unable to find Levinskaia, another colleague Goroshko mentioned. It is possible that the interrogator miswrote her name for Levenson or Lebedinskaya, both of whom appear in the programmes of the time. Vasyl' Turkevych of the National Theatre of Opera and Ballet in Kiev helped me greatly in my pursuit of Goroshko's career.

20. See Chapter 2.

21. CAW, I:303.4.1929. I am grateful to Timothy Snyder for providing me with this report.

22. Snyder, *Sketches from a Secret War*, 87.

23. TsDAHO, f. 263, op. 1, spr. 65587pf, ark. 25, 29. Hereafter references are made to this archival source in the main text with the folio number.

24. Politisches Archiv des Auswärtigen Amts, Berlin, R 142489, I M 3807/22 (14 July 1922 note by Siegfried Hey to the German Foreign Ministry). I owe thanks to Dr Martin Kröger of the archive for tracking down this information.

25. The immigration records of Canada list one Franz Huth, thirty-five years of age, a German, arriving from Liverpool in Saint John, New Brunswick, on 26 January 1930 by the Canadian Pacific steamship *Montrose*. This is almost certainly the same individual; at least their ages match. Huth is listed in the Canadian records as 'born in "Prieschib" [probably a variant spelling of Prischib, Altnassau, Crimea], Russia', single, a wine-grower, a German citizen who spoke Russian and German and intending to reside in Canada permanently. He paid his way to Canada, travelling third class with a passport issued in Berlin. He had $150 in his possession when he arrived in Canada. He had a brother, Woldemar Huth, in Dresden-Wachwitz, Germany, and a friend, Fred Kammerloch, in Grandview, Manitoba, who appears to have come from Russia in 1926 with his family. Huth intended to engage in farming in Canada. (See Library and Archives Canada, Ottawa, Canada, RG76, C–1–C, 1930, v. 1, p. 111.) I have been unable to find any information on his subsequent fate.

26. *Pravo na repressii. Vnesudebnye polnomochiia organov gosudarstvennoi bezopasnosti (1918–1953)* (Moscow, 2006), 187.

27. Rozhenko, *Sosny Bykivni svidchat'*, 89.

28. For Japan, see Chapter 7.

Chapter 2: Informers

1. Sheila Fitzpatrick and Robert Gellately (eds), *Accusatory Practices: Denunciation in Modern European History, 1789–1989* (Chicago, Ill., 1997), 9.
2. *Lubianka. Organy VChK-OGPU-NKVD-MGB-KGB 1917–1991* (Moscow, 2003), 571, 574.
3. Timothy Garton Ash has written a history of his own case: *The File: A Personal History* (London, 1997).
4. 'Agent Volodia: Neizvestnye fakty iz biografii Imre Nadia (1930–1941)', *Istochnik*, 1993, no. 1.
5. *Delo provokatora Malinovskogo* (Moscow, 1992).
6. Irma Kudrova, *The Death of a Poet: The Last Days of Marina Tsvetaeva*, tr. Mary Ann Szporluk (London, 2004).
7. *Głos Radziecki*, published until 1936 under the title *Sierp* ('Sickle'), had a circulation of 3,000 to 10,000. It ceased publication in January 1941. See Mikołaj Iwanow, *Pierwszy naród ukarany: Stalinizm wobec polskiej ludności kresowej (1921–1938)* (Warsaw, 1991), 98.
8. TsDAHO, f. 236, op. 1, spr. 64028fp., ark. 9–10, 30–31, 32, 50. Hereafter references to this archival source are made in the main text, with the folio number.
9. See Chapter 12.
10. On the other hand, it is conceivable, albeit unlikely, that her command of Polish was far better than her Russian or Ukrainian and that she therefore sometimes misunderstood her non-native languages. It is also possible that she understood all three well.
11. Janusz M. Kupczak, *Polacy na Ukrainie w latach 1921–1939* (Wrocław, 1994), 61.
12. Iwanow, *Pierwszy naród ukarany*, 143.
13. Edward Walewander (ed.), *Polacy w kościele katolickim w ZSRR* (Lublin, 1991), 96, Iwanow, *Pierwszy naród ukarany*, 123, and Kupczak, *Polacy*, 288.
14. Iwanow, *Pierwszy naród ukarany*, 83. Iwanow mistakenly states that the PIP was abolished in 1936. It was actually closed in late 1935.
15. Mykola Rozhenko and Edit Bohats'ka, *Sosny Bykivni svidchat': zlochyn proty liudstva*, vol. 1 (Kiev, 1999), 28, 303, 492.
16. *Z arkhiviv VUChK-HPU-NKVD-KHB*, 2003, no. 2, 172–76, 241, 244, 396–97.
17. This is vividly described in Antoine Wenger, *Rome et Moscou 1900–1950* (Paris, 1987), especially 372, and *idem*, *Catholiques en Russie d'après les archives du KGB 1920–1960* (Paris, 1998).
18. TsDAHO, f. 263, op. 1, spr. 54948fp, ark. 83, 85, 87 (file of Mariia Stanislavovna Ditkovskaia, see Chapter 9), Rozhenko and Bohats'ka, *Sosny Bykivni svidchat'*, 17, 203, 490, and Roman Dzwonkowski, *Losy duchowieństwa katolickiego w ZSSR 1917–1939. Martyrologium* (Lublin, 1998), 317–20, and *idem*, *Kościół katolicki w ZSSR 1917–1939: Zarys historii* (Lublin, 1997), 155, 236.
19. Neveu was operating under the Vatican's Russian hand, Michel d'Herbigny. See Paul Lesourd, *Entre Rome et Moscou: le Jésuite clandestin. Mgr Michel d'Herbigny* (Paris, 1976), Wenger, *Rome et Moscou* and Patrick A. Croghan, *The Peasant from Makeyevka: Biography of Bishop Pius Neveu, A. A.* (Worcester, Mass., 1982).
20. Wenger, *Catholiques en Russie*, 127, and Aleksei Iudin, '"Ia gotov na liubye zhertvy": rasstrel'noe delo arkhiepiskopa Varfolomei (Remova)', *Istina i zhizn'*, 1996, no. 2, 37.

21. Wenger, *Catholiques en Russie*, 116.

22. *Ibid.*, 122.

23. *Ibid.*, 135 and Wenger, *Rome et Moscou*, 329.

24. Unlike the Russian Orthodox Church, the splinter group of 'Renovationists' allowed its bishops to marry. On the Renovationist Church, see Edward Roslof, *Red Priests: Renovationism, Russian Orthodoxy, and Revolution, 1905–1946* (Bloomington, Ind., 2002).

25. Wenger, *Catholiques en Russie*, 142–43.

26. *Ibid.*, 116, 125–26.

27. Iudin, '"Ia gotov"', 37.

28. *Ibid.*, 39, and Wenger, *Catholiques en Russie*, 132, 150, 162.

29. Wenger, *Rome et Moscou*, 58–59.

30. *Z arkhiviv VUChK-HPU-NKVD-KHB*, 2003, no. 2, 328, Dzwonkowski, *Losy duchowieństwa katolickiego*, 482–83, *idem* (ed.), *Skazani jako 'szpiedzy Watykanu'. Z historii Kościoła katolickiego w ZSSR 1918–1956* (Warsaw, 1998), 94–96, and Wenger, *Catholiques en Russie*, 167–69.

31. Oleksandr Klimentii Sokolovs'kyi, *Tserkva khrystova 1920–1940: peresliduvannia khrystyian v SRSR* (Kiev, 1999), 205.

32. Kuromiya, *Freedom and Terror in the Donbas: A Ukrainian–Russian Borderland, 1870s–1990s* (Cambridge, 1998), 285–86.

Chapter 3: A Monarchist's Swan Song?

1. Isaiah Berlin and Ramin Jahanbegloo, *Conversations with Isaiah Berlin* (New York, 1991), 4.

2. Iaroslav Tinchenko, *Golgofa russkogo ofitserstva v SSSR. 1930–1931 gody* (Moscow, 2000).

3. TsDAHO, f. 263, op. 1, spr. 63605fp, ark. 1, 4, 5, 7, 18–19, 73zv. Hereafter references to this archival source are made in the main text with the folio number. Note that her name is sometimes misspelled in her file as Zheliakhovskaia or Zheliukhovskaia. Likewise, in one document, her birth date is mistakenly given as 1874.

4. There are legions of similar cases. See, for example, Chapters 1 and 8. In one case, Iuliia Vasil'evna Borichevskaia-Lemlein, a Russian in Kiev, was accused of being a believer in 'mysticism' (probably theosophy), which the NKVD took to be counter-revolutionary. She was executed in December 1937 as part of the Polish Operation. See TsDAHO, f. 263 op. 1, spr. 66180fp.

5. Mykola Rozhenko, *Sosny Bykivni svidchat': zlochyn proty liudstva*, vol. 2 (Kiev, 2001), 163.

6. Torgsin (*Torgovlia s inostrantsami*, 'Trade with Foreigners') refers to 'closed shops' which sold items, including foodstuffs, otherwise unobtainable in the Soviet Union in the 1920s and 1930s, in return for foreign currency and precious metals such as gold.

7. The reference to the Council of Old Siberian Robbers is a pun on the acronym of the Soviet Union (SSSR). Such puns were widespread throughout the Soviet period.

8. TsDAHO, f. 326, op. 1, spr. 45568fp, ark. 1–2, 12, 19–20, 26–28, 29–31. At one point, she is described as a Russian (14).

Chapter 4: 'The NKVD is Satan'

1. RGASPI, f. 629, op. 1, d. 54, l. 29.
2. Iu. A. Zhdanov, *Vzgliad v proshloe: vospominaniia ochevidtsa* (Rostov na Donu, 2004), 172. See also my *Stalin* (London, 2005), 138.
3. Gregory L. Freeze, 'The Stalinist Assault on the Parish, 1929–1941', in Manfred Hildermeier (ed.), *Stalinismus vor dem Zweiten Weltkrieg: Neue Wege der Forschung* (Munich, 1998), 230.
4. Felix Corey, 'Believers' Responses to the 1937 and 1939 Soviet Censuses', *Religion, State and Society*, 22:4 (1994), 407. For more detail, see *Vsesoiuznaia perepis' naseleniia 1937 g. Kratkie itogi* (Moscow, 1991), 106–7.
5. Quoted in my *Freedom and Terror in the Donbas* (Cambridge, 1998), 236.
6. See Edward Roslof, *Red Priests: Renovationism, Russian Orthodoxy, and Revolution, 1905–1946* (Bloomington, Ind., 2002) and *Memoirs of Peasant Tolstoyans in Soviet Russia*, tr., ed. and with an introduction by William Edgerton (Bloomington, Ind., 1993).
7. See Chapter 2.
8. Corley, 'Believers' Responses', 409.
9. See Rolf Binner and Marc Jung, 'Vernichtung der orthodoxen Geistlichen in der Sowjetunion in den Massenoperationen des Großen Terrors 1937–1938', *Jahrbücher für Geschichte Osteuropas*, 52:4 (2004).
10. O. B. Mozokhin, 'Statistika repressivnoi deiatel'nosti organov VChK-OGPU (1934–1940 gg.): 1937 god', *Voenno-istoricheskii arkhiv*, 2005, no. 4, 185.
11. TsDAHO, f. 263, op. 1, spr. 59783fp, ark. 17, 19–20. Hereafter references to this archival source are made in the main text with the folio number.
12. M. N. Tukhachevskii (1893–1937) and I. E. Iakir (1896–1937), both prominent military leaders, were falsely charged with foreign espionage and executed in 1937.
13. His last name may be wrong; it is often difficult to decipher handwritten records.
14. Mykola Rozhenko and Edit Bohats'ka, *Sosny Bykivni svidchat': zlochyn proty liudstva*, vol. 1 (Kiev, 1999), 33, 492.
15. It was founded as a civil cemetery. Only later was a church built in the ground. It would have been odd had the atheist government used a Christian cemetery for burial unless it meant to respect those it executed!
16. From 1933 onwards, one needed both a passport and a residence permit to live in a city like Kiev. This was meant to regulate the movement of the population. Because passports were not issued to rural residents, their mobility was severely restricted: they, like the serfs before 1861, were virtually bound to their lands.
17. TsDAHO, f. 263, op. 1, spr. 61619fp, ark. 4, 8, 12, 44–49. Hereafter references to this archival source are made in the main text with the folio number.
18. *Nakazannyi narod. Repressii protiv rossiiskikh nemtsev* (Moscow, 1999), 55–56.
19. See Mykola Rozhenko, *Sosny Bykivni svidchat': zlochyn proty liudstva*, vol. 3 (Kiev, 2002) and vol. 4 (Kiev, 2003).
20. Having workers make compulsory purchases of state bonds was widely practised in the 1930s in order to finance economic development.
21. Rozhenko and Bohats'ka, *Sosny Bykivni svidchat'*, 45, 183–84, 235, 347, 492, 525.

22. This is supported by the example of Voronezh, Russia, as well. See Youngok Kang-Bohr, *Stalinismus in der ländlichen Provinz. Das Gebiet Voronež 1934–1941* (Essen, 2006), 234–35. Iryna Boshko, 'Rik 1938–i, Kyiv, Luk'ianivs'ka v'iaznytsia', *Ukraina* (Kyiv), 1989, no. 20, 3 discusses a woman arrested in 1938 for begging at a Polish church in Kiev.

23. Quoted in V. N. Khaustov, 'Deiatel'nost' organov gosudarstvennoi bezopasnosti NKVD SSSR (1934–1941 gg.)' (Doctoral thesis, Akademiia federal'noi sluzhby bezopasnosti, Moscow, 1997), 334.

Chapter 5: Ukrainian Peasants and Kulaks

1. For this exodus, see *Dokumenty vneshnei politiki SSSR*, vol. 13 (Moscow, 1967), 148–49, *The Times* (London), 3 March 1930, 14, 4 March 1930, 15, and *The New York Times*, 2 March 1930, 1, 7 March 1930, 7.

2. One such case in 1930 is TsDAHO, f. 263, op. 1, spr. 66632fp.

3. See CAW, I.303.4.1964 (Dec. 1937 reports).

4. For the Tiutiunnyk army, see Oleh Shatailo, *Heneral Iurko Tiutiunnyk* (L'viv, 2000).

5. TsDAHO, f. 263, op. 1, spr. 66199fp, ark. 21–22, 86, 91. Hereafter references to this archival source are made in the main text with folio number.

6. Oddly, Mykola Rozhenko, *Sosny Bykivni svidchat': zlochyn proty liudstva*, vol. 2 (Kiev, 2001), 126 misidentifies him as a woman, 'Uliana Petrivna Horodovenko'!

7. *Pogranichnye voiska SSSR, 1919–1938* (Moscow, 1972), 77.

8. TsDAHO, f. 236, op. 1, spr. 62670fp, ark. 5–6, 21–22. Hereafter references to this archival source are made in the main text with folio number.

9. Rozhenko, *Sosny Bykivni svidchat'*, 365.

10. TsDAHO, f. 263, op. 1, spr. 61951fp, ark. 5–6, 8, 10, 12, 30–31. Hereafter references to this archival source are made in the main text with folio number.

11. The SVU (*Spilka vyzvolennia Ukrainy*, or the Union for the Liberation of Ukraine) was a 'Ukrainian nationalist organisation', allegedly headed by the Academician Serhii Iefremov (Efremov) but in fact fabricated by the secret police. The trial of the members of the SVU took place in 1930 and the defendants were sentenced to incarceration. Many were subsequently executed or died in labour camps.

12. Mykola Rozhenko and Edit Bohats'ka, *Sosny Bykivni svidchat': zlochyn proty liudstva*, vol. 1 (Kiev, 1999), 87.

13. See the case in which forty people were executed in March 1938 in the Kiev countryside: TsDAHO, f. 263, op. 1, spr. 45863fp.

14. See my 'Accounting for the Great Terror', *Jahrbücher für Geschichte Osteuropas*, 53:1 (2005).

15. Rolf Binner and Marc Junge, 'Wie der Terror "Gross" Wurde: Massenmord und Lagerhaft nach Befehl 00447', *Cahiers du monde russe*, 42:2–4 (April–Dec. 2001), 606–7, 613.

16. See Chapter 4.

Chapter 6: Ukrainian Bandurists

1. On the bandura, see Volodymyr Lutsiv, 'Kobza-Bandura and "Dumy" and their Significance in the History of the Ukrainian People', *The Ukrainian Quarterly*, 13:1

(spring 1966) and Natalie Kononenko, *Ukrainian Minstrels and the Blind Shall Sing* (Armonk, New York, 1998).

2. After the Civil War, in order to strengthen its position in the non-Russian areas, the Soviet government supported a degree of national-territorial autonomy, including the promotion of national culture.

3. See William Noll, 'The Social Role and Economic Status of Blind Minstrels in Ukraine', *Harvard Ukrainian Studies*, 17:1–2 (June 1993), 60–61. For a more detailed account, see William Noll, *Transformatsiia hromadians'koho suspil'stva: usna istoriia ukrains'koi selians'koi kul'tury 1920–30 rokiv* (Kiev, 1999).

4. Rukopysni fondy Instytutu mytetstvoznavstva, fol'kloru ta etnohrafii AN Ukrainy (RF IMFE), Kiev, Ukraine, f. 1–7/866, ark. 22.

5. *Report to Congress. Commission on the Ukrainian Famine* (Washington, D.C., 1988), 306. 'Petliurist' refers to Symon Petliura, a Ukrainian national leader in 1918–20.

6. *Ibid.*, 307.

7. *Mytsi Ukrainy* (Kiev, 1992), 224.

8. TsDAHO, f. 236, op. 1, spr. 49967fp, t. 1, ark. 5, 10. Hereafter references to this archival source are made in the main text with folio number.

9. I have found no documentary evidence to prove this claim.

10. See Thomas M. Prymak, *Mykhailo Hrushevsky: The Politics of National Culture* (Toronto, 1987).

11. See Volodymyr Prystaiko and Iurii Shapoval, *Mykhailo Hrushevskyi: sprava 'UNTs' i ostanni roky, 1931–1934* (Kiev, 1999).

12. 'Petliurite' refers to those who supported the Ukrainian national leader Symon Vasyl'ovych Petliura, who led the Ukrainian Directory in 1919–20. He was assassinated in 1926 in Paris by Sholom Schwartzbard, originally from Ukraine, who some scholars believe was a Soviet agent.

13. His name was in fact Andrei Petrovich Liubcheko. He was a member of the Borot'bists, a radical Ukrainian socialist party, and a brother of the party's leader, Panas Liubchenko, who committed suicide in August 1937.

14. *Tragediia sovetskoi derevni: kollektivizatsiia i raskulachivanie*, 5:2 (Moscow, 2006), 53.

15. Shums'kyi worked briefly as Commissar of Education in Ukraine in the 1920s, then was dismissed and exiled to Russia, where he was arrested in 1933. He miraculously survived the Great Terror in Russia, but in 1946 he decided to return to Ukraine and was murdered by the Soviet secret police under the guise of suicide. See Iu. I. Shapoval, *Liudyna i systema* (Kiev, 1994), 134–52.

16. *Ukrainian Dumy*, tr. by George Tarnawsky and Patricia Kilina (Toronto/Cambridge, Mass., 1979), 37.

17. *Ibid.*, 183. Bohdan refers to another Cossack hero from the same period, Bohdan Khmel'nyts'kyi.

18. TsDAHO, f. 236, op. 1, spr. 32387fp, t. 1, ark. 11 (hereafter references to this archival source are made in the main text with the volume and folio numbers) and *Mytsi Ukrainy*, 44.

19. 'Dumka' refers to Ukrainian lyrical and sentimental folk songs.

20. I have been unable to find any information on this composer.

21. 'Sandler' probably refers to Oskar Aronovich Sandler (1910–81) who graduated from the Kiev Conservatory in 1937.

22. *Mytsi Ukrainy*, 44.

23. *Ibid.*, 44.

24. S. V. Bashtan and L. Ia. Ivakhnenko, *Banduryste, orle syzyi: vinochok spohadiv pro Volodymyra Kabachka* (Kiev, 1995).

25. *Hnat Khotkevych. Spohady. Statti. Svitlyny* (Kiev, 1994), 73.

26. 'Hnat Khotkevych', in Anatolii Bolabol'chenko, *Vybrane* (Kiev, 2005), 119–24.

27. Caroline Brooke, 'Soviet Musicians and the Great Terror', *Europe–Asia Studies*, 54:3 (May 2002), 397.

28. Hryhory Kytasty, *Some Aspects of Ukrainian Music under the Soviets* (New York, 1954), 39–40 (in Russian).

29. Alex Weissberg, *Conspiracy of Silence* (London, 1952), 350.

30. Kytasty, *Some Aspects,* 51, 54–56.

31. *The Republic of Plato*, 2nd edn, tr. with notes and an interpretive essay by Allan Bloom (New York, 1991), 80.

Chapter 7: Koreans and Chinese in Kiev

1. *Vsesoiuznaia perepis' naseleniia 1937 g. Kratkie itogi* (Moscow, 1991), 84, 86.

2. Valentin Berezhkov, *Kak ia stal perevodchikom Stalina* (Moscow, 1993), 70, 78. For the case of 'Japanese spies' in 1934, see *Lubianka. Stalin i VChK-GPU-OGPU-NKVD. Ianvar' 1922–dekabr' 1936* (Moscow, 2003), 526.

3. V. M. Nikol's'kyi, *Represyvna diial'nist' orhaniv derzhavnoi bezpeky SRSR v Ukraini (kinets' 1920-kh–1950-ti rr.): istoryko-statystychne doslidzhennia* (Donets'k, 2003), 340.

4. Naum Korzhavin, *V soblaznakh krovavoi epokhi*, vol. 1 (Moscow, 2006), 92.

5. G. S. Liushkov, 'Soren shakaishugi hihan', *Gekkan Roshiya*, 1939, no. 5, 49–50.

6. Genrikh Liushkov, who defected to Japan in 1938, quoted in Saburō Hayashi, *Kantōgun to kyokutō sorengun* (Tokyo, 1974), 110–11.

7. US Military Intelligence Reports. The Soviet Union 1919–1941. Reel 4, frame 0976–77 (originally from the National Archives and Record Service, Washington, D.C., Record Group 165. Military Intelligence Division files: Russia). For Stalin's remarks quoted by Liushkov, see also Dirk Kunert, *General Ljuschkows Geheimbericht. Über die Stalinsche Fernostpolitik 1937/38* (Bern, 1977), 21–22.

8. See the August 1938 interview of a Korean spy: Gaimushō Gaikō Shiryō Kan (Tokyo), s.1.6.5.0–2, and the unpublished 1952 study of pre-war Japanese espionage in the Far East, 'Manshū ni kansuru yōheiteki kansatsu', vol. 10 (available at the Bōeichō Bōei Kenkyūjo Toshokan in Tokyo), 5–6, 10–11, 21–23, 25–28, 31–32, 46.

9. *Pogranichnye voiska SSSR, 1929–1938* (Moscow, 1972), 432, 433, 436–37.

10. Hata Ikuhiko, 'The Japanese–Soviet Confrontation, 1935–1939', in James William Morley, *Deterrent Diplomacy: Japan, Germany, and the USSR, 1935–1940* (New York, 1976), 133.

11. N. I. Dubinina, 'Tragediia lichnosti', *Dal'nii vostok*, 1989, no. 7, 130.

12. 'Iaponskii shpionazh v Rossii v period russko-iaponskoi voiny', *Shpion*, 1994, no. 3, and V. P. Iampol'skii, 'Iaponskaia razvedka protiv SSSR v 1918–1945 gg.', *Voenno-istoricheskii zhurnal*, 1991, no. 11.

13. For vivid descriptions of Soviet and Japanese espionage in the Far East, see 'Manshū ni kansuru yōheiteki kansatsu'; Nakano Kōyūkai (ed.), *Rikugun Nakano Gakkō* (Tokyo, 1978), a privately published study by alumni of the former Japanese

spy school; and Tadakuma Iwai, *Rikugun himitsu jōhō kikan no otoko* (Tokyo, 2005), 65–66.

14. *Koreitsy. Zhertvy politicheskikh repressii v SSSR 1934–1938*, vol. 3 (Moscow, 2004), 67, vol. 2 (Moscow, 2002), 60.

15. *Rasstrel'nye spiski*, vol. 2 (Moscow, 1995), 258. For another case involving Zaen Kim, who was executed in July 1934, see *Lubianka*, 545. He and seven others who were executed were subsequently rehabilitated.

16. Nikol's'kyi, *Represyvna*, 340.

17. TsDAHO, f. 263, op. 1, spr. 54745fp, t. 2, ark. 10zv. and 14. Hereafter references to this archival source are made in the main text with the volume and folio numbers. His name is also sometimes spelt Ben-shchu Kim.

18. For the Polish–Japanese collaboration, see Ewa Pałasz-Rutkowska and Andrzej T. Romer, *Historia stosunków Polsko-Japońskich 1904–1945* (Warsaw, 1996). At the height of the Great Terror in December 1937, Poland and Japan held a joint military intelligence conference in Warsaw to assess the Soviet situation. Archiwum akt nowych (Warsaw), Sztab Główny, 616/249 (10–13 December 1937). I am grateful to Andrzej Pepłoński for this information.

19. See RGASPI, f. 17, op. 162, d. 12, l. 107. See also the 1932 Polish intelligence report: RGVA, f. 308k, op. 3, d. 299, ll. 75–76, and the Soviet intelligence report sent in 1932 to Stalin about the 'secret agreement' signed in 1931 between Poland and Japan. RGSPI, f. 558, op. 11, d. 185, l. 65.

20. Yuriko Onodera, *Barutokai no hotori nite. Bukan no tsuma no Daitōa sensō* (Tokyo, 1985), 51–53.

21. *Idem*, 'Onodera Makoto rikugun shōshō no jōhō katsudō 1935–46' (manuscript available at the University of Tokyo Historiographical Institute), 34–35, 60.

22. See the 1936 'highly secret' mission given to the Berlin office, quoted in the statement the former Japanese intelligence expert Makoto Onodera made to US authorities in 1946. The US National Archives and Records Administration (College Park, Maryland), RG 263, 2002/A/10/3, vol. 1, 'Secret Control. Central Intelligence Group. Japanese Wartime Military Missions in Europe'.

23. See, for example, Kentarō Awaya and Kei Takeuchi (eds), *Tai So jōhō sen shiryō*, vol. 4 (Tokyo, 1999), 436 (1934 intelligence plan), vol. 2 (Tokyo, 1999), 453 (1936 instructions to the military attaché in Paris) and Lev Sotskov, *Neizvestnyi separatizm na sluzhbe SD i Abvera. Iz sekretnykh dos'e razvedki* (Moscow, 2003), 75–81. Poland watched the Japanese–Ukrainian connection with much interest. RGVA, f. 308k, op. 3, d. 456, ll. 4–5 (1935 report). Oleg Mozokhin, *VChK-OGPU* (Moscow, 2004), 387, 403–4 also suggests that the Soviet secret police suspected Japanese interests in Ukraine.

24. See a memorandum from Ukrainian nationalists to the Japanese military attaché in Istanbul, quoted in V. K. Bylinin and V. I. Korotaev, 'Portret lidera OUN v inter'ere inostrannykh razvedok (Po materialam AP RF, GARF, RGVA i TsA FSB RF)', in *Trudy Obshchestva izucheniia istorii otechestvennykh spetssluzhb*, vol. 2 (Moscow, 2006), 122–26.

25. Wojciech Włodarkiewicz, *Przed 17 września 1939 roku: Radzieckie zagrożenie Rzeczypospolitej w ocenach polskich naczelnych władz wojskowych 1921–1939* (Warsaw, 2002), 132.

26. 'Tai So rajio gyōmu no hōkoku no ken' (7 Nov. 1938), in *Rikugun mitsu dai nikki*, 1938, vol. 16 (available at Bōeichō Bōei Kenkyūjo Toshokan, Tokyo), 1423.

27. Poland monitored these programmes carefully. See, for example, RGVA, f. 308k, op. 6, d. 21, ll. 151–53 (15 April 1935).

28. Korzhavin, *V soblaznakh*, 92.

29. TsDAHO, f. 263, op. 1, spr. 62830fp.

30. *Pravo na repressii. Vnesudebnye polnomochiia organov gosudarstvennoi bezopasnosti (1918–1953)* (Moscow, 2006), 160. See also RGASPI, f. 17, op. 162, d. 22, l. 114 (31 Jan. 1938 decision by the Politburo of the Communist Party).

31. TsDAHO, f. 263, op. 1, spr. 48968fp.

32. TsDAHO, f. 263, op. 1, spr. 57082fp, ark. 1–6. Hereafter references to this archival source are made in the main text with the folio number.

33. See cases in Siberia discussed in Aleksei Tepliakov, 'Sibir': protsedura isploneniia smertnykh prigovorov v 1920–1930 godakh', in *Golosa Sibiri*, vol. 4 (Novosibirsk, 2006).

34. For the 'ethnic cleansing' of the Crimean Tatars and Chechens, see Norman M. Naimark, *Fires of Hatred: Ethnic Cleansing in Twentieth-Century Europe* (Cambridge, Mass., 2001), ch. 3.

Chapter 8: Foreign Connections

1. See, for example, Ronald J. Vossler (ed.), *We'll Meet Again in Heaven: Germans in the Soviet Union Write their American Relatives 1925–1937* (Fargo, N. Dak., 2001).

2. Ingeborg Fleischhauer and Benjamin Pinkus, *The Soviet Germans: Past and Present* (New York, 1986), 34, 91.

3. See Kuromiya, *Stalin* (Harlow, 2005), 115.

4. See *Stainskie deportatsii 1928–1953. Dokumenty* (Moscow, 2006).

5. See Terry Martin, *The Affirmative Action Empire: Nations and Nationalism in the Soviet Union, 1923–1939* (Ithaca, N.Y., 2001), 333.

6. See *Tak eto bylo*, vol. 1 (Moscow, 1993), 253.

7. TsDAHO, f. 263, op. 1, spr. 63942fp, ark. 5–6, 18–20, 30, 32. Hereafter references to this archival source are made in the main text with the volume and folio numbers.

8. Paulits is probably her brother-in-law and Alberts one of his relatives.

9. There was Order No. 49990 on the Latvian Operation dated 30 November 1937, but this was not used. For the order, see *Pravo na repressii. Vnesudebnye polnomochiia organov gosudarstvennoi bezopasnosti (1918–1953)* (Moscow, 2006), 188.

10. Mykola Rozhenko, *Sosny Bykivni svidchat': zlochyn proty liudstva*, vol. 2 (Kiev, 2001), 230.

11. TsDAHO, f. 263, op. 1, spr. 63446fp, ark. 23. Hereafter references are made to this archival source in the main text with the volume and folio numbers.

12. Rozhenko, vol. 3 (Kiev, 2002), 42.

13. See the case of Emma Adamovna Neiber, a Latvian who was executed in January 1938, and others described in her file; TsDAHO, f. 263, op. 1, spr. 64003fp.

14. See TsDAHO, f. 263, op. 1, spr. 65803fp.

15. TsDAHO, f. 263, op. 1, spr. 62836fp, ark. 38–39. Hereafter references are made to this archival source in the main text with the volume and folio numbers.

16. TsDAHO, f. 263, op. 1, spr. 63407fp, ark. 6, 10, 41–43, 40a, 40b. Hereafter references are made to this archival source in the main text with the volume and folio numbers.

17. Rozhenko, *Sosny Bykivni svidchat'*, vol. 2, 289.

18. TsDAHO, f. 263, op. 1, spr. 59512fp, ark. 14, 30. Hereafter references are made in the main text to this archival source with the volume and leaf numbers.

19. *Pravo na repressii*, 175, 176–77.

20. Rozhenko, *Sosny Bykivni svidchat'*, vol. 2, 319, and *Pam'iat' Bykivni. Dokumenty ta materialy* (Kiev, 2000), 288.

21. TsDAHO, f. 263, op. 1, spr. 65628fp, ark. 18. Hereafter references are made to this archival source in the main text with the volume and folio numbers.

22. Rozhenko, *Sosny Bykivni svidchat'*, vol. 2, 251–52, 431.

23. Valentin Berezhkov, *Kak ia stal perevodchikom Stalina* (Moscow, 1993), 13.

24. *Ibid.*, 92, 134.

Chapter 9: Consular Affairs

1. See Timothy Snyder, *Sketches from a Secret War: A Polish Artist's Mission to Liberate Soviet Ukraine* (New Haven, Conn., 2005), 86.

2. For such a list, see the captured Polish document RGVA, f. 308k, op. 3, d. 257.

3. Andor Hencke, *Erinnerungen als Deutscher Konsul in Kiew in den Jahren 1933–1936* (Munich, 1979), 16, 23–25. The Soviet secret police suspected that Hencke was a favourite of Alfred Rosenberg, a Nazi ideologue. (See *Lubianka. Stalin i VChK-GPU-OGPU-NKVD. Ianvar' 1922–dekabr' 1936* [Moscow, 2003], 495.) Subsequently Hencke became a distinguished diplomat under Hitler.

4. Snyder, 124–25.

5. Quoted in *Nakazannyi narod. Repressii protiv rossiiskikh nemtsev* (Moscow, 1999), 47, and Vadim Abramov, *Kontrrazvedka. Shchit i mech protiv Abvera i TsRU* (Moscow, 2006), 105.

6. Kenrō Nagoshi, *Kuremurin himitsu bunsho wa kataru: yami no nisso kankei shi* (Tokyo, 1994), 187–91.

7. *Nihon gaikō monjo: Shōwa ki II*, pt 2, vol. 1 (Tokyo, 1991), 396. In 1934 three Soviet citizens working in Western Siberia were accused of spying for Japan and executed. Oleg Mozokhin, *VChK-OGPU* (Moscow, 2004), 401–6.

8. Hencke, *Erinnerungen*, 8, 11.

9. Born in 1884 to a German family in Latvia, then under Russian rule, Grosskopf served as German consul in Novosibirsk from 1923 to 1936. In 1936 he was appointed by Hitler to be consul-general in Kiev. While in Kiev, he was accused of having led German espionage activity in Siberia. After Kiev, he served as consul-general in Moscow until October 1939. Thereafter, Grosskopf served as a Russian specialist for the Nazi ideologue Alfred Rosenberg in preparation for war and occupation. He died in Berlin in 1942. Larissa Belkowez and Sergej Belkowez, *Gescheiterte Hoffnungen: das deutsche Konsulat in Sibirien 1923–1938* (Essen, 2004), 19, 93, 109–10, 122, and *Biographisches Handbuch des deutschen Auswärtigen Dienstes 1871–1945*, vol. 2 (Paderborn, 2005), 114–15.

10. L. P. Belkovets and S. V. Belkovets, 'Konsul'skie otnosheniia Germanii i Sibiri v 1920–1930-e gg.', in *Nemetskii etnoc v Sibiri: Al'manakh gumanitarnykh issledovanii*, vol. 1 (Novosibirsk, 1999), 78.

11. TsDAHO, f. 263, op. 1, spr. 63645fp, ark. 26. Hereafter references are made to this archival source in the main text, with the folio number.

12. L. P. Belkovets, *'Bol'shoi terror' i sud'by nemetskoi derevni v Sibiri (konets 1920-kh–1930-e gody)* (Moscow, 1995), 236–70.

13. Mykola Rozhenko, *Sosny Bykivni svidchat': zlochyn proty liudstva*, vol. 2 (Kiev, 2001), 162.

14. TsDAHO, f. 263, op. 1, spr. 62581fp, ark. 8zv., 12zv. Hereafter references to this archival source are made in the main text, with the folio number.

15. Rudolf Sommer, born in 1877 in Naumburg, was vice-consul in Kharkiv in 1924–25, in Vladivostok in 1925–28, and then in Kiev in 1928–33. In 1933 he was transferred to Leningrad. *Degeners Wer ist's?*, vol. 10 (Berlin, 1935), 1515.

16. Andrzej Pepłoński, *Wywiad polski na ZSRR 1921–1939* (Warsaw, 1996), 48, 119, 127.

17. Rozhenko, *Sosny Bykivni svidchat'*, vol. 2, 404–5.

18. TsDAHO, f. 263, op. 1, spr. 54948fp, ark. 18, 116. Hereafter references to this archival source are made in the main text, with the folio number. Ditkovskaia seems to have signed her name as 'Didkovska'.

19. See Pepłoński, *Wywiad polski*, 48, 119, 127.

20. *Vsesoiuznaia perepis' naseleniia 1937 g. Kratkie itogi* (Moscow, 1991), 94.

21. 'Iaponskii shpionazh: istoricheskii ekskurs', *V mire spetssluzhb*, 2004, no. 6, 13.

22. See a 1935 report by the Japanese military attaché in Tehran to Tokyo, intercepted by the Soviet secret service and quoted in Arekusei [Aleksei] Kirichenko, 'Kominterun to Nihon, sono himitsu chōhōsen o abaku', *Seiron* (Tokyo), 2006, no. 10, 108.

23. See my *Freedom and Terror in the Donbas: A Ukrainian–Russian Borderland, 1870s–1990s* (Cambridge, 1998), 233. For more comprehensive data as of 10 September 1938 in the Soviet Union as a whole, see *Pravo na repressii. Vnesudebnye polnomochiia organov gosudarstvennoi bezopasnosti (1918–1953)* (Moscow, 2006), 186. The death-sentence rates of several key national groups are 62 percent (out of 30,938) for *Kharbintsy*, 78 percent (out of 31,753 cases) for Germans, 79 percent for Latvians (out of 17,581 cases), 79 percent (out of 106,666) for Poles, 83 percent (out of 11,261 cases) for Greeks and 88 percent (out of 5,880) for Finns.

24. Ivan Dzhukha, *Grecheskaia operatsiia. Istoriia repressii protiv grekov v SSSR* (St Petersburg, 2006), 51.

25. TsDAHO, f. 263, op. 1, spr. 47394fp, ark. 4, 7–10. Hereafter references are made to this archival source in the main text, with the folio number.

26. Mykola Rozhenko and Edit Bohats'ka, *Sosny Bykivni svidchat': zlochyn proty liudstva*, vol. 1 (Kiev, 1999), 38, 83, 282, 331–32, 388, 491, 492.

27. *Lubianka. Stalin i VChK-GPU-OGPU-NKVD. Ianvar' 1922–dekabr' 1936* (Moscow, 2003), 613–16, 620–25, 654–57, 670–71. The writer Konstantin Simonov describes the deportation of his own relations from Leningrad (his mother was of noble origin): see K. M. Simonov, *Glazami cheloveka moego pokoleniia. Razmyshleniia o I. V. Staline* (Moscow, 1988), 50, 54.

28. TsDAHO, f. 263, op. 1, spr. 63170fp, t. 1, ark. 16. Hereafter references are made to this archival source in the main text, with the folio number of volume one (volume two contains little information of interest for this story).

29. Rozhenko, *Sosny Bykivni svidchat'*, vol. 2, 82, 430, and Rozhenko and Bohats'ka, *Sosny Bykivni svidchat'*, 36, 104.

30. Pepłoński, *Wywiad polski*, 124–25.

31. *Nisso kōshō shi* (Tokyo, 1942), 408–24. Italy appears to have maintained its consulate in Odesa until the end of 1938, however. See RGASPI, f. 17, op. 162, d. 24, l. 65.

Chapter 10: Across the Borders

1. The best literature on the subject comes from Poland: Andrzej Pepłoński, *Wywiad polski na ZSRR 1921–1939* (Warsaw, 1996) and *idem, Kontrwywiad II Rzeczypospolitej* (Warsaw, 2002).
2. See Chapter 1.
3. TsDAHO, f. 263, op. 1, spr. 57731fp, ark. 6. Hereafter, references to this archival source are made in the main text, with the folio number.
4. Mykola Rozhenko and Edit Bohats'ka, *Sosny Bykivni svidchat': zlochyn proty liudstva*, vol. 1 (Kiev, 1999), 519, and Mykola Rozhenko, *Sosny Bykivni svidchat': zlochyn proty liudstva*, vol. 2 (Kiev, 2001), 143.
5. TsDAHO, f. 263, op. 1, spr. 34114fp.
6. *Ibid.*, spr. 34113fp.
7. TsDAHO, spr. 65873fp, ark. 6, 18–19, 25. Hereafter references to this archival source are made in the main text, with the folio number.
8. Rozhenko, *Sosny Bykivni svidchat'*, vol. 2, 412, 435, and *Pam'iat' Bykivni. Dokumenty ta materialy* (Kiev, 2000), 207.
9. TsDAHO, f. 263, op. 1, spr. 64635fp, ark. 6–7. Hereafter references are made to this archival source in the main text, with the folio number.
10. Roman Dzwonkowski, *Losy duchowieństwa katolickiego w ZSSR 1917–1939. Martyrologium* (Lublin, 1998), 505–6.
11. Rozhenko and Bohats'ka, *Sosny Bykivni svidchat'*, 28, 62–63, 488, and Rozhenko, *Sosny Bykivni svidchat'*, vol. 2, 52.
12. Singer was a large and prominent company in Imperial Russia. It was in December 1937, after Al'bova's arrest, that the NKVD issued an order to arrest all those who had worked for foreign concerns before the Revolution and foreign concessions after the Revolution. See V. N. Khaustov, 'Deiatel'nost' organov gosudarstvennoi bezopasnosti NKVD SSSR (1934–1941 gg.)' (Doctoral thesis, Akademiia federal'noi sluzhby bezopasnosti, Moscow, 1997), 305.
13. Dzwonkowski, *Losy*, 214, 505–6.
14. *Ibid.*, 462–64, and Oleksandr Klimentii Sokolovs'kyi, *Tserkva khrystova 1920–1940: peresliduvannia khrystyian v SRSR* (Kiev, 1999), 240. See also *Lubianka. Stalin i VChK-GPU-OGPU-NKVD. Ianvar' 1922–dekabr' 1936* (Moscow, 2003), 752.
15. See Hiroaki Kuromiya, 'Les années staliniennes à la lumière de la glasnost', *Revue des études slaves*, 64:1 (1992), 131–41.

Chapter 11: Husbands and Wives

1. *The Diary of Georgi Dimitrov, 1933–1949* (New Haven, Conn., 2003), 65.
2. 'Memorial' Archive in Moscow, f. 2, op. 1, d. 118 (Zinaia Danilovna Usova's memoir), l. 42.
3. TsDAHO, f. 263, op. 1, spr. 39045fp, ark. 5, 6, 7, 12–13, 15, 27, 35–36.
4. TsDAHO, f. 263, op. 1, spr. 63554fp, ark. 6. Hereafter references to this archival source are made in the main text, with the folio number.
5. TsDAHO, f. 263, op. 1, spr. 63947fp, ark. 5, 6–6zv, 12. Hereafter references to this archival source are made in the main text, with the folio number.
6. Mykola Rozhenko and Edit Bohats'ka, *Sosny Bykivni svidchat': zlochyn proty liudstva*, vol. 1 (Kiev, 1999), 20, 22, 160.

7. TsDAHO, f. 263, op. 1, spr. 49682fp, ark. 18–19, 20, 37. Hereafter references are made to this archival source in the main text, with the folio number.
8. Hereafter references are to Sosnovskii's file.
9. Rozhenko and Bohats'ka, 404, 493, 520
10. TsDAHO, f. 263, op. 1, spr. 60730fp, ark. 9–11, 12zv, 22–23. Hereafter references are made to this archival source in the main text, with the folio number.
11. Mykola Rozhenko, *Sosny Bykivni svidchat': zlochyn proty liudstva*, vol. 2 (Kiev, 2001), 519.
12. TsDAHO, f. 263, op. 1, spr. 33950fp, ark. 2. Hereafter references are made to this archival source in the main text, with the folio number.
13. TsDAHO, f. 263, op. 1, spr. 65038fp, ark. 17, 23, 27, 28. Hereafter references are made to this archival source in the main text, with the folio number.
14. Rozhenko and Bahats'ka, *Sosny Bykivni svidchat'*, 33, 71, 488, and Rozhenko, *Sosny Bykivni svidchat'*, vol. 2, 58.

Chapter 12: POW

1. V. M. Nikol's'kyi, *Represyvna diial'nist' orhaniv derzhavnoi bezpeky SRSR v Ukraini (kinets' 1920-kh–1950-ti rr.): istoryko-statystychne doslidzhennia* (Donets'k, 2003), 340–41.
2. Like Koreans, Jews, a diaspora nation par excellence, did not have their own country at the time. Yet they were not regarded by the Soviet government as particularly suspect. Their share in the population of Ukraine and among the arrested in 1937–38 in Ukraine was 5.2 and 2.6 percent respectively. *Ibid.*
3. For this, see Louis Fischer, *Russia's Road from Peace to War: Soviet Foreign Relations 1917–1941* (New York, 1969), 222.
4. Janusz M. Kupczak, *Polacy na Ukrainie w latach 1921–1939* (Wrocław, 1994), 61.
5. On the POW and the Polish intelligence in Ukraine, see Timothy Snyder, *Sketches from a Secret War: A Polish Artist's Mission to Liberate Soviet Ukraine* (New Haven, Conn., 2005) and Andrzej Pepłoński, *Wywiad polski na ZSRR 1921–1939* (Warsaw, 1996).
6. Two of them, Wiktor Steckiewicz and Igancy Dobrzyński, were arrested in 1920 by the Soviet authorities and then recruited personally by the then Soviet secret police chief, Feliks Dzerzhinskii, a Pole, to become prominent Soviet secret police operatives, as Viktor Kiiakovskii and Ignatii Sosnovskii respectively. Dobrzyński/Sosnovskii, however, was arrested in 1936 and executed in 1937 in Moscow as a 'Polish spy'. After Stalin's death, he was rehabilitated. See Pepłoński, *Wywiad polski na ZSRR*, 232–34, A. Papchinskii and M. Tumshis, *Shchit, raskolotyi mechom. NKVD protiv VChK* (Moscow, 2001), 243–45, 284–85, and N. V. Petrov and K. V. Skorkin, *Kro rukovodil NKVD 1934–1941. Spravochnik* (Moscow, 1999), 390–91. Steckiewicz/Kiiakovskii was the architect of 'Trest' ('Trust'), a brilliant Soviet counter-intelligence operation in the 1920s which set up a fake anti-Soviet underground organisation. He died in the line of duty in 1932 in Mongolia. Papchinskii and Tumshis, *Shchit, raskolotyi mechom*, 244, 250, 330, and *Razvedka i kontrrazvedka v litsakh* (Moscow, 2002), 229.
7. See Snyder, *Sketches from a Secret War*.
8. RGVA, f. 308k, op. 3, d. 230.
9. RGASPI, f. 558, op. 11, d. 185, l. 73.

10. See Nikolai Ezhov's account in 1937 in *Voprosy istorii*, 1994, no. 10, 22. Ezhov complained that Sosnovskii did not acquire 'Russian citizenship' until 1935. Ibid., 1995, no. 2, 19.

11. TsDAHO, f. 263, op. 1, spr. 64738fp, vol. 1, ark. 13, 23. Hereafter references are made to this archival source in the main text with the volume and folio numbers.

12. *Polacy na Ukrainie. Zbór dokumentów 1917–1939*, vol. 1 (Przemysl, 1998), 282–83.

13. Mikołaj Iwanow, *Pierwszy naród ukarany: Stalinizm wobec polskiej ludności kresowej (1921–1938)* (Warsaw, 1991), 141–44.

14. For 'Borovskaia' (Borowska), see Kupczak, *Polacy*, 213, 239.

15. For the Marchlevs'k Polish Autonomous District, see Kate Brown, *A Biography of No Place: From Ethnic Borderland to Soviet Heartland* (Cambridge, Mass., 2004). For its destruction, see also Iwanow, *Pierwszy*, 146–48.

16. *Pam'iat' Bykivni. Dokumenty ta materialy* (Kiev, 2000), 90.

17. TsDAHO, f. 263, op. 1, spr. 61750fp, ark. 11, 13–14, 26–27. Hereafter references to this archival source are made in the main text with the folio number.

18. See my *Freedom and Terror in the Donbas: A Ukrainian–Russian Borderland, 1870s–1990s* (Cambridge, 1988), 210.

19. TsDAHO, f. 7, op. 1, spr. 1115, ark. 15.

20. See, for example, Gábor T. Ritterspon, 'Formy obshchestvennogo obikhoda molodezhi i ustanovki sovetskogo rezhima v predvoennom desiatiletii', in Timo Vihavainen (ed.), *Normy i tsennosti povsednevnoi zhizni* (St Petersburg, 2000).

21. Naum Korzhavin, *V soblaznakh krovavoi epokhi* vol. 1 (Moscow, 2006), 85, 146.

22. TsDAHO, f. 7, op. 1, spr. 1115, 1276.

23. *Pam'iat' Bykivni*, 223–24.

24. TsDAHO, f. 263, op. 1, spr. 36260fp, v. 1, ark. 61–75. This massive file consists of three volumes with a total of approximately 1,050 pages (folios). Hereafter references to this archival source are made in the main text with the volume and folio numbers.

25. Roman Dzwonkowski, *Losy duchowieństwa katolickiego w ZSSR 1917–1939. Martyrologium* (Lublin, 1998), 341–42 and Wojciech Materski (ed.), *Wymiana więźniów politycznych pomiędzy II Rzecząpospolitą a Sowietami v okresie międzywojennym* (Warsaw, 2000), 230, 238–39.

26. Mykola Rozhenko and Edit Bohats'ka, *Sosny Bykivni svidchat': zlochyn proty liudstva*, vol. 1 (Kiev, 1999), 52.

27. A. N. Dugin, *Neizvestnyi GULAG. Dokumenty i fakty* (Moscow, 1999), 76.

28. *Lubianka. Stalin i Glavnoe upravlenie gosbezopasnosti 1937–1938* (Moscow, 2004), 359.

29. *Katyn'. Mart 1940 g.–sentiabr' 2000 g.* (Moscow, 2001).

30. *Lubianka*, 660.

Chapter 13: The Case of a Trotskii

1. *The Diary of Georgi Dimitrov, 1933–1949* (New Haven, Conn., 2003), 65.

2. Roman Dzwonkowski, *Losy duchowieństwa katolickiego w ZSSR 1917–1939. Martyrologium* (Lublin, 1998), 486–88, and Wojciech Materski (ed.), *Wymiana więźniów politycznych pomiędzy II Rzecząpospolitą a Sowietami v okresie międzywojennym* (Warsaw, 2000), 230, 238–39

3. I. I. Osipova, 'Skvoz' ogn' muchenii i vodu slez': goneniia na istinno-pravoslavnuiu tserkov' po materialam sledtsvennykh i lagernykh del zakliuchennykh (Moscow, 1998), 331.

4. Ostannia adresa. Do 60-richchia solovets'koi trahedii, vol. 1 (Kiev, 1997), 246, and Leningradskii martirolog, 1937–1938, vol. 3 (St Petersburg, 1998), 610.

5. Leningradskii martirolog, 1937–1938, vol. 4 (St Petersburg, 1999), 478.

6. Mykola Rozhenko, Sosny Bykivni svidchat': zlochyn proty liudstva, vol. 3 (Kiev, 2002), 284–85.

7. The following discussion is based on his personal file: TsDAHO, f. 263, op. 1, spr. 62062fp. Hereafter references to this archival source are made in the main text with the folio number.

8. Translated by the author and Naomi Kuromiya.

9. Holod 1932–1933 rokiv v Ukraini: prychyny ta naslidky (Kiev, 2003), 462.

10. See my Freedom and Terror in the Donbas: A Ukrainian–Russian Borderland, 1870s–1990s (Cambridge, 1998), 166.

11. Ibid., 176. 'Hopak' is the traditional Ukrainian peasant dance.

12. 'Fol'klor 1920–1930-kh godov v zapisiakh A. I. Nikiforova', Zhivaia starina, 1994, no. 2, 46.

13. Smertiu smert' podolaly. Holodomor v Ukraini 1932–1933 (Kiev, 2003), 27.

14. It goes too far, therefore, to speak of a 'spirit of rebellion', as Gábor T. Rittersporn does in his 'Le régime face au carnaval. Folklore nonconformiste en URSS dans les années 1930', Annales, 2003, no. 2 (March–April), 496.

15. Quoted in Feliks Chuev, Molotov. Poluderzhavnyi vlastelin (Moscow, 1999), 663. M. I. Kalinin, often referred to as the 'All-Union Elder', was the nominal head of the Soviet government at the time.

16. Quoted in Oleg Troianovskii, Cherez gody i rasstoiania. Istoriia odnoi sem'i (Moscow, 1997), 86.

Epilogue

1. Vladimir N. Khaustov, 'Razvitie sovetskikh organov gosudarstvennoi bezopasnosti: 1917–1953 gg.', Cahiers du monde russe, 42 (2001), nos 2–4, 370.

2. Iu. I. Shapoval, Ukraina XX stolittia. Osoby ta podii v konteksti vazhkoi istorii (Kiev, 2001), 107, 108, 122. See also I. V. Stalin, Sochineniia, vol. 11 (Moscow, 1952), 328.

3. 'Moskovskii dnevnik Romena Rollana', Voprosy literatury, 1989, no. 3, 221–22.

4. See, for instance, J. Arch Getty, '"Excesses are not permitted": Mass Terror and Stalinist Governance in the Late 1930s', Russian Review, 61:1 (2002), 113–38. On 'dissent' and 'resistance', see Sarah Davies, Popular Opinion in Stalin's Russia: Terror, Propaganda and Dissent, 1934–1941 (Cambridge, 1997) and Lynne Viola (ed.), Contending with Stalinism: Soviet Power and Popular Resistance in the 1930s (Ithaca, New York, 2002).

5. On this point, see my 'Why the Destruction of Orthodox Priests in the Soviet Union in 1937–38?', Jahrbücher für Geschichte Osteuropas, 55:1 (2007).

6. Recorded in a diary by a Moscow schoolgirl whose father had been arrested. Khochu zhit' ... Iz dnevnika shkol'nitsy. 1932–1937. Po materialam sledstvennogo dela sem'i Lugovskikh (Moscow, 2003), 6, 55. She was arrested in 1937 but survived the Stalin years in the Gulag. There is an English translation: Nina Lugovskaya, I

Want to Live: The Diary of a Young Girl in Stalin's Russia, tr. by Andrew Bromfield (London, 2006).

7. See Orlando Figes' forthcoming book *The Whisperers*.

8. See, for example, Jochen Hellbeck, *Tagebuch aus Moskau 1931–1939* (Munich, 1996).

9. Oleg Kharkhordin, 'Reveal and Dissimulate: A Genealogy of Private Life', in Jeff Weintraub and Krishan Komar (eds), *Public and Private in Thought and Practice: Perspectives on a Grand Dichotomy* (Chicago, Ill., 1997), 359–60.

10. From Stalin's 1934 letter to Kaganovich in R.W. Davies et al. (eds), *The Stalin–Kaganovich Correspondence, 1931–1936* (New Haven, Conn., 2003), 256.

11. *Voprosy istorii*, 1992, no. 10, p. 34.

12. His 2 June 1937 speech in *Istochnik*, 1994, no. 3, 79–80.

13. *Memoirs of Nikita Khrushchev*, vol. 1 (University Park, Penn., 2004), 117.

14. V. A. Boburenyofu (Bobrenev), *Shiberia yokuryū hishi* (Tsuruoka, 1992), 342–43. In 1949 Akikusa died in captivity in Vladimir, Russia.

15. See, for example, Etsuo Kōtani, 'Manshū ni okeru jōhō kinmu', available at the Bōeichō Bōei Kenkyū jo Toshokan in Tokyo.

16. A.V. Solov'ev, *Trevozhnye budni zabaikal'skoi kontrrazvedki* (Moscow, 2002), 203–8, and I. A. Damaskii, *Stalin i razvedka* (Moscow, 2004), 138–39.

17. Like that of Akikusa, Pickenbrock's testimony was taken while he was in captivity in the Soviet Union. Pickenbrock sought to use as informers many German specialists who worked in the Soviet Union, but they refused to accept the Abwehr's assignments. All the same, after their return to Germany, they were debriefed, and their information proved very useful. See Aleksandr Govorov, 'Gans Pikkenbrok daet pokazaniia', *V mire spetssluzhb*, 2006, no. 5, 24.

18. Artem Sergeev and Ekaterina Glushik, *Besedy o Staline* (Moscow, 2006), 74–75.

19. RGASPI, f. 17, op. 162, d. 21, l. 30.

20. See my 'Accounting for the Great Terror', *Jahrbücher für Geschichte Osteuropas*, 53:1 (2005), 96.

21. *Sto sorok besed s Molotovym* (Moscow, 1991), 439–40.

22. Vitalii Vezhnin, 'Nakanune', *V mire spetssluzhb*, 2005, no. 1, 28–29.

23. See my *Freedom and Terror in the Donbas: A Ukrainian–Russian Borderland, 1870s–1990s* (Cambridge, 1998), 283–84.

24. *Ibid.*, 288–94.

25. For an important analysis of collaborators in eastern Ukraine, see Tanja Penter, 'Die lokale Gesellschaft im Donbass unter deutscher Okkupation 1941–1943', in *Kooperation und Verbrechen. Formen der Kollaboration in Südost- und Osteuropa 1939–1945*, Beiträge zur Geschichte des Nationalsozialismus, Band 19 (Göttingen, 2003).

26. TsDAHO, f. 263, op. 1, spr. 66555fp, ark. 1, 25–26, 44. According to 6zv., Vikhoreva was arrested on 30 June 1941. Hereafter references to this archival source are made in the main text with the folio number.

27. Stalin was so taken aback by Hitler's invasion that he could not at first muster the courage to speak to the nation. He suggested that Molotov, then the Commissar (Minister) of Foreign Affairs, make an address instead. Molotov did so at 12.15 p.m. on 22 June. It was eleven days before Stalin made a radio address about the situation.

28. See the account of the German consul in Kiev: Andor Hencke, *Erinnerungen als Deutscher Konsul in Kiew in den Jahren 1933–1936* (Munich, 1979), 31, 45, 46.

29. Mykola Rozhenko and Edit Bohats'ka, *Sosny Bykivni svidchat': zlochyn proty liudstva*, vol. 1 (Kiev, 1999), 119.

30. See the account of a former senior secret police official who hanged himself after Stalin's death, quoted in Nadezhda Mandelstam, *Hope against Hope: A Memoir*, tr. Max Hayward (Harmondsworth, 1975), 56.

Index

Adamenko, B. D., 230–37
Adamenko, B. F., 230–37
Adamenko, D. F., 230–37
Adamenko, S. A., 230–37
Adjara, 95
Afghanistan, 182
Aizenberg, E. I., 212–13
Akikusa, Shun, 256, 287n. 14
Alaska, 41
Al'bov, V. Ia., 192–97
Al'bova, M. V., 192–97
Aleksandrovsk, 182
Alexander II, 255
Altnassau (the Crimea), 41, 272n. 25
Al'tzitser, M. A., 21
American Society for Scholarly
    Assistance, 181
An, Nikolai, 131
Andrienko, P. I., 230–37
Andrienko, S. I., 230–37
Angel'chik, Ch. N., 221–26
anti-Semitism, 70, 120, 122, 204, 205,
    212, 213, 215, 216, 222, 228
Antoshchenko, M. V., 235
Arkhangel'sk, 101
Aronskii, Z. A., 118

Bagniuk, G. Z., 214–17
Balatskii, D. Ie., 117–24
Balitskii, V. A., 18, 40
Bandurists, 108–24
beggars, 90–92, 276n. 22
Beitel'spakher, 166–67

Belarus, 14, 94, 98, 131, 183, 214, 230,
    237
Belarusans, 131, 174, 214, 219, 237
Berdebes, D. D., 178–79
Berezhkov, V. M., 160–61
Beria, L., 207
Berlin, 131, 149, 179
Bessarabia, see Moldova
Bigotskii, N. V., 101–5
Bila Tserkva, 23, 55
Blagoveshchensk, 182
Bohun, Ivan, 116
Borichevskaia-Lemlein, Iu. V., 274n. 4
Britain, 28, 32, 182
Budzko, Witalij, 96
Bukharin, N. I., 8–9
Bulgakov, Mikhail, 15, 24, 253
Bulgaria, 179
Bunge, N. N., 180–82
Bur'iats, 94, 127
Bykivnia, see mass graves
Bylov, Stepan, 164

Canada, 41, 42, 45, 272n. 25
Catholic Church, 49, 58, 163, 194–95,
    223
census (1937), 13, 76, 173
Chechens, 237
Cherniak, A. A., 236
Chernigovka, 128, 129
Chernihiv, 66, 110
Chernomorets, E. V., 168–70
Chicago, 191

China, 2, 16, 94, 127, 134
Chinese, 125–26, 129, 132, 134–35,
    174, 218–19
Chita, 16, 182
Choibalsan, Horloogiin, 2
Civil War, 14, 28, 65, 66, 94, 95, 99,
    111, 117, 125, 127, 170, 184, 186,
    212, 253
Colombia, 221
concessions, foreign, 283n. 12
confessions
    analysis of, 7–8, 11–12
consulates, 16–17, 30–40, 41–45,
    58, 129, 132, 144–45, 147–48,
    162–82, 177–79, 186, 191, 200–4,
    214–16, 224, 271n. 6, 282n. 31,
    287n. 28
Cossacks, 108–9, 116, 123, 246
Czechoslovakia, 271n. 6
Czechs, 159

Davidiuk, N. P., 225–26
Days of Turbins, see White Guard, The
'De Securi', 181
Denikin, Anton, 192–93
Denmark, 182
Ditkovskaia, M. S., 170–73
Dobrzyński, Ignacy, 221, 284n. 6
Donbas, 62, 138, 174
Doroshko, F. V., 110–16
Doroshko, I. T., 112–16
'Dreamers', operation, 256
Dub-Dubowski, I., 196
Dubovoi, V. A., 236
Dunaev, A. I., 236–37
dvoika, see troika
Dzerzhinskii, F., 183
Dzevitskaia, A. M., 202–4
Dzevitskii, S. M., 200–4
Dzhuzha, P. I., 69
Dziubenko, A. T., 118, 120, 122
Dzvinchuk, Iu. G., 184–90
Dzvinchuk, P. A., 184–90

Efron, Sergei, 48
emigration, 184
England, see Britain
Estonia, 131, 141, 142, 182

ethnic cleansing, 140
Eshchenko, N. K., 165–67
Eshchenko-Monarshukova, T. S., 165–67
Ezhov, N. I., 17, 118, 213, 221, 222,
    238, 246, 285n. 10

famine, 53, 78, 87, 94, 101, 107, 144,
    148, 150, 153, 163, 185, 198, 218,
    245, 246
Fastiv, 209, 211, 212
Fibich, Friedrich, 161
Finland, 141, 182, 259
Finns, 140, 142, 237, 282n. 23
Fraiman, D. B., 190–92
France, 28, 32
Franko, Ivan, 124

Galicia, 41, 102, 118, 184, 186, 190
Gdańsk, 146, 182
Georgia, 30, 95
German Operation, 86, 159, 201–2,
    203, 256
Germans, 141–2, 161, 218, 282n. 23
Germany, 2, 29, 30, 41–45, 86, 94, 99,
    114, 130, 182, 257
Glazko, Mariia, 172
Glembotskii, B. A., 234
Glenbotskii, M. B., 230–37
Głos Radziecki, 49, 51, 52, 55
Gorbachev, M. S., 242, 243
Gorodovenko, U. P., 95–99
Goroshko, V. E., 29–40
Great Famine, see famine
Great Terror
    statistics on, 1, 218, 238, 282n. 23
Greek Catholics, see Uniates
Greeks, 142, 173–77, 218, 282n. 23
Grigor'ev, N. N., 69
Grinevich, N. E., 65
Grosskopf, G. W., 165–67, 281n. 9
Gurnevich, P. V., 230–37
Gut, Franz F., 41–45
Gutkin, I. Ia., 208
Guzerchuk-Manchenko, E. I., 184

Haidamaks, 120, 123
Hata, Hikosaburō, 220–21
Hencke, Andor, 30, 163, 281n. 3

d'Herbigny, Michel, 273n. 19
Hey, Siegfried, 41
Hitler, A., 150, 160–61, 259
hooliganism, 91–92
Hrushevskii, M., 111
Huth, Franz, *see* Gut, Franz, F.

Iagoda, G. G., 92
Iakir, I. E., 78, 120, 169, 211
Iatskevich, E. K., 226–29
Il'nitskii, Ts. I., 229–37
informers, 47, 53, 55–56, 87–88, 203,
    222, 251, 258
Inquisition, records of, 6
interrogation records
    analysis of, 10–11
Iranians, 142
Irkutsk, 256
Istanbul, 279n. 24
Italy, 29, 164, 182, 282n. 31
Ivankiv, 229
Ivano-Frankivs'k, 184
Ivanov, V. T., 18

Jankowski, Henryk, 168–69, 170, 171,
    172, 173
Japan, 2, 17, 94, 110, 112, 125, 126,
    127, 131, 132, 133, 134, 164, 174,
    256, 257
    and Poland, 131, 141, 183, 219, 232,
    279n. 18
Jews, 16, 53, 70, 95, 126, 154, 159, 174,
    204, 206, 221, 229, 284n. 2

Kabachok, V. A., 123
Kaganovich, L. M., 15, 100, 255, 257
Kalinin, M. I., 252, 286n. 15
Kalisz, 95, 106, 190
Kamerer, E. Kh., 166–67
Kan, Khai-ron, 128
Kapshuk, I. V., 80
Karaganda, 154, 207
Karszo-Siedlewski, Jan, 30, 271–72n. 10
Kas'ian, F. M., 215
Kawabe, Torashirō, 220–21
Kazakhs, 94
Kazakhstan, 119, 137, 154
Khabarovsk, 136, 182

Khalkin Gol, 127
Kharbintsy, 126, 256, 282n. 23
Kharkiv, 15, 41, 42, 72, 165, 187, 247,
    270, 271–72n. 10, 282n. 15
Khasan, Lake, 127
Khmel'nyt'skyi, 56
Khmel'nyts'kyi, Bohdan, 116, 277n. 17
Khong-Yi-Pe, Nam-yang, 135
Khoroshun, I. G., 235
Khotkevych, Hnat, 123
Khrapinskii, M. A., 236
Khrushchev, N. S., 14, 119, 120, 121,
    256
Khvilia, A., 118–19
Kiev, 12–18, 132, 133, 270nn. 24, 25,
    29, 37
    consulates in, *see* consulates
    gaols in, 17–19
    Lysa Hill in, 248
    mass graves in, *see* mass graves
Kiev Institute of Economic
    Administrators, 150
Kiev Pedagogical Institute, 154
Kim, Agaf'ia, 137
Kim, Ben-shu, 128–38
Kim, Ben-sun, 127
Kim, El'-bon, 138–40
Kim, En-ke, 138
Kim, Ivan, S., 134
Kim, Tiu-er, 127
Kim, Zaen, 279n. 15
Kiprova, G. P., 241, 242, 244
Kirov, Sergei, 59, 106, 180, 221,
    227–28
Knol', Filitsiia, 171
Knol', Gabriel', 170
Koestler, Arthur, 8–9
Kogai, Sen-un, 134
Kogan, Regina, 53, 54
Kolumbis, D. P., 178–79
Kolyma, 134
Komsomol, 101, 128, 134
Kondratenko, V. A., 225–26
Kononenko, A. N., 115–16, 122
Konoplianik, L. Ia., 260–61
Kopan, G. Ia., 113–17
Korea, 126, 127, 128, 129, 132, 134,
    138

Koreans, 125–40, 174, 218–19
Korzhavin, Naum, 132, 228
Kosakovskii, I. M., 180
Kosior, S. V., 237, 248
Kostiatiuk, I. I., 234
Kostis, K. K., 178
Kotusenko, N. A., 235
Koziuba, F. M., 112–16
Kravchenko, N. R., 83–92
Kreiman, M. P., 153
Kremenchuk, 109, 149
Krikun, I. Ia., 204–5, 208
Kronberg, L. E., 143–49, 254
Krylov, I. A., 82
'Kulak Operation', 77, 105
kulaks, 86, 87, 99, 93–107, 110, 229–37,
    257
Kulibina, O. N., 72
Kurdik, Ia. A., 236
Kurdistan, 95, 140
Kurovskii, T. F., 209–13
Kurovskaia, A. P., 209–13, 217
Kuznetsov, K. F., 129–30, 137
Kvasnevskii, S. K., 56–59, 172

Latvia, 94, 141, 142, 143–54, 182, 257,
    281n. 9, 282n. 23
Latvian Club (Kiev), 153
Latvian Operation, 280n. 9
Lenin, V. I., 5, 48, 70, 239
Leningrad, 13, 16, 35, 36, 64, 74, 94,
    128, 239, 240, 270–71n. 46
Leplevskii, I. M., 18
Levina, Z. M., 74–75
Ligai, I. N., 132–33
Lisponenko, P. D., 120
Lithuania, 94, 141, 183, 257
Litvin, E. O., 235–36
Litvinov, A. M., 159–60
Liubchenko, A., 112
Liushkov, G., 126, 278n. 6
Loba, I. V., 235
Lomatkin, T. E., 101–4
Łódź, 149, 153, 191
Łomża, 97
Lublin, 200
Luhans'k, 62, 257
Luk'ianivka cemetery, 83, 85, 88, 89

Lutaenko, V. I., 118
Lutheran Church, 143, 161
L'viv, 182, 184
Lysenko Music and Drama Theatre, 117,
    118
Lysianka, 168

Mahilioŭ, 62, 66
Makariv, 192, 194
Maki-Mirage, Operation, 256
Malinovskii, Roman, 48
Managi, Takanobu, 131
Manchukuo, 2, 16, 126, 127, 164, 182,
    256, 257
Manchu-li, 17
Marangos, I. Kh., 174–79
Marchlevs'k, 224
marginal people, 91–92
Markov, F. I., 130, 136
mass graves (Bykivnia), 21–24, 39, 45,
    56, 57, 58, 68, 83, 91, 97, 99,
    100, 105, 136, 149, 153, 158, 160,
    167, 169, 181, 187, 192, 195, 209,
    216, 224, 229, 233, 234, 264,
    265
Mel'nikova, D. F., 214, 216
Metal'nikova, S. S., 180
Mikheev, M., 164
Milovetskaia, A. F., 195
Minsk (Mensk), 173, 182
Mishchenko, Iu. Kh., 199, 217
Mishchenko, S. V., 199, 217
Mogilev, see Mahilioŭ
Moldova, 142, 154, 158, 159
Molotov, V. M., 100, 255, 257, 266
monarchism, 64
Mongolia, 2, 94, 284n. 6
Moshinskaia, Ia. F., 49–56, 62
Moscow, 13, 16, 18, 23, 26, 35, 36,
    38, 48, 94, 99, 128, 131, 144–46,
    153, 175–77, 230, 246, 252, 263,
    271–72n. 10
Moscow Theological Seminary, 58
Mruvko, I. F., 172
Murashko, T. V., 248, 249–51
Musorks'kyi, M. Sh., 21
Muspenko, I. B., 236
Mykola Prytyska Church, 83, 84

Nademskii, A. G., 78–83, 254
Nagornyi, I. H., 21
Nagy, Imre, 48
Natanzon, F. G., 154–60
Navrotskii, A. D., 229–37
Navrotskii, V. D., 229–37
Neiber, E. A., 280n. 13
Nemyriv, 56
Neveu, Pius, 58, 60, 61
Niezbrzycki, Jerzy, 39–40
Nikel'berg, G. L., 20
Nikolai, Archbishop, 60–61
Nishchenko, N., 247, 249–51
NKVD, 18–19, 22, 54, 55–56, 78, 82,
        100, 105, 120, 122, 138–40, 153,
        163, 166–67, 175, 213, 231, 234,
        235, 246, 247, 251, 252, 257, 262
    informers for, see informers
    interrogators
        Dobryk, 51, 52, 54–55
        Dolgushev, 236
        Gofman, 260, 261
        Kamenev, 244
        Kniazev, 244, 248
        Kornberg, 244, 248, 249
        Mushkin, 68, 69
        Novgorodskii, 236
        Pavlov, 194
        Shchitnov, 191
        Smol'nyi, 199
    military tribunal of, 262
    Orders
        00439, see German Operation
        00447, see Kulak Operation
        00485, see Polish Operation
        00606, 45, 158, 167, 233
        00693, 134
        49990, 280n. 9
    Special Board of, 246, 251
    Third Department of, 181
Norway, 182
Novhorod-Volyns'kyi, 87
Novosibirsk, 16–17, 164

Odesa, 62, 122, 132, 168, 174, 182,
        240, 282n. 31
Okha, 182
Olekh, A. P., 205, 208

Olev'sk, 97
Onodera, Makoto, 279n. 22
Orthodox Church, 58, 59, 60
    Renovationist Church, 60, 274n. 24
    'Living Church', 77
Ōta, Hideo, 164

Pankevych, I. I., 150–51
Paplomantopulo, K. A., 178–79
Paris, 179, 180, 221
Pavlichev, L. M., 236
Pepłoński, Andrzej, 279n. 18
Perepechai, A. Iu., 260
Petliura, Symon, 94, 95, 277n. 5
Petrograd, see Leningrad
Petropavlosk, 182
Petrovskii, V., 164
Philadelphia, 155
Pickenbrock, Hans, 257, 287n. 17
Piłsudski, Józef, 220
Plastunova, S. K., 158–59
Pliats, E. V., 150, 152, 154–55
Podniak, Ia., 221
Pokhil, V. S, 116
Poland, 2, 29, 30–40, 58, 94, 97, 112,
        114, 117, 180, 185, 256, 257
    and Japan, 131, 141, 183, 219, 232,
        279n. 18
Poles, 218–19, 282n. 23
    in Ukraine, 52
Polish Operation, 30, 38, 56, 66, 74,
        149, 153, 159, 169, 170, 178, 181,
        187, 195, 202, 204, 211, 214, 224,
        229, 237, 238, 274n. 4
Polish Pedagogical Institute (in Kiev),
        50, 51, 52, 53, 54, 55, 221, 222,
        224, 226, 227
Polish secret police, 191
Polishchuk, A. K., 83–92
Poltava, 122, 123
Ponomareva, E. N., 263
Popsueva, Muza, 128, 135
'POW' (Polish Military Organisation),
        51, 218–38
prisoners of war, 41, 84, 112–13, 187
Proskuriv, see Khmel'nyts'kyi
Pushkin, Aleksandr, 244
Pustotin, I. S., 82

Rava Rus'ka, 41
rehabilitation, 11
Remov, Nikolai F., *see* Varfolomei
Repik, I. I., 230–37
Repik, L. I., 230–37
Reshetilo, M. L., 112–15
Riaboi, I. D., 236
Riga, 131, 142, 149
Rogov, G. N., 129–30, 137
Rogova, Z. Ia., 129–30
Romania, 141, 142, 154–60
Rozanov, Nikolai F., *see* Nikolai
'Ruslan and Liudmila', 244, 247
Russia, 14, 41, 48, 58, 64, 70, 100, 111,
    125, 149, 200, 218, 221, 228, 245,
    257
Russians, 14, 16, 127, 218, 256
Russo-Japanese War, 174
Rybinskaia, E. A., 51, 53–54
Rzhyshchiv, 184, 226

Sakhovskii, N. I., 227–28
Salonika, 194
Sandler, O. A., 277n. 21
Sataniv, 225
Savorovskii, G. O., 260
Scientific Research Institute of
    Electrical Welding, 129
Sergeev, Artem, 257
Serikova, L. S., 228–29
Shapiro, I. V.-M., 212–13
Shashkov, A. G., 20
Shevchenko, Taras, 108
Shirer, Kh. Sh., 190–92
Shlepchenko, 21
Shlepchitskii, L. Ia., 204–5, 208
show trials, 8, 9, 269n. 19
Shtern, D. M., 156, 157
Shugial'ter, A., 146
Shukovak, M. Ia., 259
Shums'kyi, O., 113, 277n. 15
Sia, Sa-bo, 135
Simonov, K., 282n. 27
Sin, Don, 135
Singaevskii, N. I., 230–37
Singer Company, 192, 283n. 12
Skarbek, B., 222
Skliaruk, A., 80–82

Skoropads'kyi, Hetman, 94, 113
Skvyr, 95, 97
Snezhnyi, I. G., 112
Snyder, Timothy, 163, 272n. 21
Socrates, 124
Solovki Islands, 61, 194, 240, 245
Sommer, Rudolf, 168, 282n. 15
Sosnovskaia-Budnitskaia, F. M., 206–9,
    217
Sosnovskii, I. F., 204–9
Spain, 82
Spring, Operation, 65
Stalin, I. V., 3, 5, 48, 124, 142, 221,
    239, 254, 257, 267, 287n. 27
    and Bulgakov, 253
    and executions, 269
    on diplomats, 28
    on Japan and Korea, 126, 253
    on kins, 198, 217
    on Poles, 238
    on power, 255
    on religion, 76
    on spies, 29
    on torture, 268–69n. 13
    on truth, 256
Stashchenko, S. P., 99–100
State Model Bandura Chorus, 117, 118
Steckiewicz, Wiktor, 284n. 6
Stolypin, Petr, 40
Stpiczyński, Aleksander, 30, 33, 35, 37
Strauss, M. E., 143–44
Sviatoshyne, 101
'SVU', 103, 107, 184, 220, 276n. 11
Sweden, 182
Switzerland, 75
Sysoev, G. N., 136
Szczepaniuk, N. W., 195–97

Tavda, 241
Tolstoi, Nikolai A., 61–62
theosophy, 274n. 4
Tolstoi, Lev, 77
Torgsin, 68, 72, 245, 274n. 6
torture, 6, 19–20, 173, 175, 191, 199,
    203, 217, 234, 236, 244, 248, 258,
    268–69n. 13, 270nn. 37, 38
Trest (Trust), Operation, 256, 284n. 6
troika, 2, 4, 20, 82, 84, 99

Trotskii, D. V., 240, 270n. 30
Trotskii, F., 240
Trotskii, I. M., 240
Trotskii, L. D., 239–40
Trotskii, L. P., 241–52, 254
Trotskii, M. N., 240
Trotskii, V. V., 240
Tso, Don-bin, 138
Tsudzinovich, V. I., 234
Tsutsarina, N. I., 175, 179
Tsvetaeva, Marina, 48
Tukhachevskii, M. N., 65, 78, 169, 211
Turkey, 32, 94, 95, 141
Tver', 60, 84, 240

Ukraine, 14, 17–18, 95, 108, 118–19, 218
    Central Rada of, 110, 112
    and Japan, 131–32
    and music, 109–110, 124
Ukrainian Pedagogical Institute, 221–22
Ukrainians, 14, 15, 16, 105, 109, 114, 116, 120, 124, 218, 230, 237
    in the Far East, 132
    in Poland, 183, 186
Ukrainisation, 109, 114, 160
Uman', 23
Uniates (Greek Catholics), 61, 196
United States, 2, 28, 182
Uspenskii, A. I., 18
UVO, 123, 151

Varfolomei, 58–60
Vasilenko, G. G., 102
Vasil'eva, O. S., 41–45
Veres, V. R., 230–37
Vidubychi, 78–83
Vikhoreva, Z. G., 257–66
Vil'ner, D. S., 137

Vilnius, 179
Vinnytsia, 24, 270–71n. 46
Vishnevskaia, G. V., 195
Vladimir, 287
Vladivostok, 182, 256, 282n. 15
Vol'chak, M. M., 129–30, 136
Vologda, 259
Voronezh, 276n. 22
Voroshylovhrad, see Luhans'k
Vorov'ev, P. P., 84, 86
Vorobiov, N. I., 20
Vyshinskii, P. F., 112, 113

Warsaw, 32, 39, 54, 96, 106, 170–71, 174, 180, 200, 204, 221, 222, 225, 230, 279n. 18
Wąsowicz, B., 194–97
Western Ukraine, 14, 23, 118, 124
White Guard, The, 15, 24, 251
white/émigré Russians, 48, 72, 98, 118, 127, 142, 181, 192, 220, 256
Wilner, L., 190
World War I, 41, 84, 112, 113, 142, 149, 192, 219, 238
World War II, 24, 62, 73, 208, 235, 257, 259, 270–71n. 46

Zagreb, 179
Zaichenko, V. G., 235
Zakharevich, V. A., 83–92
Zaleski, Wiktor, 30–40, 96, 106, 225, 271n. 8
Zbruch River, 225
Zeibert, E. T., 149–54
Zhelikhovskaia, A. I., 66–75, 254
Zhelikhovskii, G. I., 72, 73
Zhukov, L. A., 39
Zhytomyr, 23, 56, 97, 196
'Zionists', 159
Zubovskii, A. P., 62
Żych, Zygmunt, 231, 236